The Strategic
Project Office

CENTER FOR BUSINESS PRACTICES

Editor

James S. Pennypacker

Director
Center for Business Practices
West Chester, Pennsylvania

The Superior Project Organization: Global Competency Standards and Best Practices, Frank Toney

The Superior Project Manager: Global Competency Standards and Best Practices, Frank Toney

PM Practices

The Strategic Project Office: A Guide to Improving Organizational Performance, J. Kent Crawford

Project Management Maturity Model: Providing a Proven Path to Project Management Excellence, J. Kent Crawford

ADDITIONAL VOLUMES IN PREPARATION

Managing Multiple Projects: Planning, Scheduling, and Allocating Resources for Competitive Advantage, James S. Pennypacker and Lowell Dye

The Strategic Project Office

A Guide to Improving Organizational Performance

J. Kent Crawford

Project Management Solutions, Inc.
Havertown, Pennsylvania

MARCEL DEKKER, INC. NEW YORK · BASEL

ISBN: 0-8247-0750-8

This book is printed on acid-free paper.

Headquarters
Marcel Dekker, Inc.
270 Madison Avenue, New York, NY 10016
tel: 212-696-9000; fax: 212-685-4540

Eastern Hemisphere Distribution
Marcel Dekker AG
Hutgasse 4, Postfach 812, CH-4001 Basel, Switzerland
tel: 41-61-261-8482; fax: 41-61-261-8896

World Wide Web
http://www.dekker.com

The publisher offers discounts on this book when ordered in bulk quantities. For more information, write to Special Sales/Professional Marketing at the headquarters address above.

PRINTED IN THE UNITED STATES OF AMERICA

Series Introduction

THE ORGANIZATIONAL ENVIRONMENT NEEDED FOR project success is ultimately created by management. The way that the managers define, structure, and act toward projects is critical to the success or failure of those projects, and consequently the success or failure of the organization. An effective project management culture is essential for effective project management.

This Center for Business Practices series of books is designed to help you develop an effective project management culture in your organization. The series presents the best thinking of some of the world's leading project management professionals, who identify a broad spectrum of best practices for you to consider and then to implement in your own organizations. Written with the working practitioner in mind, the series provides "must have" information on the knowledge, skills, tools, and techniques used in superior project management organizations.

A culture is a shared set of beliefs, values, and expectations. This culture is embodied in your organization's policies, practices, procedures, and routines. Effective cultural change occurs and will be sustained only by altering (or in some cases creating) these everyday policies, practices, procedures, and routines in order to impact the beliefs and values that guide employee actions. We can affect the culture by changing the work climate, by establishing and implementing project management methodology, by training to that methodology, and by reinforcing and rewarding the changed behavior that results. The Center for Business Practices series focuses on helping you accomplish that cultural change.

Having an effective project management culture involves more than implementing the science of project management, however — it involves the art of applying project management skill. It also involves the organizational changes that truly integrate this management philosophy. These changes are sometimes structural, but they always involve a new approach to managing a business: projects are a natural outgrowth of the organization's mission. They are the way in which the organization puts in place the processes that carry out the mission. They are the way in which changes will be effected that enable the organization to effectively compete in the marketplace.

We hope this Center for Business Practices series will help you and your organization excel in today's rapidly changing business world.

James S. Pennypacker
Director, Center for Business Practices
Series Editor

Preface

"100% of everyone's time should be taken up by projects."
—Tom Peters, in *Circle of Innovation*

IF YOU WERE INSPIRED to pick this book up off the shelf, chances are you already have some idea of the importance of good project management to today's organizations. What industries like construction have long known—that managing an endeavor with a fixed deadline, a unique product, and a budget cap is a very specialized art/science— is now being discovered by every industry where new products are the lifeblood of competition. In software development and other IT/ IS application areas in particular, the value of sound project management has never been more in the public consciousness, thanks to studies by the Standish Group, the Gartner Group, and other IT research firms.

But even sound project management of individual projects is no longer enough. While there still are some instances in which a company is almost entirely focused on one or two major projects at a time— small software development firms or capital construction firms come to mind—the reality in most businesses is that dozens of projects exist throughout the company in various stages of completion (or, more commonly, of disarray). It wouldn't be at all uncommon for a company to have several new product development projects in process, along with a process reengineering effort, a TQM initiative, a new marketing program in the works, and a fledgling e-business unit. Widen the scope of your thought to take in facilities, logistics, manufacturing, and public relations and you begin to understand why most companies have no idea how many projects they have going at one time. And when you consider that technology plays a role in almost all changes to organizations these days, and that technology projects have an abysmal record of failure, the light begins to dawn: unless all the projects that a company engages in are conceptualized, planned, executed, closed out, and archived in a systematic manner—that is, using the proven methodologies of project management—it will be impossible for an organization to keep a handle on which activities add value and which drain resources.

You can't manage what you can't measure, the old saying goes, and unless all the projects on the table can be held up to the light and compared to each other, a company has no way of managing them strategically, no way of making intelligent resource allocation decisions, no way of knowing what to delete and what to add. And the only way to have a global sense of how a company's projects are doing is to have some sort of project focus point: the project office.

Call it what you will—Center of Excellence, Project Support Office, Program Management Office, or Project Office—a home base for project managers and project management is a must for organizations to move from doing a less-than-adequate job of managing projects on an individual basis, to creating the organizational synergy around projects that adds value, dependably and repeatably.

Why This Book Now?

Imagine for a moment your organization without a financial management system:

- No documented procedures or systems

- No common understanding of processes

- No shared vocabulary

- No standards

- No data collection or reporting

- No knowledge transfer or management in the financial practice

- No history.

Nightmarish? Definitely. But this is how most organizations operate today with respect to project management. In fact, in some ways the state of project management is even worse. Whereas our imaginary company with no financial processes in place would at least have entry-level employees with a four-year degree in accounting or finance, project managers are often crowned overnight, often with no clear training plan for the future in mind. Even if a company has standardized on a project management tool across the enterprise, providing access to the methodologies inherent in that tool, it's unlikely that everyone who works on project teams has had adequate training to make the best use of it. Even good project managers within a system like this are flying blind, with no way of knowing how the project they are working on fits into the whole. Thus the frustration of many project managers who bring projects in on time, on budget, and to specifications—only to find they have a failure on their hands, since the customer requirements were wrong, or the market research was inadequate, or company strategy has changed since inception.

This is undoubtedly why the Gartner Group has predicted that through 2004 companies that fail to establish a project office will experience twice as many major project delays, overruns, and cancellations as will companies with a PO in place.

Who Is This Book For?

The content of this book is relevant to three principal segments of the project management community within an organization:

- Executive management
- Project office directors
- Managers of project managers
- Project managers.

It is our hope that the book will make the rounds of all four groups because without buy-in on all levels, the project office culture is very difficult to instill in an organization. Project managers need to understand the big picture of how their project fits into the organization as a whole, as a piece of the portfolio, and as a part of the strategy. Managers of project managers and the project office director need a game plan whereby they can improve project and project manager performance and take the lead in disseminating project knowledge throughout the company culture. Those who have already been tasked with the responsibility of spearheading the project office will have a handbook to lead them.

How to Use This Book

First, read the introductory chapters for background on the project office and its association with project management maturity and with project portfolio management. Then, do the organizational quick assessment in Chapter 2 to find out what level of project office is right for your organization. But don't set your sights too low. Our objective in writing this book is to help more organizations move to the most effective model of the project office: the Strategic Project Office.

We have seen companies fail in project office implementations because executive leadership hands off the job of "creating a project office" to one individual. But the implementation of a PO is less like a solo and more like a five-act production with a cast of thousands. The entire organization has to get involved. Therefore we've provided suggested types of meetings or trainings, most of which include a checklist of who should ideally be involved.

WE AGREE WITH TOM Peters: everyone should be working within the project paradigm. But that's not enough. Just putting 50 ballerinas on stage and yelling, *Everybody dance!* does not make it *Swan Lake*, no matter how good their individual skills may be.

Everyone within a company and, to some extent, within that company's vendors, alliance partners, and other external stakeholders, needs to be working to the same beat. If Stephen Covey is right, and interdependence is the name of the game, then the project office concept is the way for people throughout your company to recognize and capitalize on their interdependencies, to manage and transfer project management knowledge, and to get into step with each other for the benefit of all.

Where do you start? Just turn the page.

Postcript: A Research Appeal to Readers

Like many of the lessons learned and best practices discovered in business and industry, the experiences—both positive and negative—that companies have had in implementing project offices are shrouded in the mist called "proprietary information." One of the hurdles the project management discipline faces in collecting objective information about the various techniques that are available for continuous improvement in project processes is that companies who fail in the implementation of a project technique are loath to go public with that information; while companies who succeed jealously guard the story of how they did so from their competitors. This, we believe, is a mistake.

A better strategy for both the discipline of project management and for the companies whose prosperity depends on the effective practice of it, would be for information on best practices and lessons learned to flow freely from practitioners to the larger community, including research organizations, both academic and professional, other practitioners, and organizations. The Center for Business Practices, the research and publishing arm of our own firm, Project Management Solutions, Inc. has numerous research studies underway but the value of the results of such studies depends in large part upon participation from practitioner companies. A rising tide floats all boats, as the saying goes, and we encourage companies dependent on good project management to participate in such studies ... and see how high we can rise, together. For information about CBP research currently underway, ontact the Center for Business Practices at cbp@pmsolutions.com or visit www.cbponline.com.

Acknowledgments

THIS BOOK MAY PROVE TO be the exception to the old rule about writing by committee. As such, it's a great example of the efficacy of one of project management's signal features: the creative team. As with any product that distills the experience and knowledge of many people working together over time, it is a little hard to give all credit where it is due. I will do my best to name names here, with the uncomfortable feeling that someone is bound to be inadvertently left out. For any oversight, I apologize in advance.

My deepest thanks must first go to my wife Linda and to my children who tolerated my sabbaticals and many hours set aside to focus on drafting, revising, and completing this book.

A heartfelt thanks and "well-done" to Jeannette Cabanis-Brewin, editor-in-chief of the Center for Business Practices, the research and publishing division of Project Management Solutions, Inc. for her journalism, significant contribution, and countless hours in polishing my rough materials into a well-organized and readable book.

Curtis R. Cook, PMP, Ph.D., served as a subject matter expert and content consultant on the final draft of the manuscript. His input was invaluable.

Materials concerning the PM Solutions Project Management Maturity model, while the product of the efforts of many PM Solutions associates over the past four years, were prepared for publication by David Yosua, PMP, Product Integration Manager, Project Management Solutions, Inc. Also involved in our project to create a maturity model were Karen White, PMP, Managing Consultant, Project Management Solutions, Inc. and Dianne Bridges, PMP, Managing Consultant, Project Management Solutions, Inc.

The writings of C.J. Walker, PMP, Managing Consultant, Project Management Solutions, Inc. on change management were used as the foundation for chapter ten.

Jim Pennypacker, director of the Center for Business Practices, was invaluable as a source on project management research and also kept our relationship with Marcel Dekker seamless.

Thanks to Debbie Bigelow, PMP, Executive Vice-President, Jim Oswald, PMP, Vice-President of Professional Services, Bruce Miller, PMP, Vice-President of Business Development, and Lori Gipp, Vice-President of Marketing and Alliances, all of PM Solutions, and Jimmie West, Ph.D., PMP, of PM College, who so effectively managed the ongoing operations of these businesses during the writing of this book.

Finally, I can't forget the many current and former associates of PM Solutions and the PM College who by their work on behalf of clients in the field have helped to develop and refine our project office deployment processes, strategies, and knowledge. Thanks also to our many Project Office classroom participants and clients—they have participated in knowledge development along the way and contributed their experience and wisdom to the collective mind of our company.

Contents

List of Figures and Tables

The Strategic
Project Office

CHAPTER **1**

The Project Office Concept

W E'VE HEARD SO MUCH IN the past few years about the project office that it's hard to believe there was a time, not long ago, when the idea of an organizational center for project management was way out there on the fringe. But project management wandered rootlessly throughout the organization for about a quarter-century before it became fashionable to build it a home in the project office (PO). Let's examine how the management of individual projects evolved naturally into a project management center.

Early Days

Project management has been around for decades—some may argue for centuries. In the construction industry in particular, the idea of a work effort with a specific set of requirements and a deadline had been business as usual since the days of the pyramids. However, the concept of the project as an organizing principle and a management specialty—with its own techniques, tools, and vocabulary—had its beginnings in the 20th-century military. Like many other features of post-WWII America, the project and its supporting software and techniques were a spin-off of the first truly modern war effort.[1]

These military origins help to explain why the initial focus in projects was on planning and controlling. In fact, control might be considered the *raison d'etre* for project management: control of schedules, costs, and scope on endeavors that otherwise might career over budget or time and/or fail to meet specifications.

That "out-of-control" feel to projects has its roots in the way projects were superimposed on existing bureaucratic structures, with their bulky communications mechanisms. Imagine the highly hierarchical

1

command-and-control management of a military organization—and then imagine a short-term, deadline-sensitive effort with budget, personnel, and other resources drawn from multiple departments, divisions, and even branches of the service. Obeying the strictures inherent in the hierarchy and at the same time acting for the best interest of the project under such conditions would have been difficult at best—and was often downright impossible. But this is the model we began from in project management. No wonder projects felt uncontrolled, mysterious; no wonder project management developed a reputation as both science and "art." It is interesting to note that the military was also the first to react to this situation, creating system program offices with semi-autonomous program managers empowered to plan, execute, and complete projects (subject to "higher authority" such as the U.S. Congress). These system program offices were the precursors of today's project offices in the private sector.

An Evolving Structure

When project management's early tools—Gantt charts, network diagrams, PERT—began to be used in private industry, the new project managers faced a similar hurdle: business was also fashioned on the command-and-control model. Putting together an interdisciplinary team was a process fraught with bureaucratic roadblocks. The earliest uses of project management—in capital construction, civil engineering, and R&D—imposed the idea of the project schedule, project objectives, and project team on an existing organizational structure that was very rigid. Without a departmental home or a functional silo of its own, a project was often the organizational stepchild—even though it may have been, in terms of dollars or prestige, the most important thing going on. Thus was born the concept of the "matrix organization"—really a stopgap way of defining how projects were supposed to get done within an organizational structure unsuitable to project work. It was a "patch," to use a software development term—not a new version of the organization.

Today, those rigid, pyramid-shaped structures are changing shape. "Flattening" the organization means erasing the boundaries between functional silos. This trend is driven by both market imperatives and by the seamless communication made possible by modern communications technology. Multidisciplinary, team-based endeavors are now recognized as the only way to stay adaptive and flexible enough to succeed in a changing marketplace.[2] Many organizations that host projects now take a different tack: rather than forcing projects to fit within a bureaucratic structure, they embrace projects as an organizing principle.[3] Projects are no longer "something extra"—they are the way work gets done at an increasing number of companies, from small start-ups to the likes of Hewlett-Packard, IBM, USWest, Motorola, ABB and many others. (For a more complete list, see Chapter 1 "Talking Points.")

But such change doesn't come easy. To take it out of the management context and put it in political terms, reorganizing a company's work around projects is the equivalent of moving from a feudal system to participatory democracy. Many of the participants in the Project Office Implementation courses I teach come from companies that have started "management by projects" initiatives in the past and failed— sometimes more than once.

Many times these failures are a result of the organization misjudging the magnitude of the change they were about to undergo. From many teaching engagements centered around implementing the project office, my impression is that most of my students hold the misconception that a project office is merely a project controls office that focuses on scheduling and reports. At one time, of course, this was true: in the old matrix organization, if a project was lucky to have a "project office," it was usually nothing more than a "war room" with some Gantt charts on the walls and perhaps a scheduler or two— people gifted with the ability to run the project management scheduling software of the day. This simple single-project control office is what I'll call a Level 1 project office (see Chapter 3 for a full discussion of these levels).

A Level 2, or "business unit," project office may still provide support for individual projects, but its primary challenge is to integrate multiple projects of varying sizes within a division (such as IT), from small, short-term initiatives to multi-month or multi-year initiatives that require dozens of resources and complex integration of technologies. With a Level 2 PO, an organization can, for the first time, integrate resources effectively, because it's at the organizational level that resource control begins to play a much higher-value role in the payback of a project management system.

For an organization without any repeatable processes in place—such as the majority of software development organizations, which are at the first, or Initial Level on the Software Engineering Institute's Capability Maturity Model[4]—these levels of project office organization are beneficial. At Level 1, or the individual project level, applying the discipline of project management creates significant value to the project because it begins to define basic processes that can later be applied to other projects within the organization. At Level 2 and higher, the PO not only focuses on project success, but also migrates processes to other projects and divisions, thus providing a much higher level of efficiency in managing resources across projects. A Level 2 PO allows an organization to determine when resource shortages exist and to have enough information at their fingertips to make decisions on whether to hire or contract additional resources. And at Level 3, the Strategic Project Office applies processes, resource management, prioritization, and systems thinking across the entire organization. The development of each of these types of project infrastructure provides a significant boost to process maturity (for a fuller discussion of the relationship between POs and project management maturity, see Chapter 2).

But it's at Level 3—the Strategic Project Office—that the value-adding mechanisms of a PO really reach warp speed. At the corporate level, the PO serves as a repository for the standards, processes, and methodologies that improve individual project performance in all divisions. It also serves to deconflict the competition for resources and identify areas where there may be common resources that could be used across the enterprise. More important, a corporate PO allows the organization to manage its entire collection of projects as one or more interrelated portfolios. Executive management can get the big picture of all project activity across the enterprise from a central source—the project office; project priority can be judged according to a standard set of criteria, and projects can at last fulfill their promise as agents of enterprise strategy. The Gartner Group has identified five key roles for a project office,[5] all of which are most effectively carried out at Level 3:

- Developer, documenter and repository of a standard methodology: a consistent set of tools and processes for projects

- Resource evaluator: Based on experience from previous projects, the PO can validate business assumptions about projects as to people, costs, and time; also a source of information on cross-functional project resource conflicts or synergies.

- Project planner: a competency center and library for previous project plans

- Project management consulting center: providing a seat of governing responsibility for project management; perhaps staffing projects with project managers or deploying them as consultants.

- Project review and analysis center: a knowledge management center where information on project goals, budgets, progress, and history are stored—both during the project life cycle and after, in the form of lessons learned.

Thus, more than a place or a set of people, the project office is "a shared competency" designed to integrate project management within an enterprise. A Level 3 PO can promote enterprise competency in project analysis, design, management, and review. And, says Gartner, "given the appropriate governance, it can improve communication, establish an enterprise standard for project management and help reduce the disastrous effect of failed development projects on enterprise effectiveness and productivity."

Although admittedly many companies today still struggle to implement even Level 1 project offices, the focus of this book is on the Level 3 Strategic Project Office. Why? Because that's where organizations can get more bang for their buck—and realize organizational dreams at the same time. Like the matrix organization, lower-level project offices are a waystation: a stage between the old-style organization and the new, project-based enterprise.

Why the Project Office Matters *Now*

There's been a tremendous resurgence in interest in the discipline of project management in the last few years. The reason: information technology, information services, and new product development organizations have "discovered" project management. A traditional part of the toolkit for construction and large government projects, project management now sparks interest wherever compressing time-to-market cycles is an issue—in other words, throughout the modern marketplace. As industries work hard to compress product life cycles, to reduce costs, and to improve the quality of their deliverables, they are increasingly turning to project management.

Thus, the extensively practiced and researched discipline of project control systems and schedule development have now come to find a home in less traditional areas, such as high-tech industries, where organizations are under increasing pressure to utilize product development funds more efficiently. There's been a shift of focus toward the business side of delivering high-tech products and services: a focus on the *process* and the *business* of managing projects.

With this microscope turned on the business side of IT projects comes the bad news: most of them are not managed very well. In all fairness, project success rates in other industries may not be that great either, but they have not been subjected to the intense scrutiny that technology projects have been, for the simple reason that high-tech is the biggest wealth-creating sector in the economy this decade—the primary driver of economic prosperity.[6] America spends over $275 billion each year on about 200,000 software development projects, many of which fail. As IT moves out of the back office and into more mission-critical business processes like customer relationship management and e-commerce, the line between IT and other types of projects is blurring.

Failure: A Wake-Up Call

We alluded briefly in the preface to the weighty evidence we now have of persistent management problems with projects. Most readers are probably familiar with the dismal technology project failure statistics that have been kept since 1994 by The Standish Group International Inc., a research firm in Dennis, MA.[7] To summarize, their latest survey indicates that 46% of IT projects were over budget and overdue, while 28% failed altogether. Another, earlier study cites even grimmer success rates: only 24% of IT projects undertaken by Fortune 500 companies will be completed successfully.

Standish isn't the only source of dire project statistics. A survey of project managers conducted in 1999 by Robbins-Gioia Inc. found that 90% of them often underestimate project size and complexity. Nearly half (44%) have cost overruns of 10 to 40%, and only 16% consistently meet scheduled due dates.[8]

In construction—widely held to be the most mature industry in terms of project management—there was the loudly publicized failure of the Boston Central Artery/Third Harbor Tunnel (Big Dig) project in Boston, which featured then-presidential candidate Senator John McCain dressing down the project manager in front of the Senate Committee on Commerce, Science and Transportation. At its inception, the project was expected to cost $2.6 billion, but a federal estimate in February 2000 put the actual price tag at $13.6 billion—a cost overrun of more than 500%.[9]

In the consulting field, such industry giants as Deloitte Consulting, PeopleSoft, Andersen Consulting, and SAP became targets of lawsuits in 1999 by companies furious that ERP and HR system implementations had dragged on for years, run millions over budget, and created a culture of dependency on the consulting firm.[10]

Project failure, as Standish Group chairman Jim Johnson has noted, "is everyone's problem."[11]

The Gartner Group proposes, as a "Strategic Planning Assumption" for companies, that through 2004, IS organizations that establish enterprise standards for project management, *including a project office with suitable governance*, will experience half as many major project cost overruns, delays, and cancellations as those that fail to do so. They also note that the IT software development project as presently managed is often 170–180% over budget.[12]

Why is this so important? Because time is money: if a project is late for an amount of time equal to 10% of the projected life of the project, it loses about 30% of its potential profits.[13] A study by McKinsey & Company has shown that high-tech products lose 33% of after-tax profits when they are late to market, but lose only 4% when they are on time—even if they are 50% over budget.[14]

Failure: A Learning Experience

The good news in those bad statistics is that there is a trend toward improvement. In 1999, the Standish Group reported that project failure rates are falling.[15] Based on an examination of 23,000 software projects in companies of all sizes, in many industries since 1994, their research shows that project success rates are up, while cost and time overruns are down. In 1994, only 16% of application development projects met the criteria for success—on time, on budget, and with all the features originally specified. By 1998, 26% were successful. Large companies have made the most dramatic improvement. In 1994 the chance of a Fortune 500 company's project coming in on time and on budget was 9%; its average cost, $2.3 million. In 1998, that same project's chances of success had risen to 24%, while the average project cost fell to $1.2 million.

Johnson believes three factors explain these encouraging results: 1) a trend toward smaller projects, which are more successful because they are less complex; 2) better project management; and 3) greater use of "standard infrastructures"—such as those instituted through a project office.

Another benefit of this research has been the collection of an enormous amount of data on why projects fail.

Why Projects Fail

Infoweek magazine put it succinctly in their August 1996 issue: "The major cause of project failure is not the specifics of what went wrong but rather the lack of procedures, methodology, and standards for managing the project." The project manager who is asked to manage a project with no methodology, no procedure, no process to support them is going to be very challenged to keep that project under control. Some reasons for failure that are directly related to lack of a project office include:

- Project managers who lack enterprise-wide multi-project planning, control, and tracking tools often find it impossible to comprehend the system as a whole.[16]

- Ranges of acceptable project variances against key baselines are not established during project initiation or planning; thus a kill or recover decision is not made early enough.[17]

- Poor project management/managers. Most of the reasons technology projects fail are management-related rather than technical. The old paradigm of promoting the best technical personnel to project manager level didn't work, since technical ability is a poor indicator of project management ability, yet many enterprises have no processes in place to ensure that project managers are appropriately trained and evaluated.[18]

- There is a high correlation between lack of clear project sponsorship and failure. Executive support for/understanding of projects is lacking in many organizations.[19]

- Accurate project resource tracking is imperative to successful project management, but many organizations are hampered by awkward or antiquated time-tracking processes.[20]

What We Can Do About It

Interestingly, many of the best practices for preventing failures are also directly related to project offices:

- Enterprises that hold post-implementation reviews, harvest best practices and lessons learned, and identify reuse opportunities are laying the necessary groundwork for future successes.[21]

- A project office shines as the repository for best practices in planning, estimating, risk assessment, scope containment, skills tracking, time and project reporting, maintaining and supporting methods and standards, and supporting the project manager.

- Sound project plans are realistic, up to date, and frequently reviewed; reviews focus not just on what has been done, but look forward to identifying risks and opportunities.

- Project metrics and milestones are defined, measured, and reported.[22]

- Experienced sponsors and project managers develop and maintain a "go/no go" cancellation strategy. They don't hesitate to kill a project that becomes a liability—without indulging in blame and punishment.[23]

- Monitoring critical dates is imperative, and enterprise time-tracking software—usually Web-based for ease of use—has become a necessity for larger projects, multi-project environments and dispersed project teams.[24]

- The project manager must be competent and experienced. Benefits of having a good project manager include reduced project expense, higher morale, and quicker time to market. The skills most executives cite as desirable in a project manager are technology and business knowledge, negotiation, good communications (including writing ability), organization, diplomacy, and time management. Understanding the business is more important than understanding technology. They must be able to define requirements, estimate resources, and schedule their delivery, budget and manage costs, motivate teams, resolve conflicts, negotiate external resources, manage contracts, assess and reduce risks, and adhere to a standard methodology and quality processes. Such project managers are not accidental: they are grown in an environment that trains, mentors, and rewards them based on performance in projects.

- Best-in-class enterprises have a process of due diligence to turn ideas into projects, using a standard checklist, addressing such issues as sponsorship, project plan, roles and responsibilities, and finance. Based on this checklist, a project is either given the go ahead, further researched, or rejected.

- Projects should be carried out in a standard, published way, with a project method that sets planning and control standards, review points, the nature and frequency of project management meetings, and change control procedures. Project methods can be short and high-level, but they must be clear and up to date.[25]

Most organizations believe that their solution to problems in managing projects can be found by investing in project management software and/or training. Yet a look back at our accounting systems analogy in the Preface will tell you that software and training alone do not make a sound organizational system for managing the enterprise. While appropriate software and adequately trained personnel are certainly important pieces of the puzzle, these pieces must be implemented within some sort of process framework: and that framework is the project office.

The Challenges of Implementing a Project Office

So many times people will sign up for a project office seminar thinking, *Just tell me how I can set up this administrative structure and I will go deploy a PO.* They appear to believe the project office is a clerical function, or that they can bring a small staff to bear to do administrative functions and *voila!* they have project management. Or, if their think-ing is a bit more advanced, they perceive it as a project controls func-tion—controlling cost, time, and resources within the individual projects. Unfortunately it isn't that simple, because you are dealing with people, you are changing culture, building new processes, creat-ing new approaches, integrating these elements across business units, and coordinating with teams of all sizes, technologies, complexities, and business interests. It's a worthwhile goal but by no means a simple one to achieve.

The project office is a function designed to facilitate the manage-ment of projects on one level and to improve management of the en-tire enterprise via project portfolio management and linking projects to corporate strategy. More than establishing an office and creating reports, it is infusing a cultural change throughout the organization.

Culture Change

It is a tremendous challenge to deploy and effectively apply these systems. Our work is cut out for us on so many fronts—both in system deployment and the educational arena—in order to get the best re-sults from a project office. The complexity and magnitude of the effort of developing, designing, and deploying a full PO is too often under-estimated. Let's look briefly at eight key areas of cultural change that the project office initiation will require. (For a full discussion of chang-ing the corporate culture, see Chapter 10.)

Speed—and Patience

Years ago I studied and worked under Oliver Wight, the guru of Manufacturing Resources Planning and MRP2. He had charted a num-ber of MRP deployments and found that while you could never do one in less than 12 months, if you took much longer than 18 months the failure rates dramatically increased. This pertains to deploying the project management culture throughout the organization. The Standish Group has found the longer the project duration, the greater the chance of failure.[26] Building a project management culture takes time. On the other hand, it is critical to meet clear objectives during deployment of the project office or you risk the possibility of a failed project office project, with the participants losing sight of added value that project management practices can bring.

So the basic premise behind deploying a project office is *move forward quickly*—show results within six months; really begin changing the culture within the first year; and begin showing corporate results within a two-year time frame. But be prepared that it will most likely take anywhere from two to five years to fully deploy a project office.[27] (For a full discussion of how to structure the project office rollout to show immediate benefits, see Chapter 5.)

Leadership from the Bottom Up

Technology organizations are taking these studies that have been conducted by Gartner, Standish, and McKinsey very seriously. They see that their time-to-market is slow compared to either industry average or best-practice companies. They are finding that the only way they can improve quality, improve time-to-market, decrease costs, improve timing, and improve deliverables is to bring a new process to bear—something different from what they have used in the past.

IT processes and failures have been thrown into the spotlight not just because of the research studies but because of high-profile projects like Y2K and the Euro conversion. So there is a tremendous amount of pressure on IT and other technology development projects to improve performance. They feel this pressure internally—but the failure data has also become a whipping stick with which other operational units to punish internal technology organizations. Project performance has become a significant driver for people's careers and even for the existence of some internal IT departments. They must bring the organization to a position where it is actually delivering projects on time and within budget and with the quality that is desired by the customer.

Therefore, unlike most organizational change projects of the past, we typically see the initiative to formalize project management begin on the department level, even on the project level. As technology efforts begin to show results, two things happen: one, all the other business units begin to come into the project teams as stakeholders of the organization, and two, those business units see improved delivery performance on technology projects and ask themselves, *What can we do to improve our own performance? What are they doing right that we can adapt to our own projects?*

As IT brings project management to the organization, it's a grassroots change process quite different from anything traditional companies are used to.

A Systems Thinking Perspective

To effectively deploy project management throughout an organization, all the players must be on board. Everyone from the project team member on up to the executive sponsors of projects must understand what is happening with project management. This translates to an organizational setting in which virtually everyone who is touched by a project is impacted by what happens with the project management initiative. Ultimately this impact sweeps across the entire corporation. That's why effective POs are located at the corporate level, providing data on total corporate funding for projects, the resources utilized across all corporate projects, capital requirements for projects at the corporate level, materials impact, supplies impact, and the procurement chain impacts. To achieve corporate strategic goals, there will be strategic programs that generate strategic projects, and those projects will of necessity reach across multiple divisions of the organization and pull selected resources in to achieve that overall corporate objective. When corporate executives can effectively prioritize projects and make fact-based decisions about initiation, funding, and resources, they will be in a position to apply systems theory to their organization—to optimize the system (corporation) as a whole, rather than just tinkering with the parts (projects and departments). At this point, most corporations haven't yet achieved that level of sophistication.

Enterprise-wide Systems

Taking the need for common corporate data on resource projections as an example, we can see that all of the planning must be accomplished in a common database so that those resource projections can be summarized at the project level, then at the organizational level, on up to the corporate level, in order to understand the impacts of individual projects or new programs on the overall corporate resource pool.

For this to be possible, common systems must be established that integrate data and provide summarized integrated reporting in a timely fashion—not just with regard to resources but also in the areas of capital funding, budgeted expenses, and the like.

At the organizational level, effective, integrated resources management, cost planning, and time tracking require integration with corporate procurement systems, financial systems, time collection systems, and human resources systems. Systems integration at this level of complexity requires detailed specifications development and planning of its own accord.

Knowledge Management

A whole new set of procedures and standards need to be established along with a common mechanism for storing and sharing that information. Along with this goes the training process and data collection routine that must be established to get information into this database, before knowledge transfer can take place.

One difficulty organizations face is that project management is a fairly new discipline in terms of the knowledge base and standards that exist to support practitioners. What standards exist can be found in *A Guide to the Project Management Body of Knowledge (PMBOK® Guide)*[28], but these are limited primarily to the management of individual projects, not of an entire project-based organization. Few organizations have kept a history of lessons learned on projects done in-house or possess standards for data collection of this kind. So most organizations are very new to this business of project management and are unable to rapidly develop this complex, integrated system that is necessary for accurate data collection and reporting.

Managers and project managers and program managers will make good decisions with good data. Without good data, decisions are going to be very poor: the organization is faced with a very complex integrated system and process, but very little knowledge about how to deploy it. That's why the Gartner Group recommends incorporating a contractor or consultant in the implementation strategy. It's necessary to get folks in who have actually done systems deployment in the past so that the probability of success has to be much higher.[29]

Learning—and Learned—Project Organizations

If your company has a system in place for educating, mentoring, and evaluating project personnel, you are in the minority. When I work with customers, I often ask who is currently engaged as a project manager, project leader, team member, project support staff, and other key positions. I get many positive responses. But when I ask how many have a college or university degree in project management, only a few respond positively—and those individuals usually have a master's certificate in project management. The skill set and knowledge you need to effectively deploy a project management initiative rivals the knowledge set of an MBA in terms of complexity and integration. Yet we ask project teams and project managers to effectively execute without having the requisite education or, in many cases, experience to deploy these very complex systems and processes. Learning has to take place enterprise-wide for the project office to be most effective.

Open Communication

Communication—a sticky issue even within project teams—must now become free-flowing not just within but between projects and up and down the organizational levels. Why is this so important? Because 80% of what we call the "art" of project management is just communication and all the traits that good communicators display: trust, integrity and honesty. We spend a great deal of time teaching the science of project management—how to develop project plans, how to do Gantt charts and WBSs and estimating and so forth—but these things are actually fairly straightforward. The real challenge comes in blending the art of project management into the science.

Through new channels of communication set up by the project office, it will become possible for the entire organizational culture, from chief executives all the way through project teams to communicate in a common language and work together to understand the issues surrounding how projects are faring and how the issues on one project affect other projects and, ultimately, the organization.

The Objective: Results, and Fast

All this costs money, so at the end of the day, it is absolutely essential that an organization is able to quantify the value that project management brings. What does success look like? How will you know when you have arrived? Dr J. Davidson Frame, PMP, of the University of Management and Technology in Washington, D.C. has performed research[30] that identifies the "traits of competence" exhibited by successful organizations:

- Top management understands project management basics

- Activity-based costing systems are in place

- Effective order processing systems are in place

- Effective training programs are in place

- Up-to-date tools are provided for staff

- Clear project management systems and processes have been established.

In addition, a research study sponsored by PMI and the University of California at Berkeley identified the following organizational benefits:

- Improved coordination of inter-group activities

- Enhanced goal focus on the part of employees

- Elimination of redundant or duplicate functions

- Centralization of expertise

- A standardized management approach.[31]

The key question is how can the initiative show results fast enough to avoid top management loss of interest? Dianne Bridges, PMP, writes that there are two ways to demonstrate the immediate value of the project office: through short-term initiatives and project mentoring.[32] The short-term initiatives provide solutions to immediate concerns and take care of issues surfaced by key stakeholders. These are items that can be implemented quickly while at the same time they take care of organizational top-priority concerns. Examples include support for new projects and projects in need; an inventory of projects (new product development, information technology, business enhancements, etc); summary reports and metrics; informal training lunches; project planning or project control workshops; templates.

In conjunction with the short-term initiatives, project mentoring is an excellent way to provide immediate project management value to projects that are in the initial start-up phase or are in need of support, without waiting for the implementation of formal training programs or process roll-outs.

AT THIS WRITING, the Center for Business Practices is engaged in a research project that we hope will help to further quantify the benefits of project management, and this is only one of many initiatives under way throughout the profession. Already the existing research tells us that without proper project management, failure is in the forecast. The implementation of a project office takes the successes of managing projects properly a step further by standardizing project management throughout an organization—one of the hallmarks of a mature project management capability.

Executive Tipsheet

Projects are:

- Temporary endeavors undertaken to create a unique product or service[33]

- Activities organized to deliver something of value to a customer (and therefore to your organization)

- The building blocks in the design and execution of your organization's strategies.

Project management is:

- The application of knowledge, skills, tools, and techniques to project activities in order to meet or exceed stakeholder needs and expectations of a project. Meeting or exceeding stakeholder needs and expectations invariably involves balancing competing demands.[34] These demands include scope, time, quality, and cost; identified requirements (needs); and unidentified requirements (expectations).

Management by projects or strategic project management is:

- A system that integrates all the project activity within an organization and links it to organization-wide strategies, priorities, and resource pools. The most common infrastructure to support management by projects is the project office.

What value can an organization expect to derive from implementing a project office?

- Research shows that establishing a project office is predictive of success in IT projects: the Gartner Group states that companies with a PO will experience half the delayed and cancelled projects as compared to companies without a PO.

What challenges will the organization face?

- Changes in organizational culture including new information systems, altered communications channels, and new performance measurement strategies.

Talking Points

Make points by citing the research covered in this chapter:

1. The Gartner Group has published the following Strategic Planning Assumptions:

- Through 2004, IS organizations that establish enterprise standards for project management, including a project office with suitable governance, will experience half the major project cost overruns, delays and cancellations of those that fail to do so.

- Through 2004, IS organizations with no strategy for blending internal and external resources to achieve "best-in-class" staffing will incur 25% higher labor costs than those that do (0.7 probability).

- Through 2003, organizations using rigorous gating criteria to move projects from the requirements phase to the development phase will save more than 25% in organizational costs for canceled projects.

- Through 2004, without significant changes to its project management processes, a [development] organization of 100 developers can expect to spend more than $10 million on canceled software projects.

- IS organizations that lack stringent risk assessment procedures will continue to cancel more than 20% of [development] projects in the execution phase through 2002. [35]

2. The Standish Group has found that:

- 46% of IT projects come in over budget and overdue, while 28% fail altogether.

- Only 24% of IT projects undertaken by Fortune 500 companies will be completed successfully.

- When failure rates improve, they do so because of "better project management" and the use of "standard infrastructures."

3. Tom Peters has written that "Projects are the nuggets . . . the atoms . . . the basic particles. . . . Take whatever you are working on right now and begin today to shape it into a scintillating project."[36] and "The model for the future is the [project-based] professional services firm [which can] organize in project teams that change shape with regularity. It's a creativity-based world, a talent-based world. That logic is absolutely unstoppable."[37]

Endnotes

1. Francis Webster, "Setting the Stage for a New Profession," *PM Network*, April 1999.
2. Glenn M. Parker, *Handbook of Best Practices for Teams*, Human Resource Development Press, March 1996.
3. Paul Dinsmore, *Winning in Business Through Enterprise Project Management*, AMACOM, 1998.
4. Software Engineering Institute, "Capability Maturity Model for Software Development," 1993.
5. M. Light and T. Berg, "The Project Office: Teams, Processes and Tools," *Gartner Strategic Analysis Report*, 1 August 2000.
6. U.S. Dept of Commerce, www.ecommerce.gov
7. The Standish Group, *The Chaos Report*, 1999. See www.standishgroup.com.
8. Robbins-Gioia. 1999. See www.pmblvd.com.
9. Associated Press wire release, Feb. 20, 2000. See also www.bigdig.com.
10. Andrew Osterland, CFO, April 2000.

11. Jim Johnson "Turning CHAOS into SUCCESS," *Software*, Dec. 1999.

12. Berg, op. cit.

13. Preston Smith and Donald Reinertsen, *Developing Products in Half the Time*, Van Nostrand Reinhold, 1991.

14. Brian Dumaine, "How Managers Can Succeed Through Speed," *Fortune*, Feb. 13, 1989. Charles House and Raymond L. Price, "The Return Map: Tracking Product Teams," *Harvard Business Review*, Jan.-Feb. 1991.

15. Johnson, op. cit.

16. Lauren Gibbons Paul, "Turning Failure into Success: Maintain momentum," *Network World*, Nov. 22, 1999.

17. Richard W. Bailey, II, "Six Steps to Project Recovery," *PM Network*, May 2000.

18. Paul, op. cit.

19. J. Roberts and J. Furlonger, "Successful IS Project Management," Gartner Group, April 18, 2000.

20. C. Natale, "IT Project Management: Do Not Lose Track of Time," Gartner Group, May 9, 2000.

21. Bailey, op. cit.

22. Paul, op. cit.

23. Bailey, op. cit.

24. Natale, op. cit.

25. Furlonger, op. cit.

26. Johnson, op. cit.

27. Dianne Bridges and Kent Crawford, "How to Startup and Rollout a Project Office," *Proceedings of the PMI Annual Seminars and Symposium*, PMI, 2000.

28. PMI Standards Committee, *A Guide to the Project Management Body of Knowledge*, PMI, 1996.

29. Furlonger, op. cit.

30. J. Davidson Frame, "Understanding the New Project Management," Presentation to Project World, Washington, DC, Aug. 7, 1996.

31. C.W. Ibbs and Young-Hoon Kwak, "Benchmarking Project Management Organizations," *PM Network*, Feb. 1998:49-53.

32. Bridges, op. cit.

33. PMI, op. cit.

34. PMI, op. cit.

35. Berg, op. cit.

36. Tom Peters, *Circle of Innovation*, Knopf, 1997.

37. Tom Peters, quoted in "Passion Beats Planning ... ,"Jeannette Cabanis, *PM Network*, Sept. 1998.

Chapter 2

The Starting Gate: Assessing Your Current Condition

H OW MANY PROJECTS ARE UNDER way right now in your organization? How many people do you have with project management skills and knowledge? How is that competence documented? Is there a formal career path established for them? What are the project management needs of all your business units and departments—not just IT and the other project-oriented ones, but all of them—and what specific skills are they most in need of?

If this barrage of questions elicits some head-scratching, don't feel bad. Joel Koppelman, CEO of project-management software vendor Primavera, estimates that very few companies can even answer the first one. In fact, documentation of project activity is so poor in most organizations that they don't even realize that most of their value-added is generated by the project engine.

Thus, like any process improvement initiative, the drive toward a project office must begin with assessing your current condition—establishing a baseline. While no industry standard yet exists for baselining the capabilities of an organization's project management functions, several models exist designed to measure project management maturity, most based on the IT-industry standard Software Engineering Institute Capability Maturity Model for Software Development. Let's look at how one model, the one developed and used in the field by my own firm, and discuss how maturity modeling assists the organization in answering the questions, *How are we doing? And do we need a project office?*

Maturity and the Project Office

Maturity modeling for project management is a huge topic, one which has consumed a great deal of energy by many skilled and thoughtful project management practitioners for the past several years. So much is involved in determining all aspects of a fully mature project office that what follows should be regarded as no more than a quick study of the subject.

A Maturing Profession

Project management is known as the "accidental profession." How many project managers can actually say they planned to be a project manager when they were in grade school, or even college? Not many. Chances are that your first project management job involved rescuing some undertaking that was out of control. It was probably not even called a project, and you may have been referred to as a troubleshooter. If you were successful in pulling that first endeavor back from the brink of disaster, you were rewarded with—you guessed it—another opportunity to excel. Before long, other people began to ask you about your keys to success. This process was repeated across the nation and around the world. As time went on, the literature began to reflect this troubleshooting effort as project management.

In his most recent book, project management expert Paul Dinsmore describes the discipline[1] as one that "grew up from the grassroots" in most organizations, rather than being imposed from above. For this reason, its role, benefits, and productivity have been hard to assess. Project management in many firms has been outside the mainstream of measurement and reward systems. Now that research has shown that it is an important factor in competitive success, companies are scrambling to figure out how to make the best of this productive resource.

Here's a quick overview of the thought process behind maturity modeling.

Defining Maturity and Capability

Thanks to a decade of work by the SEI, sponsored by Carnegie Mellon University, we have a much better understanding today of the areas of expertise necessary in order for an organization to consistently produce quality software products. Since it describes a project-driven business, the software model provides project management with a handy springboard to begin constructing a set of process measures for the discipline. Just as a recap, SEI sets five levels of capability (see Appendix A, Figure A.1)—which they define as:

1. *Initial.* The software process is ad hoc and occasionally even chaotic. Few processes are defined, and success depends on individual heroics.

2. *Repeatable.* Basic project management processes are established to track cost, schedule, and functionality. The necessary process discipline is in place to repeat earlier successes.

3. *Defined.* The software process for both management and engineering activities is documented, standardized, and integrated into a standard software process for the organization. All projects use an approved, tailored version of this standard process for developing and maintaining software.

4. *Managed.* Detailed measures of the software process and product quality are collected. Both the software process and products are quantitatively understood and controlled.

5. *Optimizing.* Continuous process improvement is enabled by quantitative feedback from the process and from piloting innovative ideas and technologies.

From experience as a project consultant, I can verify that the lower the level of maturity, the greater the failure rate on projects. Project management must exist as a repeatable, quantifiable process, found in levels three and above of the maturity model, for there to be any real chance of consistently bringing in projects on time, within budget, and according to customer expectations. The project management methodology must make the measurement of scope, quality, and cost a natural part of running projects. Perhaps most important, the processes must be *institutionalized*, that is, supported by upper management of the organization and applied uniformly throughout the organization—most easily done under the auspices of a project office. Thus the measurement of project management maturity "plugs in" to other product development and service delivery process maturity models, whether for software or systems or any other development effort we would care to document and measure.

The challenge that has faced project management practitioners has been to develop a maturity model that is appropriate for all industries, whether it be telecommunications, insurance, banking, finance, or any of the other industries in which project management is applied.

The Role of Metrics. One of the ways we gauge the maturity of, for example, our children, is with numbers: we measure height, weight, SAT scores, and the like. But as any parent knows, these numbers barely scratch the surface. So while gathering metrics to describe the project process is useful, qualitative research into how the people side of the organization functions can be just as important to the organizational assessment phase of determining maturity. Luckily, the PM Maturity Model and assessment tool described in this chapter covers both quantitative and qualitative measures of success.

What are some typical quantitative metrics used to assess project management maturity? For the answer to that question we go back to the project "triple constraints" of time, cost, and technical aspects/ scope. A less mature organization would consistently miss scheduled milestones and completion dates. This would show up quantitatively as large schedule variances, rescheduled shipments, missed product introductions, and customer complaints. Likewise, cost performance would be poor. This would surface as large cost variances, overruns, requests for additional funds, and shrinking profit margins. And on the technical aspects/scope side, the two primary measures most frequently associated with lack of process are runaway scope growth and low customer satisfaction. All these are easy to spot during even a cursory audit of project performance within a single project, a division, or the entire organization.

Taking metrics to the project office level, the scope broadens. The basic functions of a project office, such as methodology development, providing expertise to the organization, facilitating project planning sessions, and helping define the corporate software standards, are used to measure effectiveness. A simple yes/no checklist can be used in some cases. For example, does a project management methodology exist? Yes or no? If the answer is yes, you are at least thinking about level two maturity. The next question would be whether the methodology is mandatory or voluntary. If it's mandatory, you may be near level three maturity. If it is voluntary, obviously project performance will be spotty across the organization, indicating a less-mature project office. Another example is the level of training and development of project managers. Has the project office established a training curriculum for project managers? Yes or no? Does it lead to professional certification? And for a final measure of the effectiveness of the training program, has project schedule, cost, and technical performance improved as a result of the training? Obviously for some of these metrics a sophisticated assessment tool is not needed. But for a comprehensive assessment of project management maturity, a systematic examination of the practice should be undertaken. More on this later (see Chapter 5).

Be careful that you do not attempt to define organizational maturity and capability in terms of financial and other numerical metrics only, as this may give an unbalanced picture. Numbers can only reflect what has already happened—not why it happened and not what is possible for the future.

On the qualitative side of the ledger, a company may want to develop metrics to gauge employee satisfaction, customer satisfaction, and stakeholder value. Creating value to stakeholders within and outside of the organization is key to organizational success. Financial measures alone do not present a clear picture of value. They are too unreliable as either a clear gauge of success or a clear picture of the value. Companies that stress shareholder, customers, and employees outperform firms that do not.[2]

Metrics development and tracking is a big subject: we'll come back to it in subsequent chapters when we discuss goal-setting (Chapter 5) and performance measurement (Chapter 9). For now, the important thing to focus your attention on is the fact that doing maturity assessment is a combination of quantitative and qualitative research and, as such, it requires a fairly labor-intensive period of questioning, interviewing, and evaluating people's responses. If the organization were mature enough to have readily available project metrics adequate to describe process maturity, well, you probably would not be reading this book.

One Example of a Maturity Model. *The Amercan Heritage Dictionary* defines *mature* as "having reached full natural growth or development" or "to bring to full development." To define and measure maturity in project management we must therefore specify levels of growth and development in the requisite skills. Thus the identification of project manager skills and competencies must be an integral part of any effort to measure the maturity of the processes within which he or she functions. Obviously, this is a complex undertaking.

Table 2.1 Project Management Process Groups

- **Initiating:** Tasks and activities that conceptualize and/or authorize the project or phase.
- **Planning:** Tasks and activities that define and refine objectives and select the best of the alternative courses of action to attain the objectives that the project was undertaken to address.
- **Executing:** Tasks and activities that coordinate people and other resources to carry out the plan.
- **Controlling:** Tasks and activities that ensure that project objectives are met by monitoring and measuring progress regularly to identify variances from plan so that corrective action can be taken if necessary.
- **Closing:** Tasks and activities that formalize the acceptance of the project or phase and bring it to an orderly end.

Source: Adapted from *A Guide to the Project Management Body of Knowledge*, Project Management Institute, 2000.

The Project Management Maturity Model uses as a starting point and underlying structure the nine knowledge areas of the Project Management Institute's *Guide to the Project Management Body of Knowledge* (1996). Why? Because the *PMBOK® Guide* contains two frames of reference for addressing the whole project management body of knowledge:

- *PM Processes.* This approach looks at the management of projects as a set of five tightly integrated, repeatable processes (see Table 2.1 for a full description of these). These processes can be decomposed into a set of Activities and Tasks necessary to successfully manage a project. This hierarchy of processes and activities forms the basis for a project management methodology.

- *PM Knowledge Areas.* This approach looks at the management of projects as a set of eight interwoven sets of skills/expertise, with a ninth set (Integration Management) which binds them all to-

Table 2.2 The Nine Organizational Knowledge Areas

Project Integration Management: How well are the various project processes coordinated? Is there a smooth process for making tradeoffs among competing objectives and alternatives? Is the work of the project integrated with the ongoing operations of the performing organization?

Scope Management: Are processes in place to ensure that the project includes all the work required to complete the project successfully? Scope management is primarily concerned with defining what is and isn't included in the project work.

Cost Management: Are processes in place to ensure that the project is completed within the allowed budget? Processes for resource planning, cost estimating, and cost control fall within this knowledge area.

Time Management: Are processes in place to make sure the project is completed on time? This includes the estimation and scheduling of project activities.

Quality Management: Are processes in place to ensure that the project meets the requirements or satisfies the needs for which it was undertaken? This includes quality policy, assurance, and control.

Human Resource Management: Are processes in place to make the most effective use of all the people involved in the project—not only team members but sponsors, customers, and other stakeholders? This includes identifying, documenting, and assigning roles and responsibilities as well as developing individual and team competencies to enhance performance.

Communications Management: Are processes in place for timely and appropriate management of project information? Determining communication needs, distributing information, establishing reporting mechanisms fall within this knowledge area.

Risk Management: Are processes in place for the systematic identification, analysis, and mitigation or other response to project risks? Both quantitative and qualitative risk analysis are included.

Procurement Management: Are processes in place for planning the solicitation and procurement of goods and services? For the proper management of the associated contracts?

Source: Adapted from *A Guide to the Project Management Body of Knowledge,* Project Management Institute, 2000.

Figure 2.1 Mapping CMM to PMMM

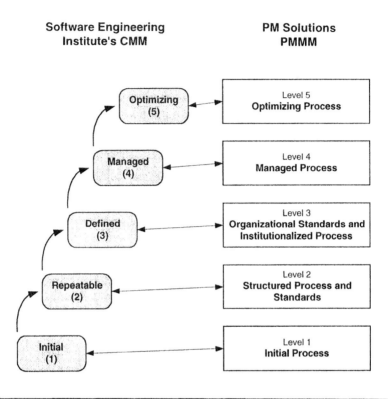

Software Engineering
Institute's CMM

PM Solutions
PMMM

gether. A project manager needs to wear each of these nine "hats" at some time throughout the project and needs knowledge/expertise in all areas—almost as if she or he is nine different virtual people.

It is this second, knowledge-area approach, focusing on knowledge, skills, and expertise, in which the real engine of increasing process maturity lies. In other words, as the project managers within an organization increase their expertise, knowledge, and skills in each of these areas, the organization overall becomes more *mature* in its practice of project management (see Table 2.2 for a breakdown of these knowledge areas).

The Project Management Maturity Model (PMMM) decomposes the knowledge areas into their major areas of focus (which we will call Components) and then defines the levels of project management maturity within each Component. Since the industry-standard Software Engineering Institute's Capability Maturity Model (SEI CMM) for software development is generally used as a guide in the creation of a maturity model, the PMMM mirrors the SEI model's five-level structure (see Appendix A).

SEI's CMM says: "Maturity Levels 2 through 5 can be characterized through the activities performed by the organization to establish or improve the software process, by activities performed on each project, and by the resulting process capability across projects."[3]

This project-oriented language leads one to infer that direct connections between the CMM and project management maturity can be mapped. SEI goes on to say: "Software process improvement occurs within the context of the organization's strategic plans and business objectives, its organizational structure, the technologies in use, its social culture, and its management system."[4]

In our own work with maturity modeling, we have mapped the levels of the CMM to our model for project management maturity, which we call the PMMM, as shown in Figure 2.1.

Cut to the chase. In practical terms, what all this means is that when an organization wants to improve project management processes, it can start by baselining what exists. It then compares that baseline to an existing maturity model to determine where the organization stands in terms of generally accepted process standards in the project management discipline.

In order to create that baseline study, you break your organization's processes down into knowledge areas, those knowledge areas into components, and each component into a list of tasks, activities and characteristics about which you can ask a series of simple, practical questions (see Table 2.3 for a sample of these questions broken out for two knowledge areas: scope and time management). The advantage of using an existing standard, such as the PMMM, is that it incorporates thousands of hours of research, years of project office deployment experience, and countless lessons learned. Now, let's walk through, in simplified form, the steps of baselining your organization's process maturity.

Table 2.3 Examples of Assessment Considerations

SCOPE MANAGEMENT

The overall purpose of scope management is to ensure that the project includes all the work required, and only the work required, to complete the project successfully.

Requirements Definition (Business)

1. The organization uses a standard documented process of gathering and documenting business requirements, which includes obtaining user sign-off of those requirements.

2. The business requirements serve as the basis of project estimation activities (schedule, budget, and other resources).

Requirements Definition (Technical)

3. The organization uses a standard documented process to translate business requirements into technical requirements.

Deliverables Identification

4. The project has developed a product breakdown structure (PBS) which is integrated into the project's work breakdown structure (WBS).

5. All project deliverables are identified in coordination with client and quantified in terms that are measurable.

6. All project management products, such as status reports and quality control reports, are included in the product breakdown structure.

Scope Definition

7. The organization has a standard documented process, including templates, for developing a project charter. The process includes all stakeholders and is used for all projects.

8. Project scope is monitored as part of the project management activity, with deviations being anticipated, documented, and addressed through the change control process/WBS.

9. The project has a work breakdown structure, with interim milestones and schedules identified that is of sufficient detail to support project planning and control.

Scope Change Control

10. The organization uses a defined documented process, which includes all stakeholders and the project plan, to manage scope change. The process defines the forms and approvals that must be obtained prior to the changing of a project's scope.

Table 2.3 (continued)

TIME MANAGEMENT

The overall purpose of time management is to develop the project schedule, manage to that schedule, and ensure the project completes within the approved timeframe.

Activity Definition

1. All work on the project (business, technical, and management) is included in the project work breakdown structure.

2. Schedule constraints driven by customer, technology, supplier, resource availability, or management requirements are identified and clearly documented.

Activity Sequencing

3. Dependencies between activities and between products are clearly identified.

4. Organizational standards and templates are used to identify activities, products, and their dependencies.

Schedule Development

5. The project schedule, including all identified constraints, is developed based upon the initial work breakdown structure.

6. The project schedule is resource loaded and resource leveled. Conflicts are identified, addressed, and resolved.

Schedule Control

7. A schedule baseline is used to measure and report variances between planned and actual progress.

8. The project manager maintains the project schedule on a periodic basis, capturing actual hours and progress metrics for each activity.

Schedule Integration

9. All project components and sub-components (e.g., software development, hardware procurement, and sub-contractor activities) are integrated into the project schedule.

10. The project schedule is integrated into a higher-level schedule (program or organizational) so that the impact of schedule change can be fully assessed.

Pre-Assessment Evaluation

Before making a commitment to engage in a formal project management maturity assessment, your organization should endeavor to gauge its readiness for the process. This is important because it helps establish a baseline for both the organization and any third party from whom you might request assistance in the assessment process. It also sets the stage for determining what you want to receive from an assessment and how you plan to use the information to benefit the organization and your project management efforts.

For some this might be an extensive and lengthy process, for others only an update of what has been documented and tracked. Here are some questions to consider:

- As an organization, what knowledge about project management do we possess?

- How was this knowledge acquired?

- What individuals or group of individuals possess this knowledge?

- What is our "basic" approach to organizing, planning and managing projects?

- How successful do we think we have been?

- What factors or information form the basis the measure of success?

- What formal internal assessments have been conducted within the organization?

- Who conducted the assessment?

- What was the focus and content of the assessment?

- What were the conclusions and recommendations?

- Was any action taken based upon the recommendations? Describe.

- What support for project management exists within the organizations (both business and IT)? Determine and document the level of support among senior executives, mid-level management, project managers, and technical staff.

- How does the executive level view the success of current project management practices? What do they say they want changed? In what timeframe?

- Do you believe you will receive support (in terms of people and funding) for entering into a formal assessment process and implementing changes as a result of the assessment and recommendations?

- What risks are associated with the assessment process and implementation of changes?

- What benefits are anticipated from the assessment process?

- Do you want to share any of the internal assessment information with a third party? What information? What are the potential risks of sharing that information—and the risks of *not* sharing it? Are there any contractual considerations? For example, your firm may have proprietary rights in data that must be protected. Suitable contract provisions must be written protecting those rights if you plan to involve consultants or other contractors.

Even though you might consider internal assessment information proprietary in nature, it would be worthwhile to evaluate the risks and benefits of sharing or not sharing internal assessment information before entering into any discussions with a third party about performing an assessment. The advance preparation will help you hit the ground running when and if you do decide to bring in a consultant. Companies sometimes hamstring themselves—in the effort to avoid disclosing too much to an outside party, they disclose too little and wind up wasting time and money working with consultants who don't have the information they need to do a good job. Eventually, you will have to treat consultants doing the assessment as members of the organization and provide full disclosure. Otherwise, the assessment will not be accurate and you will have wasted time and money in the process.

And while the pre-assessment can easily be done in-house, doing a serious assessment of the maturity of your project management processes really requires the skills of an experienced assessor. The assessor should be a certified Project Management Professional, and must understand project initiation, planning, execution, control, and the integration of all knowledge areas in the practice of project management. Further, he or she must be able to accurately assess your level of development and maturity in all these processes and areas. The evaluator must be articulate in writing a development plan for the organization and project office, clearly stating explicit steps that need to be taken to achieve higher levels of maturity. And he or she must have a grasp of the business and cultural issues within the organization.

Baseline Maturity Assessment

Any assessment of a company's or a department's processes—not just project management processes, but any processes—must begin with a firm understanding of the organization's business goals. Without this kind of high-level roadmap, any changes to processes or procedures are done in the dark. Unfortunately, as the Balanced Scorecard Collaborative has found in the course of their research into strategic planning, the majority of companies do very poorly at aligning business activities to corporate strategy. In fact, according to their research, 80-90% of strategies set by top management never come to fruition, in part because they are not communicated with the employees who carry it out and because the company's projects, measurements, and reward system are not aligned with the strategies.[5] If you are considering implementing a project office—or any major organizational change—you would do well to first inspect the alignment of corporate strategy to the daily activities of employees. Do they have a firm understanding of the organization's business goals? (For a full discussion of aligning corporate strategy with project activities, see Chapter 9: The Strategic Project Office.)

Once it is clear what business objectives the organization is striving toward, the assessment can proceed. We've found that a two-step assessment process incorporating questionnaires and interviews—a process we call a PM HealthCheck[SM]—serves very well to uncover an organization's strengths and weaknesses. This process is briefly described here.

PM HealthCheck—Understanding an Organization's Project Management Maturity

PM Solutions' PM Assessment starts with an understanding of an organization's business goals. We use the unique assessment tool, PM

HealthCheck, to understand organizational strengths and identify areas for improvement. The result of the PM Assessment is analysis, documentation, and a project management improvement plan.

The PM HealthCheck incorporates feedback from all stakeholders in the project management process. It is a two-step process of questionnaires and interviews designed to maximize the amount of information and minimize the time commitment of people within the organization.

The analysis and findings are mapped against the PM Solutions PM Maturity Model matrix, which illustrates current positioning and the steps necessary to reach project management maturity. It is also used for measuring the progress of the organization's project management initiative.

Deliverables. Deliverables from a project management assessment are:

- PM assessment report

- Project management improvement plan.

The PM Assessment report incorporates goals and information gathered from the PM HealthCheck. The information is mapped against the PM Maturity Model continuum, which helps identify gaps and a path for improvement.

The project management improvement plan is a series of action steps and activities needed to close the gap and achieve the organization's desired level of project management maturity. When building the plan, we keep the following principles in mind:

- Build on strengths

- Augment with best practices

- Teach and apply new skills

- Provide appropriate support structure

- Keep it simple

- Integrate back into the organization

- Add value quickly.

Participants. The PM Assessment is led by a senior member of the analysis team. Input from all stakeholders is essential to an accurate assessment. Questionnaires are given out ahead of time and follow-up interviews are scheduled in groups to maximize information and minimize the time commitment of client employees. The PM Assessment requires input from:

- Executive management
- Customers/users
- Key middle managers
- Project managers
- Resource/functional managers
- Project office director(s)
- Team leaders
- Project team members
- Project support staff
- Technical and other support staff.

The effectiveness of the PM Assessment hinges on getting candid input from representatives of all areas that are involved in the project. PM Solutions will work with the client in initial meetings to identify the appropriate individuals and schedule their time efficiently.

Research. The PM HealthCheck questionnaire has nine sections, based on the Project Management Institute's *A Guide to the Project Management Body of Knowledge (PMBOK® Guide)* best practice principles:

- Project scope management
- Project time management
- Project human resource management
- Project communication management
- Project risk management
- Project quality management

- Project cost management

- Project procurement management

- Project integration management

Findings and the Path Forward. Client goals and current capabilities are mapped against the PM Maturity Model. The PM Assessment report presents the findings of the PM HealthCheck and the gap between current capabilities and goals. The gap provides the starting point for building the project management improvement plan.

The PM Assessment and project management improvement plan establish the direction for implementing strategic project management in the organization.

Artifacts to be Reviewed as Part of an Assessment. These items are selected from a set of projects that represent the full range and complexity of organizational initiatives throughout the enterprise:

- Project Charter. A document issued by senior management, which authorizes the project manager to use corporate resources to fulfill the purpose of the project

- Statement of Work. A document describing the expected outcome of the project, including the deliverables to be produced.

- Success Criteria. A document describing the factors by which project success will be measured. These could include schedule and budget performance, ROIs to be achieved when developed product is deployed, and a measure of user satisfaction.

- Project Organization Chart. A pictorial representation of the project team structure. It should include position titles and names of individuals assigned to those positions. It should also identify all user and support personnel. Another related document is the Responsibility Matrix, a matrix indicating who on the project team is responsible for what and job descriptions for each position on the project team.

- Corporate Organization Chart. A pictorial representation of the corporate structure. It should include position titles and names of individuals assigned to those positions.

- Work Breakdown Structure. A hierarchical representation of all work to be performed as part of the project. The document should also include the WBS dictionary, with definitions of each work element.

- Product Breakdown Structure. A hierarchical representation of the products to be produced by the project.

- Estimating Standards. The estimating guidelines and actual data used by the project management team to estimate the level of effort needed to complete the project. The standards should identify the type of estimation performed (i.e., lines of code, function point analysis, size of documentation) and any tools used in the estimation process.

- Project Schedule, Including Baselines. The documentation that informs all concerned parties when various project activities will begin and end. The schedule should identify who is doing what work and the dependencies within the activities.

- Weekly Time/Activity Status Reports. The data used by the project management team to status the project.

- Last Six Internal Project Status Reports, including Project Variance Reports. Any reports produced for distribution internally within the project team that communicate project status.

- Last Six External Project Status Reports. Any reports produced for distribution external to the project team that communicate project status.

- Project Financial Reports, Including Budget Baselines. The data used by the project management team to status the project's finances.

- Project Plan, Including Cost and Schedule Management Plans. The document(s) that identifies how the project will be managed and what the final product developed will be. This document is usually developed during the project planning activities. It should include a detailed description of the deliverables sign-off process. It should also include a discussion of how the project will be closed down upon completion of all deliverables or upon cancellation. The document is a management document, not a technical document.

- Product/Software Development Life Cycle Documentation. Any documentation supporting the development life cycle for the project. This might include items such as a design document template, guidelines for user documentation, and release notes instructions.

- Project Communications Plan. The document that describes how communications (which includes project status reports) will occur.

- Risk Identification and Mitigation Plan. The document that describes the project risks, their probabilities and the strategies that will be used to mitigate those risks. It should also describe how risks are identified and quantified on the project.

- Requirements Management Plan. The document that describes how requirements will be defined and managed throughout the project's life cycle.

- Quality Assurance Plan. The document that describes how the corporation will evaluate the project's performance to ensure that the project will meet corporate quality standards. The quality assurance manager should be identified.

- Quality Management Plan, including Testing Documents. The documents that describe how the project will meet corporate quality standards. The document should include a discussion of all quality control activities including peer reviews and audits. It should identify those resources specifically charged with quality control activities.

- Quality Control Plan. The documents that describe how the project will implement quality control activities including peer reviews and audits. It should identify those resources specifically charged with managing and conducting these activities. As an example in software development, it should include standards to be used in the activities, including forms, coding standards, definitions of defects, and severity codes, plus any reporting standards applicable.

- Change Control Plan. The document that describes how changes to the project's scope will be managed. The make-up of the change control board, including how often it convenes, should be discussed in the plan.

- Change Requests and Log. The documents used in the project's change control process.

- Peer Review Reports. Minutes and notes from peer review sessions.

- Action Items Tracking Documents. The documents used to track action items for the project.

- Project Office Charter. The document that describes the roles and contributions of the project office.

- Sub-Contractor Contracts. The legally binding document describing the statement of work, including terms and conditions, applicable to sub-contractors used on the project.

- Project Team Training Plan. The document describing any training to be provided by the project to team members.

- Lessons Learned Reports. Any post mortems that have been performed on the project to date.

- Miscellaneous Project Documentation. This umbrella category includes the following artifacts: project status meeting agenda, project meeting minutes, kick-off meeting agenda and minutes.

- Time Reporting System SOP and Timecard Data. The documentation that describes how time charged to a job is recorded and used to report project status. Timecard data should be reviewed to determine how actuals have been used to modify estimating standards.

- Visibility (War) Room and Procedures. Any documentation supporting the project's visibility room, if one exists.

Interview Checklists. Once the artifacts are gathered, interviews begin, using comprehensive checklists for each knowledge area. Upon completion of a review of the artifacts and compilation of interview data, a reasonably accurate picture of the organization's current condition emerges. But the assessment in and of itself is just the beginning. The assessment report points you toward an understanding of your maturity level. Fully assessing maturity is a far more complex proposition than most companies who are just looking to launch a project management initiative fully realize. What the assessment does, in a fairly quick manner, is indicate where the immediate problems are and generate a hit list of issues that can be addressed to immediately improve the project management processes.

Deliverables and Results. The deliverables of an assessment effort such as PM HealthCheck include the assessment report, detailing the quantitative and qualitative results of the survey, and the project management improvement plan. These documents include a summary of the conditions, strengths and weaknesses within the organization and recommendations for improvement, along with a plan for how to proceed with these improvements. Examples of a comprehensive PM Assessment report and project management improvement plan can be found in Appendix B.

It is up to senior management to choose which level of maturity is desired and how much of the improvement plan to implement. Naturally, the more comprehensive the effort, the greater the cost and time required for implementation.

Sometimes after completing an assessment and reading the improvement plan, an organization is unwilling to devote the time and resources necessary to reach project management maturity Level 5. To progress from Level 1 or 2 to Level 5 will divert scarce resources and management attention away from the primary business objectives. For this reason, implementation plans must be tailored to fit the amount of change the organization is ready to accept, which is usually something less than what it would take to leapfrog to the highest maturity level. And, in fact, it may not make sense to attempt such an effort in the short term. It's important to keep your eye on the prize, and the prize is better-run projects and more repeatable processes—not a plaque with a certain maturity model level engraved on it. The modeling process is merely a tool that allows us to work toward the end of improving processes and thereby improving productivity and, ultimately, profitability.

41

Identification of Issues and Risks

Now that you have done the assessment and better understand the maturity model itself, you are prepared to look at the key issues and risks that the organization is facing. In order to move forward with a project management improvement plan, what issues will have to be dealt with? What risk events may occur that could derail the effort? While many issues and risks will have been identified in the project management improvement plan, the task now is deciding how to deal with these issues in such a way that will ensure a smooth transition to full-scale implementation of project management. Let's look at a case study—The Money Super Market, Ltd. Case—to reinforce some of these issues. Read the case in Table 2.4, then refer to Table 2.5 for a list of implementation issues from a meeting convened for issue identification.

We have found in working with a number of customers that the same issues found in our case study arise in many organizations. The important thing at this point is to invite participation of all stakeholders in the change process, and to conduct the meeting in such a way as to ensure the free flow of ideas. You might consider using your assessment consultant for this purpose to remove any bias that might creep in from the stakeholders. See Table 2.6 for a few helpful tips on facilitating issues identification meetings.

Keep in mind that the issues list doesn't die once implementation of the recommendations to improve project management practices begins. Once your implementation plan is developed you will want to backtrack and do a "sanity check" against the issues list to ensure that the plan has adequately covered all the issues identified in this brainstorming session. If the issues have not been adequately addressed in the implementation plan, the choice may be made to replan or to table the issue for the time being. The issues list is both a planning tool and a quality check.

Gap Analysis

A gap analysis is simply a tool to identify the gaps between the desired level of maturity and current capability—basically a statement of where the organization is versus where the organization desires to be. The gap analysis helps the organization define a path forward. For each organizational entity shown in the gap analysis chart, present and desired future functions are identified. Key stakeholders in the

---

Table 2.4 Case Study: Money Super Market, Ltd.

Background

The Money Super Market, Ltd. (MSM) is a large financial institution that was founded in the early 1950s. MSM revenues grew conservatively for 40 years under the direction of its founder, Ross T. Nichols. Under new, aggressive management, since the founder's death in 1989, MSM has undergone major changes in business direction as new opportunities developed as a result of deregulation. However, the majority of MSM's growth came mainly from acquisitions in the 1990s.

Although MSM's financial performance in the 1990s was astounding for investors, it took its toll on the infrastructure as costs rose at a higher rate than revenues. The many acquisitions resulted in duplicative functions and systems. Systems maintenance and enhancement costs consumed 80% of the IT $10 million annual budget. In the last few years, investors have grown leery of MSM's ability to sustain its financial performance as aggressive competition erodes its market share.

Today, only 20% of the IT budget can be devoted to supporting new business opportunities, resulting in lost opportunities and revenue. The business unit managers are very upset with the IT organization. They see the IT organization as providing little or no value to MSM's business. The pressure was intense on the CIO, Mr. Justin Time, to provide more IT support for new business initiatives. Three months ago, he resigned in disgrace.

Current Situation

A new CIO, Mr. I. M. Miracle, has been on board for one month. Mr. Miracle comes from a small but aggressive company, Dollar Deli Inc. (DDI), which uses project management as a competitive edge. Before assuming the position of CIO at DDI, he led major IT projects to successful completion. He gained his Project Management Professional (PMP) certification in 1992. Mr. Miracle is a member of the Project

---

Table 2.4 continued

Management Institute and is a strong believer in project management. During this month, he has discovered the following about the MSM IT organization:

- The MSM IT organization has a very poor reputation within the business units.
- There is no communication among the business units regarding project needs and priorities.
- The business unit managers have been politicking to get the COO to outsource the entire IT operation.
- The IT budget will not be increased this year.
- The IT organization has never completed a project within the triple constraints (budget, time, and specifications).
- MSM needs five new IT projects completed in 2000 to remain competitive.
- The IT organization does not have a project management methodology.
- Only a few IT managers are trained in project management.
- The morale in IT is low because of all the derogatory comments from the business units.
- Most MSM project managers came from other companies and use project management tools and techniques that worked for them in the past.
- There are no project standards in place.
- There is no standard estimating process.
- Project risks are never addressed.
- At least three different project management software products are partially used.
- The MSM IT organization is larger than most organizations of comparable size.
- No one in the IT organization knows the total number of projects.
- The IT organization does not track hours or report performance to budget.

organization, including the identified project office director or the owner of the project office process, key sponsors, as well as other stakeholders such as lead project managers who are engaged with active, successful projects should be included in the group that does the gap analysis. Once each gap is identified, a plan of action is formulated that will address the gap. At the completion of the gap analysis, the overall scope of the improvement effort will be known. Taken with the improvement plan, the implementation team can now define the scope, plan the steps necessary to accomplish the scope and objectives, and begin to execute the plan. If that sounds like project management, it is! As we will discuss in the next chapter, implementation of a project management maturity improvement plan, an element of which is the project office, can be undertaken as a project, using basic project management practices, tools, and techniques.

A completed gap analysis chart for the case study organization is shown in Table 2.7. It will give you an idea of the types of input you will receive from this exercise.

In a way, the gap analysis requires the organization to develop a kind of double vision: keeping in constant view the desired longer-term state, the higher level of maturity that is the ultimate goal, while at the same time moving the organization quickly in the short range to an added-value position by improving each of these areas of consideration.

You will be amazed at the energy that is created when the issues, short- and long-term vision, and benefits are on paper and available for all to see. That's why this process needs to be fully documented as part of project office deployment planning. When the implementation team reviews the reports and lists downstream, they will be able to validate that their efforts continue to be directed toward the objectives set early in the assessment and planning phases.

Conclusion

A note of caution: racing up the "stairs" of a model can be counterproductive. Like any other organizational development tool, a maturity model is a tool, a means to an end. As former ABT Vice-President Edward Farrelly once warned, a company must use maturity modeling as a way to meet business goals, not as a goal in itself.[6] And Bob Lewis of Perot Systems Corp. has written[7] that when it comes to an art/science like product development, we must be cautious not to standardize the life—the innovative, creative spirit—out of the orga-

Table 2.5 Sample Issues Identification List

MANAGEMENT	ORGANIZATION	PROCESS/TOOLS
Buy-in from IT department	Diverse culture	No status reporting
Improve scores in PM HealthCheck assessment	Mistrust between departments	No risk analysis
Not budgeted	Infrastructure too large	No cost tracking
Short time frame to show success	Poor communication	No standard methodology
Low morale	Overall change issues	Duplicate tools
No recognition of a problem	No accountability	No standard for estimating
Management turnover	Culture not conducive	No budget tracking
New CIO (too much, too soon)	Bad image (IT)	No standard PM software
No true project portfolio	No business unit support	No quality control
Inappropriate use of resources	Duplicative systems & functions	Improve procurement process
Unclear expectations	No true project manager	Can't incur additional expenses
Too many acquisitions	Resistance to change	Don't address risks
No clear roles	No clear roles	No project standards
Deregulation		
Losing market share		

nization through process measurement that becomes a process straight-jacket. Like any living thing, the organization needs a maturation process that develops what's best in it without stunting its growth.

An Iterative Process

Because simply by assessing organizational competence in these areas, you will direct attention to them, and create subtle energy for change—the old Hawthorne effect[8] in action—assessing your

TRAINING	CONSULTING	PERFORMANCE
Lack of PM training	Is not established as business partner	Loss of confidence from stakeholders
Poor management	Outsourcing	Limited capacity for growth
No cross-education	No PO expertise	Pressure to out-source
		Establish PO & still do business as usual
		Rapid growth
		No track record for success
		Very little PM experience
		Poor financial performance
		Competition
		No buy-in from stakeholders
No true project manager		Can't incur additional expenses
		Too many acquisitions
		80% maintenance related

organization's situation can't be done just once. Once a company enters the self-assessment mode, be prepared for all kinds of organizational changes—including the change to a "learning organization"—one that constantly reevaluates its own progress, learns from history, and refines for future growth and opportunity. I like to think of it as a similar pattern to the iterative software development model—a spiral that contains the phases of (1) assessment, (2) planning based on the results of that assessment, (3) implementation of those plans, and then

Table 2.6 Facilitation for Issues Identification

- Who should attend: Key participants should include the identified project office director, the project office sponsor, key members of the project office steering committee, and key members of the project office staff (if they have been identified).

- Provide a "seed list" of common organizational issues related to project management improvement (see Table 2.4 Case Study). The facilitator may want to analyze the data generated by the pre-assessment and the maturity assessment in order to develop a seed list tailored to the organization.

- As a group, identify which of the issues on the seed list is a reality for your organization. Cross out those issues that don't apply to the organization. (Note: consensus should be reached on this decision. Sometimes a lonely voice can, in fact, be on target in identifying a problem that others have ignored.)

- Have participants rate the remaining issues on a scale of 1 to 5 from least important to most important.

- Ask participants if there are other areas not on the seed list. Rate these areas from 1 to 5.

- Break the listed issues down into the following categories: management issues, organizational structure or culture issues, process issues, tools issues, training issues, performance issues, and issues related to external support. (See Table 2.3.)

- Break the meeting into workgroups around the issues and have them brainstorm ways to move forward. A decision not to deal with an issue is valid in some cases. The group as a whole may make a decision, for example, only to deal with issues rated 4 or 5.

- Each workgroup brings its results back to the larger group for further discussion and development of an action plan (task list). Further meetings may be scheduled at this time for development of goals and objectives on those issues that are singled out for action.

- Deliverables from the meeting should include both the task lists and a situation analysis based on the problems and solutions discussed by the workgroups.

Resource for facilitation in groups: B. Terence Goodwin, *Write on the Wall,* American Society for Training and Development, 1994.

Table 2.7 Sample Gap Analysis for Case Study Organization

PRESENT	FUTURE (3-5 years)

Methods

• Non-existent • No standards • No risk analysis • Ad hoc • Chaos (lack of under-standing of current situation) • Multiple tools and techniques • No PM methodology • No project standards • No risk management process • No portfolio manage-ment • No project selection process	• Standard project management methodology and process standards, templates, and best practices • Benchmarking • Project history • Project life cycle methodology • Website with templates, guidelines, and examples in use • Risk analysis • Method for project portfolio manage-ment (prioritizing) • Develop project resource pool • Estimating • Lessons learned repository

Training | ### Training

Training	Training
• Only a few PMs trained • None internal • Some from new hires (CIO) • Management development program • No formal project manager training • No project man-ager career path • Training & develop-ment needed quickly	• Internal certification program • A curriculum for project managers in place • Career path in place for project managers, including PMP • Project managers trained • Tracking system to identify who needs training and who has had it • Project manager's development program (curriculum) • Tools, people skills (leadership/communication) • Subjects: methodology, software tools, PMI certification, team building, facilitation • PM handbook (manual)

Table 2.7 continued

PRESENT

FUTURE (3-5 years)

Consulting

PRESENT	FUTURE (3-5 years)
• Non-existent • Flat budget, can't afford • No mentoring • No project management services provided	• Start-up and planning assistance • Project audits / reviews • Rein in runaways • Formal mentoring program • Provide services for other business units • Establish partnership with externals • Develop internal competency for consulting • Evaluations • Process support • Assessments • Manage projects • Knowledge transfer • Audit (QA)

Support

PRESENT	FUTURE (3-5 years)
• Some estimating • Project risks not addressed • No standardized tools, use at least 3 software products • No time, performance, cost, or issue tracking • No project list or database • No formal support • Heavy infrastructure • Duplicate systems • No common application of support services	• Enterprise scheduling/planning tool & procedures implemented • Status reporting • Resource & skill repository • Time & issue tracking • Current inventory • Documentation management • Resource database in place • Systems—cost accounting, estimates, and scheduling • Project database • Project portfolio • Estimates • Libraries (capitalize on experience) • Formalize management support • Standardized tools and systems • Templates • Resource repository • Project help desk

Table 2.7 continued

PRESENT	FUTURE (3-5 years)
Managers	
• Not identified	• More than 5 years experience
• No project office	• Project manager pool (bench)
• Some project management skills in new hires	• Project office in place
	• Trained project managers
• No bench	• Manager of project managers
• No evaluations	• Project manager report to manager quarterly
• Assignments made ad hoc	
• No leadership	• Organize current project manager in teams
• No formal PM job description	
	• Establish future practice
• Poor communication	• Create job description
• No bench	• Establish communications
• No database	• Sponsorship
• No evaluations	• Incentives, rewards, compensation established
• Resistance to change	
	• Role definition
	• Resource forecasting
	• Career path development
	• Formal measurement, evaluations, and accountability

continuing to circle back to reassessment, replanning, and reimplementing. As the organization and its processes mature, these iterations can take place further apart in time, but in these times, no organization should ever become complacent (see Figure 2.2).

Talking Points:

How the project office helps an organization boost maturity:

- *Project Support.* The project office can make the lives of project team members easier by assuming administrative chores in the areas of project scheduling, report production and distribution,

Figure 2.2 Assessment, Planning, and Implementation Iteration

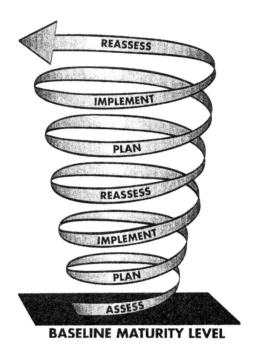

BASELINE MATURITY LEVEL

operation of project management software, maintenance of the visibility room, and maintenance of the project workbook.

- *Consulting/Mentoring.* As organizations mature in project management, the project office satisfies an increasing need for internal project management consultants. These people will provide the organization with the expert insights it needs to execute projects effectively.

- *Processes/Standards.* The project office is the unit within the organization that develops and promulgates common methodologies and standards relating to project management.

- *Training.* The project office trains project managers, team members, and clients regarding project management principles, tools, and techniques. Both training material and instructors originate in the project office.

- *Project Management.* The project office can house a group of professional project managers who can be assigned to carry out the organization's projects.

- *PM Software Tools.* As the project office matures, it becomes the focal point in the organization for software tools supporting the project management effort.

Endnotes

1. Paul Dinsmore. *Winning in Business with Enterprise Project Management,* AMACOM 1999.
2. *The Value of Project Management Study,* Center for Business Practices, 2000. See also "Why Every 21st Century Company Must Have an Effective Project Management Culture," by J. Kent Crawford, and James S. Pennypacker, PMI 2000 Proceedings CD-Rom, PMI, 2000.
3. Software Engineering Institute. *Capability Maturity Model for Software,* 1993.
4. ibid.
5. Robert Kaplan and David Norton, *The Balanced Scorecard,* Harvard Business School Press, 1996.
6. Jeannette Cabanis-Brewin, The Elusive ROI, *PM Network,* April 2000.
7. See *InfoWorld,* March 3, 1997.
8. First described by management theorist Mary Parker Follett in the early 1930s, the Hawthorne Effect refers to the tendency for any workgroup to improve its productivity simply because it is being studied; the extra attention motivates workers to do better than usual.

Chapter 3

Project Office Rationale, Organization Structure, and Functions

Where does "strategic project management" come from? How does it develop? Is it a business practice that one can purchase or go to school for? Unfortunately, the term has been loosely applied to everything from multi-project software to courses on how to start a Level 1 project office. Our definition of strategic project management (SPM) is that it is *an evolved practice*, closely paralleling the evolution of a business. We can define three stages in this evolution—individual project management, division or department level project management, and enterprise/corporate level (which we will call strategic) project management. These three stages correlate to the levels of project office (see Figure 3.1) briefly described in Chapter 1.

The Evolving Enterprise

Most businesses begin rather humbly. Even multinational corporations were once small concerns, perhaps even sole proprietorships. But like any organism, as a business grows it gains complexity and its needs change. As the organization grows in complexity, projects begin to interrelate and have impacts on each other in more subtle ways; ways that might not be understood until each project is well under way and suddenly a conflict or dependency emerges—usually an unpleasant surprise.

Here's an imaginary case study that describes how that evolution normally takes place.

Figure 3.1 Three Levels of a Project Office

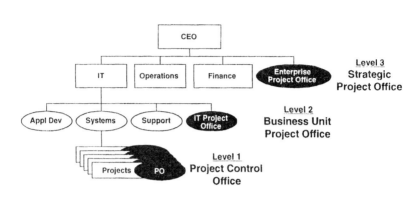

Case. In our example, Joe Merchant and his wife Jane decide to open a grocery business in Chinook, a small town in Wisconsin. They begin in a small storefront on Main St. and the locals, appreciating the prices and fresh produce, give them a good start in business.

Analysis. Does Merchant Grocery Co. need project management? Probably not. This is purely a process-oriented business: they are involved in the same procedures day after day.

Case. In two years Joe and Jane are ready to branch out, and they decide to start a second store in Walleye, the neighboring town. They purchase a new building, renovate it, stock it, hire and train clerks, and go through a start-up process much as they did in Chinook.

Analysis. Although the Merchants don't realize it, they are using project management to make this change. The new store startup is a temporary endeavor, and they are creating a unique product (the new store).

Case. The scene now jumps ahead 15 years. Joe and Jane have been very successful with Merchant Grocery. After opening their eighth store, they decided to centralize much of the operation by opening an office and warehouse facility in northern Wisconsin. The checkout lanes in all their stores are now served by computer registers and all stores are serviced by an automated inventory system. The 10-person IT staff

56

in the central office writes and maintains the shipping/receiving system, the checkout system, and other applications.

Analysis. As astute business people, the Merchants readily understand the need for control of business functions. In particular they understand that whenever changes are made around the company (whether it's building the next store or changing the shipping system) it is imperative to manage the project. At this point, the Merchants' concept of project management is on a *project-by project* basis. Projects, as they come up, are executed by individual project managers (who may not even think of themselves as such) using whatever tools they have at hand and are familiar with. Some projects are managed by the PIN method (Post-it® Note) while others may be more formally managed using concepts from the *PMBOK Guide*. But each project functions as its own entity. Changes within one project are not considered in another, unless some information gets exchanged by the water cooler.

Case. Merchant SuperStores, as the company has recently been renamed, is now a robust organization with 15 stores all over Wisconsin and northern Illinois. Joe, as President, has initiated several projects, one of which is to build a new regional distribution center along with a new warehousing system. Another project will entirely replace the shipping/receiving system in the existing warehouses. The shipping/ receiving project is in final testing before it's discovered that if the project team had accelerated the project schedule by only four moths, the new system could have easily been integrated with the new warehousing system. Unfortunately this lack of coordination will call for a rewrite of the shipping system once the warehousing system is implemented, costing the company over $100,000.

Analysis. As with most organizations that increase in complexity, Merchant SuperStores has gotten to the point where one project impacts another. At this point the organization must insist that there be some modicum of control outside each project. Generally at this point an organization directs its attention toward a project management software tool. The implementation of project management software helps to ensure that at least those projects that are managed within the tool do not conflict with each other in important ways. But there are still projects in the organization—say in merchandising, where Jane Merchant, the VP, is launching a new program for getting customer feedback—that fall outside the purview of the software. Thus project management is at a divisional or organizational level, but does not yet extend across the enterprise. At this stage, the organization (or project office) will check schedules of projects against one another. At some point, utilization of key resources (such as database analysts) between multiple projects will become enough of a consideration (read "problem") that the project office will monitor their usage, arbitrating conflicts when they arise. At this stage, many of the project managers will be keeping issue logs, instituting change management processes, etc., but there will be little consistency and no control of these things by the project office.

Case. Merchant SuperStores now has 52 stores across a five-state swath of the Midwest and four automated distribution centers in strategic locations. The IT staff has a head count of 273, including the database staff, analysts, programmers, managers, etc. They now complete some 150 projects annually and have 15 full time project managers on staff. Although these project managers report to the line of business IT teams, they are matrixed into the project office for expert support.

The project office has found it absolutely necessary to examine each project closely at initiation, sitting in on review of the stated scope and objectives with what used to be called the senior management oversight team (now renamed the "Project Office Steering Committee" at Merchant). There is now a standard PM software package in use within IT as well as other departments within the company, such as the facilities department. For this reason, the project office is now providing training on PM software internally.

Often key resources are demanded by multiple projects. In these cases the project office steps in to arbitrate the demand. This is happening more and more, now that so many projects are ongoing at the same time. Another problem that has come to the surface is that each time a resource moves from one project team to another, there is a learning curve because each project manager has his/her own ideas of what needs to be documented, how the documentation should be structured, etc.

Because Merchant IT has at least 15 projects in process at any given time, a company business unit or support department may be interacting with multiple project teams simultaneously. For example, the purchasing manager is actually working with three teams right now.

She is very confused and, frankly, angry. One of the project managers asks her for sign-off on almost everything (design documents, scope statements, test results), while another (we'll call her Jane) pretty much "wings it" — she talked to Jane for awhile and came back two weeks later with a system of screens put together on the network, which they worked together to change. The third is somewhere in the middle — he goes through a rather formal review of certain major documents and asks for sign-offs at the end of what he calls "project phases" and then seems to go away for weeks at a time.

Analysis. It should come as no surprise that the things the project office at Merchant SuperStores finds itself needing to coordinate and manage fall into the nine project management knowledge areas described in Chapter 2. Merchant has found that there are needs in each of the knowledge areas for higher-level coordination and management. They need a project office with the reach and capability to handle all the following issues:

- PM software
- Schedules
- Resource coordination
- System interfaces
- Quality
- Change control
- Human resources

- Communications
- PM methodology
- Procurement
- Training
- Cost
- Risk

As the tale of Merchant SuperStores illustrates, increasing levels of sophistication in a business call for increasing levels of integration in project processes—much the same way that more complex businesses require better financial tracking. Obviously, more work is needed at Merchant to standardize the project management process and publish a methodology. Just as a financial system rolls up expenditures and revenues across many departments into a single budget, in a strategic project management system, individual projects (Level 1) roll up into programs, programs roll up into business unit project control (Level 2), and then ultimately those programs, which in some cases may stretch across the organization, roll up into enterprise-wide, or strategic, project management. And at that point we are actually integrating a project management system that reaches across the entire enterprise, affecting all projects.

Ideally, the fully evolved Strategic Project Office operating at the enterprise level will be capable of addressing all of the issues in the bulleted list in our Merchant SuperStores example. Let's take a closer look at what's involved with each of those issues:

- **PM Software**—assessing the need for project management software, conducting research to determine the best package or suite for the organization, going through the procurement process for that software, implementing the software in the organization, training those who will use the software, coordination and administration of the software when it is in operation, and support of the people using the software after implementation.

- **Schedules**—the estimation for, creation of, and—most important in a complex organization—coordination of schedules for the various projects. At the enterprise level, it is critical to determine and track the interrelationships of tasks from one project to another.

- **Resource Coordination**—the enterprise level coordination of resources working on projects, most specifically of key resources but to some extent of all resources. Usually these will be human resources, but not always. Key resources on a construction project may be construction materials, supplies, equipment, trucks, or pieces of difficult-to-acquire equipment, for example. Key resources in event management may be conference rooms in a hotel.

- **System Interfaces**—as the organization takes a higher-level (strategic) view of projects it will become more and more important to achieve a tight interface between project management software and other administrative systems, such as:

  Financial Systems—adjusting the accounting/finance system to support project management in addition to the traditional support of functional departments; project estimates should integrate into departmental budgets; actual hours worked and other direct costs associated with project tasks should be downloaded to the project management software, enabling project managers to track variances, project material, supplies, and equipment costs must be allocated to the costs of the project.

Procurement Systems—many projects involve outsourcing of hardware, software, and services. Procurement lead time for project-related materials, equipment, and other critical items must be reported to the project manager to avoid potential negative impact on the critical path.

Human Resource Systems—a project may require resources from many areas of the company and may have a certain skill set requirement for each. A skills inventory for all people in the organization should be established in the HR system and made available to the project manager through the project management software. Project schedules must take into account planned vacations, company holidays, and other time not available for project work. A good HR system will have that information readily available. If the project management software is to keep records on actual project expenditures, it must know what each person is paid—and that information is also available in the HR system.

- **Quality**—as projects are performed within multiple departments in the organization, it becomes imperative that an enterprise-wide project management methodology be established and followed. If there is a separate quality assurance organization, that department performs process compliance audits to ensure that the PM methodology is being followed correctly. If a separate quality department does not exist, the Strategic Project Office will undertake this responsibility. Beyond process audits, quality of the deliverables themselves must be monitored and assured. The project manager relies on the quality department or technical departments for this assurance.

- **Change Control**—a rigorous change control process is a mandatory part of any project management process and is a primary element of scope management. Why does this become an enterprise level concern? Because as projects function at more of an interdepartmental level, the question of the legitimacy of scope changes must be decided from an enterprise level—that is, taking the entire organization's needs/objectives into account rather than just the sponsoring department. Only a Strategic Project Office, operating at the enterprise level, has the necessary "range of vision" to see the effect of changes relating to one project on the entire portfolio of prioritized projects.

- **Human Resources**—we covered skill inventories and accessibility of salary information under "System Interfaces." Beyond that, project management must be recognized as a career within the organization. There must be a career path for project managers, complete with competitive salaries and opportunities for professional development and promotion. Otherwise, project managers will consider project management as an additional duty to current technical responsibilities. To get promoted, they will be compelled to return to their technical departments. Project managers must have a clear promotion path to senior positions by excelling in the practice of project management. Also within the area of human resource management, project managers must understand how to motivate people and teams, not just manage the projects.

- **Communications**—communication is tough enough when projects are managed individually or within a single business unit. But when projects are managed as part of an interrelated portfolio, it is necessary that communication takes place with *all* the stakeholders in the enterprise simultaneously. Although it's not necessary or desirable for all communication to pass through the project office , certain key communications should be monitored by the project office , such as kickoff meeting notes, copies of status reports, lessons learned reports, and other data that will become part of the project management knowledge base. Each individual project plan should include a communication plan, and the project management methodology that governs project management across the enterprise should clearly state the minimum requirements for communicating with other stakeholders and the Strategic Project Office.

- **PM Methodology**—when we left our imaginary case study, Merchant SuperStores had 15 project managers working on 150 projects annually. Assume for the moment that each project manager was governed only by the triple constraints of time, cost, and technical performance and had no other process direction. It is reasonable to assume that any given customer of these 150 projects could experience five to ten different project-phase schemes, different review/sign-off requirements, different scheduling mechanisms, different control mechanisms, and a variety of team structures and project management processes. And as resources move from project to project, they will have to learn the unique processes, tools, and techniques in place on each project. More time will be spent trying to figure out how to manage and participate in projects than on the technical and creative work of solving problems and delivering value to customers. This is obviously unacceptable, yet this very situation exists in many real-world enterprises. In order to prevent this situation and bring some order to the chaos, a project management methodology must be created, deployed, and enforced across the enterprise. A good PM methodology will take into account each of the nine *PMBOK Guide* knowledge areas and will detail what is to be done and how to do it for each activity in the project life cycle.

- **Procurement**—as indicated, many projects will require the procurement of hardware, software, and other materials and services; and some projects will be performed with outside vendors. It is imperative that project budgets and actual costs be determined and documented correctly and that this information is concisely reflected in specifications and statements of work in vendor contracts. The vendor selection process is usually governed by methodology within the procurement department, not the project office. The project manager or director of the project office should ensure that the process selects the best vendor for the project in question. The individual contracts themselves should have clear performance requirements and a method for measuring contractor performance, as well as specific requirements for progress reporting, tied closely to progress payments to the contractor.

- **Training**—some project managers are smart or experienced enough to wing it and still achieve success, but the majority will do a better job if they are properly trained. Knowledge can be transferred through formal training courses, a mentoring program, project workshops, college courses, or the "school of hard knocks," otherwise known as experience. It is particularly important that the project office provide training to all project managers, team members, and senior managers on the PM methodology developed for the organization, including areas such as project leadership, the project team's role in contracting and negotiating, project budgeting and controls, along with the many additional soft skills which support effective project management. This training should be delivered in formal training courses using extensive hands-on cases and exercises. If a formal project management training program is already underway when the methodology is developed, the courses in the curriculum should be tailored to include the specific activities, templates, forms, and practices called for in the methodology.

- **Cost**—it is particularly important to elevate the coordination of cost management to the strategic level. Most project cost management is concerned with the cost of the resources needed for the project's activities. Because those resources come from multiple departments of the organization, enterprise level coordination is necessary. But there are other costs incurred in a project—hardware, software, vendors, and the like. Management techniques such as return on investment, discounted cash flow, economic value added, and payback analysis must be considered when managing a portfolio of projects across the company. The project office steering committee, to be discussed later, takes a direct interest in selecting and prioritizing projects based in large part on their return to the organization. Integrated cost estimating, forecasting, and management must be available to the steering committee to make these decisions.

- **Risk**—identification and management of risk is not a one-time event, but must continue throughout each individual project's life cycle as well as across the entire project portfolio. Not only should internal project risks be identified and managed, but also external risks, such as changing market conditions, project funding by external sponsors, political events, environmental changes,

Table 3.1 How Projects Fit into Organizations

PROJECT CHARACTERISTICS	ORGANIZATION TYPE				
	Functional	Weak Matrix	Balanced Matrix	Strong Matrix	Projectized
Project Manager's Authority	Litte or None	Limited	Low to Moderate	Moderate to High	High to Almost Total
Personnel Assigned Full-Time to Project Work	Virtually None	1–25%	15–60%	50–95%	85–100%
Project Manager's Role	Part-time	Part-time	Full-time	Full-time	Full-time
Common Titles for Project Manager's Role	Project Coordinator/ Project Leader	Project Coordinator/ Project Leader	Project Manager/ Project Officer	Project Manager/ Program Manager	Project Manager Program Manager
Project Management Administrative Staff	Part-time	Part-time	Part-time	Full-time	Full-time

and others. These external and cross-project events are clearly strategic, enterprise level considerations.

Having made the argument for enterprise level project management in complex organizations, let's move on and look at the optimal organizational structures for growing and nurturing a project office.

Organizational Structure for Projects

The cross-functional team is a central feature of project management. However, research has shown that simply creating teams within an existing functionally oriented organization will not bring about the advantages they are noted for, such as faster product development and higher success rates with new products.[1] Organizations that organized around functional areas or a weak matrix approach were less successful than projectized teams and teams employing strong matrix structures. These types of organizational structure worked equally well for both complex and simple projects (see Table 3.1 for a comparison of organizational structures).

This isn't that surprising since organizational structure is really all about how decision-making authority and responsibility are allocated. In a matrix, even though cross-functional teams may exist, the

Table 3.2 Features of the Projectized (Team-based) Organization

- Teams are accountable for performance.
- Functional managers are resource suppliers, not resource owners.
- Individual performance reviews are suspended—team performance is key.
- Professionals have a say in their assignments.
- Teams—not just managers—have access to senior management.
- Everyone is trained for team-based work.
- Team members stay with their team for the duration of the project.

Source: Adapted from Anne Donnellon, "Cross functional teams in product development: accommodating the structure to the process," *Journal of Product Innovation Management,* Nov. 1993, pp. 377-392.

functional manager still has the authority over resource assignments and the power to eventually cripple the effectiveness of the team.

Many companies have already realized the inherent problems of fitting cross-functional teams into existing functional organizations and concluded it will not work.[2] The old functional culture tends to dominate, making accountability difficult and decision-making slow. In forward-thinking companies, one solution has been to empower the program (or projects) by moving to a more projectized structure and by creating groups or centers of expertise (such as the project office) to service the programs. This changes the functional managers' role from *owners of resources* to *suppliers of people.*

Using the project or program as the basic structure of the organization has been a key to success at companies such as Microsoft, Intel, Texas Instruments, AT&T, EDS, Toyota, Ford, and others.[3] Motorola's team-based satellite communications division realized a revenue-to-employee ratio of $2 million to 1 as opposed to a ratio of $150K to 1 for other divisions in the company.[4] These companies often use projects to drive change in the organization and add core capabilities as natural byproducts of the process of delivering products. In a team- and project-based organization, project delivery is enhanced. Table 3.2 shows some of the key attributes of a "projectized" organization. It's no surprise that most, if not all, of these changes can be initiated as part of the implementation of a project office—and then effectively managed by that PO once they are in place. The PO becomes the facilitating body for cross-functional team management. It provides leadership training to project managers, provides training to the project teams, provides the guidance and direction on how to manage and direct cross-functional product/project teams, and generally helps to create an environment within the organization that is team-friendly and team-optimizing.

Culture change of this magnitude, however, is a tall order. Realistically, most companies begin by shoring up the features of projectization your organization already possesses, and working from there toward the ideal: an enterprise level project office within an organization where projects and teams—rather than functional departments—are the central organizational units. Chapter 10 covers culture change in more detail.

Where is your company on the evolutionary scale? Let's examine in detail the features of each level of evolution of the project office.

Levels of the Project Office

Not all project offices are created equal, although almost any form of PO will jumpstart incremental process improvements in organizations that have nothing at all in place. Basically, a PO is an "office"—either physical or virtual—staffed by project management professionals who serve their organization's project management needs. It also serves as an organizational center for project management excellence. A PO may exist at any one of three levels in the organization—or project offices may exist at all three levels concurrently.

Level 1: The Project Control Office

This is an office that typically handles large, complex single projects (such as a Y2K project). It's specifically focused on one project, but that one project is so large and so complex that it requires multiple schedules, which may need to integrate into an overall program schedule. It may have multiple project managers who are each independently responsible for an individual project schedule and, as those schedules, their associated resource requirements, and their associated costs are all integrated into an overall program schedule, one program manager or a master project manager is responsible for integrating all of the schedules, the resource requirements, and the costs to ensure that the program as a whole meets its deadlines, milestones, and deliverables.

Level 2: Business Unit Project Office

At the divisional or business unit level, a PO may still be required to provide support for individual projects but its challenge is to integrate a large number of multiple projects of varying sizes, from small short-term initiatives that requires few resources to multi-month or multi-year initiatives that require dozens of resources, large dollar amounts, and complex integration of technologies. The value of the Level 2 PO is that it begins to integrate resources at an organizational level. And it's at the organizational level that resource control begins to play a much higher value role in the payback of a project management system. At Level 1 or the individual project level, applying the discipline of project management creates significant value to the project because it begins to build repeatability—the project schedule, and the project plan become communication tools among the team members as well as within and among the organizational leadership. At Level 2 and higher, the PO serves that function but it also begins to provide a much higher level of efficiency in managing resources across projects. Where there are multiple projects vying for a systems designer, for example, the Level 2 PO has project management systems established to deconflict that competing need for a common resource and identify the relative priorities of projects, such that the higher priority projects receive the resources they need and lower priority projects are either delayed or canceled. A Level 2 PO allows an organization to determine when resource shortages exist and to have enough information at their fingertips to make decisions on whether to hire or contract additional resources. Since the Level 2 PO exists within a single department, conflicts that can't be resolved by the PO can easily be escalated to department management, who has ultimate responsibility for performance within the department.

68

Level 3: Strategic Project Office

Consider an organization with multiple business units, multiple support departments at both the business unit and corporate level, and ongoing projects within each unit. A Level 2 project office would have no authority to prioritize projects from the corporate perspective, yet corporate management must select projects that will best support strategic corporate objectives. These objectives could include profitability goals, market penetration strategies, product line expansion, geographic expansion, and upgrades to internal information management capability, to name just a few. Only a corporate level organization can provide the coordination and broad perspective needed to select, prioritize, and monitor projects and programs that contribute to attainment of corporate strategy—and this organization is the Strategic Project Office. At the corporate level, the Strategic Project Office serves to deconflict the need for competing resources by continuously prioritizing the list of projects across the entire organization. This cannot be done by the SPO in isolation; thus the need for a steering committee made up of the SPO director, corporate management, and representatives from each business unit and functional department. The project office steering committee looks at the contribution of each project to corporate and business unit goals. It also ensures that overlap and integration of projects are considered. For example, one well-known organization found that when it prioritized its list of 103 projects, some projects could not succeed unless other projects failed due to competing technologies. Without an integrated, prioritized list of projects, this would not have been discovered.

The Strategic Project Office operates at the appropriate level to facilitate the selection, prioritization, and management of projects that are of corporate interest. It ensures the project management methodology is tailored to the needs of the entire organization, not just one department or business unit. It is important to note in passing, however, that frequently a single methodology is not appropriate for every business unit. For example, one of PM Solutions' clients is in the petroleum exploration and processing business, as well as specialty chemicals, retail operations, asphalt production and paving, and associated businesses. It also has a large sophisticated information technology department that supports the organization and a large facilities management department. In attempting to develop a methodology that fits the needs of its entire corporate membership, it found that a significant amount of tailoring was required at the lower levels of detail in the methodology to be consistent with industry practices in their various business lines. For example, the facilities department worked with construction and its associated processes. The IT department followed software development and systems integration processes. The oil business likewise had its industry-specific project management terms, forms, templates, and practices. The overall project management process groups—initiating, planning, execution, control, and closing—applied to all projects, but many of the forms and templates supporting these processes were tailored to the business units.

Which level of project office is right for your organization? It depends on the size and complexity of the company, the interdependence of projects among business units and functions, the availability of resources, and the competence of your project managers, among other things. Large complex projects need a core team of talented individuals to manage them. This can be considered a Level 1 project office. However, if you have several complex, important projects, a Level 2 PO is called for to capture and institutionalize the best practices of the best project teams. And if the organization is large, with scarce resources and many critically important projects, a Level 3 project office is needed to ensure that corporate strategy is realized through the most effective and efficient execution of projects

Regardless of which level of project office you envision for your organization, all project offices perform the same functions to one degree or another. These core functions are reviewed here.

Functions of the Project Office

There are six primary components to any project office, and they grow in capability and complexity as the PO takes on more strategic responsibilities.

Project Support

There's a significant element of project management that requires project planning, project scheduling, cost control, administration, controls, and other detailed technical tasks—what we call the science of project management. But a much more important segment of the project manager's work deals with the art of project management—

areas like leadership, negotiation, motivation, team-building, facilita-tion, analysis, project chartering, incentive creation, and the like. To provide the appropriate level of technical support for project manag-ers so that they can focus on the things on which they have the greater impact is an important role for the PO. Project support is a specialty focus that requires considerable expertise in the specialty areas—sched-uling and project controls. These skills may take time to develop, are critical to retain, and adhere to standard processes and approaches specific to the project support function.

Documentation

The project support group performs the science of project man-agement, as opposed to the art. They are responsible for estimating and budgeting, including cost estimating and capital estimating. They develop plans and schedules. Project support works with project teams to develop a WBS, follow the WBS with the network diagram, get the network diagram into the project's scheduling software, have the scheduling software run the forward and backward pass to identify the critical path and float, and, with some additional analysis, pro-duce the final schedules. In addition they also provide status updates, pulling data from time collection, timesheets, and the financial sys-tem to update the status against the plan. They perform variance analy-sis and all the associated reporting back to the project team, up through management, and throughout the organization.

There's a significant amount of data entry involved in project sup-port, but data is the lifeblood of project control. In some cases, the status of critical projects must be updated daily, with changes to the schedule and modifications in the visibility room—once known as the war room—so key stakeholders who need the updated information can see exactly where the project is in "real time."

Change Control

Project support functions are critical to change control. Each change must be documented on a change request form, including analysis of impact on cost, schedule, and technical baselines, as well as disposi-tion of the change. Minutes from the change control board must be recorded and disseminated. A change log must be maintained show-ing status of all changes, whether approved or not approved. All this must be managed as part of a project manager's job. The project office can play a key role, and significantly eases the paperwork burden on project managers, by managing the change control process. The PO will convene change boards and take care of the resulting documentation. It ensures that approved changes are reflected in specifications and contract documents and that team members who need to be kept abreast of changes are notified in a timely manner.

Project Repository

Project support also entails keeping a project repository, which may be as simple as a book, or as complex as a knowledge management system. It's a record of all the documentation, all the plans, and an historical record to reference in the event that a project manager or team member leaves the project. This project repository helps indoctrinate new project managers to lessons learned and enables a smooth transition into and out of new and old projects.

Tracking and Reporting

Project support also maintains issues tracking. Much like change control, issues and action item tracking can be substantial depending on the number of projects and the number of people in the organization.

Project progress reports roll up into summaries for the appropriate functional areas, are further summarized for appropriate levels of the matrix organization, and so on, up to executive management. Thus the project support organization is responsible for *the executive dashboard*. That is a fancy way to say that they are responsible for executive reporting, but the dashboard typically is focused on keeping a reporting structure that is distilled to one page. Executives should look at one page of information and see that projects are on schedule as a whole or not—and if they are not, where they can go to find out what the issues are that are creating problems for the projects. So the executive dashboard might be an electronic or a paper report, but in all cases it needs to be summary level—succinct, precise, and focused specifically on the information that executives need for decision-making.

Risk Management

Project support also includes risk management. Risks in each project must be identified, analyzed, mitigated, and followed up. Plans for how to handle each high and moderate risk event must be put in place, and action taken to ensure responses are executed on a timely basis. In some cases, where the risk may be so significant as to require rebaselining the project plan, the project office works with the project manager to develop alternatives that might affect the schedule, budget, or project scope. Because risk analysis tends to be a specialty area, in terms of both software and techniques, risk analysis experts typically reside in the project support area of the project office. They provide software and technical support to project managers and frequently facilitate risk planning and replanning sessions with project teams.

Resource Repository

An organization of any size must maintain a resource repository. The resource repository is an inventory of all available resources throughout the organization or throughout the enterprise. As individuals are added to the company their profile is established in the resource repository and updated as they develop new skills. The project office, especially at Level 3, acts as a resource broker with functional heads to ensure the right resources are working on the right projects at the right time.

Cost Tracking

In organizations with mature project management processes, the accounting system may have been altered to provide actual cost data directly to the project manager via the project management software. However, this is rare. Accounting systems are slow to change due to the expense involved as well as the simple fact that they are entrenched bureaucracies themselves. If the organization does not have direct access, through integrated enterprise-wide software, to cost information at the project level, a lot of legwork is required to provide project managers with current, accurate, and complete cost information. Without this data, any attempt at assessing current and projected cost variance is an illusion. This is where the project office comes in. Members of the project support team within the project office literally "mine" the information they need from available data sources. They ask questions, visit the procurement department for information on contract costs, dig out actual hours worked from time-keeping systems, talk to resources to validate information—literally go anywhere in the organization to get the needed information. Individual project managers simply do not have the time to do this. As a result, without the project office providing this support, they have no clear idea of cost variance on their projects.

Software Support

Finally, project support handles all issues surrounding the project management software: a category of responsibility so large we have named it one of the central components of the project office.

Software Tools

The PO centralizes the establishment and maintenance of project-related software tools. With that also comes establishing and maintaining project management software standards, which will lead the organization into establishing common coding structures so that project schedules can be integrated and rolled up for management level resource, cost and schedule reporting.

Project support is responsible for acquiring project management software and supporting software, which could include time collection software, time reporting software, configuration control software, documentation software, library software, database software, spreadsheets and other software applications. The project support group identifies the needs in the software area, facilitates or performs the integration and use of that software, and then maintains and monitors its performance.

This project support group makes the ultimate decision on which project management software the project manager would use, as well as the decision on risk management software or integration software so that the tools used across the enterprise are compatible with one another. This is necessary so that resources and costs can be summarized at the enterprise level.

Project support also establishes a project help desk where project managers or other project team members can receive specialized or expert help with the project management or risk management software tools. They may need help with templates, database design, database application, spreadsheet development, spreadsheet use, template development, and so forth.

Processes, Standards, and Methodologies

The project office is also responsible for developing and maintaining processes and methodologies pertaining to the management of projects. It serves as a central library for these standards and is the expert on their deployment. The project office also incorporates lessons learned on projects nearing completion into the PM methodology.

If the PO is sizable enough, there will usually be a separate individual responsible for process development and maintenance. At a minimum, a project management methodology is developed, but other processes for which the project office may be responsible include the systems development life cycle, software development life cycle, process development life cycles, and product development life cycles. This area of the PO also functions as a keeper of standards, whether these are industry standards, such as the *PMBOK Guide*, internal company standards, or standards brought in by a consulting firm.

As the keeper of these standards, the project office also maintains the templates, forms, and checklists developed to ease the paperwork burden on project managers. In many cases the templates are an integral part of the standards themselves. The project management methodology may require, for example, a risk plan, and project managers are helped considerably if they can see a sample of a risk plan, including instructions for completing one. Templates such as the project request form, project charter form, communication plan, risk log, issues log, templates for schedules, templates for cost estimates, templates for the resource assignment matrix, and so on should be standardized across the enterprise. If basic processes are standardized, comparison and prioritization of projects becomes much easier.

Part of maintaining methods and standards is continually looking at industry to determine best practices. For example, one leading knowledge technology company did a fantastic job of establishing best practices for the product development industry. They looked at the different professional organizations and came up with a summary of best practices for new product development: use a stage/gate process, fully integrated with a comprehensive project management process. Benchmarking individual projects against other projects of like kind either within the organization or within the industry also has immediate practical application. For example, in estimating the deployment of a particular software package, rather than just pulling an estimate out of the air, the project manager can look at other organizations that have deployed a similar software package under similar conditions. Benchmarking helps to legitimize project cost, schedule, and resource requirements estimates.

Benchmarking can also take the form of contracting with a consulting firm known for expertise in your area of interest. For example, in developing a project management methodology, it makes sense to contract with a firm that has developed methodologies for other firms, both in your industry sector and outside your sector. In this way, an organization is purchasing a best practices knowledge base as part of the contract price with the consulting firm.

Whether benchmarking is done in-house or acquired from industry and association analysts such as the Project Management Institute, Gartner Group, Meta Group, National Contract Management Association, and Forrester Research, among others, the acquisition and application of industry-wide data to validate whether or not your particular processes fall within parameters commonly accepted in industry is a primary responsibility of the project office.

Building a world-class set of processes and methodologies also involves taking advantage of the lessons your own project managers learn while engaged in projects. An archive of lessons learned and methods and processes documentation is one of the project office's key contributions to standardizing methodology across the organization. This library of information and data is assembled from past projects—what worked, what didn't work, and how it can be reapplied more effectively to other projects within the organization. One strategy of software development process engineers has been to develop a process database for software development methodologies. They developed partners in the business community, customers to whom they had sold a component or process tool and as these partners used the tools and built their own templates, those templates were then provided back to the vendor who standardized them and put them in their library of approaches to planning and managing projects. Now in their process database they have methods for implementing client/server systems, for prototyping, for iterative development, for Lotus Notes deployments, SAP deployments, and so forth. Keeping a library of methods used on projects that can be readily reapplied is a time-saver and can also serve as part of the quality function.

The methods and standards area of the project office may also serve as the quality audit and continuous improvement function for project management, since they understand what should be done in terms of methodology and process and can audit against whether or not it is being done and, if it is being done, whether or not it is showing value and productivity.

The project office should also establish and manage an intranet or Web presence through which the standards and templates can be exchanged. Plans, estimates, schedules, deliverables, and project status can be integrated and communicated through a project office Web site or intranet site.

Finally, the project office methods and standards group works with the organization to manage the project portfolio. They help to establish a portfolio prioritization process by providing facilitators or consultants to structure and administer that process with the executives. They document the results of prioritization within the division and/ or within the company and communicate those results to the planning teams and integration teams. And they prepare the ongoing, regularly scheduled review that validates the portfolio. They ensure the portfolio is revisited, reviewed, revalidated, and reprioritized as necessary, and that those priorities flow over into the project planning and control process. (For more on project portfolio management, see Chapter 9.)

Training

The project office is the central focus for project manager and team training. It identifies competencies needed by high-performing project managers, and for executive awareness and team member participation. The project office participates, typically with a specialized project management training vendor, in tailoring standardized courses around the culture and methodologies that apply to the organization specifically.

Although the training department will be the coordinator of corporate training, the PO provides subject matter expertise in project management. The project office identifies the appropriate training that is required and participates in selection of the trainers. The project office also identifies the required levels of knowledge and competency and the required segments of training that are necessary in order to achieve maximum performance. Thus the PO is the focal point for measuring project manager competency. (For more on project manager competency, see Chapter 10.)

Consulting and Mentoring

When another department in the enterprise—marketing, for example—wants to manage a project themselves, the project office can provide expert assistance in the form of counseling and coaching for the staff involved in those projects. This component also provides an audit function for existing and ongoing projects to determine how effectively the project management process is being utilized and deployed within the organization.

The entire organization should view the project office as a source of specialized experts who have focused concentration and ability in project management. The leader of the marketing department's event planning team, who may not be experienced in project management, can go to the PO for startup assistance and advice. PO consultants (or coaches or mentors—the language used varies) provide counsel and conceptual understanding of what's necessary. They clearly understand the science of project management but they would also have a very solid understanding of the art of planning and managing projects, so they are able to give advice on teambuilding, leadership, communications, negotiations with clients or vendors, problem solving, facilitation, and so forth. Mentors may not be called on until a problem or challenge arises, so they should be very experienced project managers. They must know the nuts and bolts of project management—how to draft a project charter, develop and design the project plan, develop a risk plan, and rescue a project in distress.. But they must also know the business and the industry. When a project is facing challenging times and needs additional oversight and guidance to achieve project recovery, the mentor can help develop the project workaround plans, the new estimates of cost, resource reallocations, and replanning.

In addition, a project expert frequently works with a project manager and marketing manager to develop proposals for external work. Since proposals are sometimes accepted without negotiation, estimates of time and cost for the scope proposed must be accurate. This necessitates a greater level of planning earlier in the project life cycle than might be customary. If project planning is sound and estimates are accurate, profitability on contracted projects can be predicted with a reasonable degree of certainty.

In sum, the role of project mentors and consultants is to transfer the knowledge they have developed to project managers and project teams to enable them to perform better on current and future projects. Knowledge transfer is the key, since mentors are not be provided on a continuing basis.

Finally, mentors and consultants from the project office are the logical personnel to do project assessments or audits. They develop the project audit process and checklists, help determine the timing of the assessments and conduct the audits. Following the audit of a project in trouble, the auditors might themselves be the most logical experts to help the project manager get back on schedule or within budget.

Project Managers

A stable of capable, qualified, professional project managers can manage a full range of projects, from large, complex technology projects, to smaller short-term projects. To remove the functional bias that inevitably creeps into the project manager's psyche, these professionals are sometimes assigned full-time to the project office. In the fully deployed Strategic Project Office, project managers actually report to the PO and are deployed to projects either as full time managers or on a part-time basis. The PO maintains a database of project managers, their skill sets, capabilities, specialties, experience, and technical skills. Using this database, the project office steering committee discusses the needs of new projects and, in consultation with the director of the project office, recommends assignment of specific project managers to specific projects. Project managers between full-time assignments work on special projects such as developing new processes, methodologies, techniques, templates, and capabilities. A highly competent project manager is too valuable be idle just because he or she is between projects: this infrastructure development aspect of the project office allows the organization to derive full value from a project manager's expertise and experience as well as avoid the high cost of turnover.

The manager of project managers or director of the project office would be responsible for evaluating, coaching, and developing project managers and project team performance. He or she would also be responsible for managing the database of projects and project assignments and matching project requirements with project managers.

Integration of the Project Office

Since major projects usually cross all organizational divisions, the most effective use of the project management expertise resident in the project office will be made if the PO is integrated into activities such as project prioritization, budgeting, and cost allocation at the corporate level—where the strategic decisions are made as to how to allocate resources.

In other words, as projects ebb and flow, start, ramp up, and finish, the Strategic Project Office is the place where project data are collected and thus is the place in the organization best suited to track corporate trends. As they collect data on resource skills, on project tracking, and on training needs, they have data to make decisions on hiring and contracting. The SPO is the umbrella for project needs, much like the finance department acts as the organization's treasurer and accounting office. Even within a company that has a SPO, there may be individual projects that are managed internally within a single business unit, of course, but those individual projects will have the benefit of being standardized, supported, and mentored if the need arises by the SPO.

Endnotes

1. Per a best practices study of 189 firms by the Product Development Management Assn. Cited in Clark and Fujimoto, "The Power of Product Integrity," *Harvard Business Review*, Nov.-Dec. 1990. See also Ann Donnellon, "Cross Functional Teams in Product Development: Accommodating the Structure to the Process," *Journal of Product Innovation Management*, Nov. 1993; Robert G. Cooper, *Winning at New Projects: Accelerating the Process from Idea to launch, 2nd ed.,* Addison Wesley, 1993.

2. Cited in "Case Study: DFM, Simultaneous Engineering, Employee Involvement Aid Deere," *CIMWEEK*, Jan. 28, 1991. See also Cole, Clark, and Nemec, "Reengineering Information Systems at Cincinnati Milacron," *Planning Review*, May 1993; Christopher Lorenz, "Reaping the Harvest of an Integrated Team Approach," *Financial Times*, Oct. 7, 1991.

3. Cited in William Bridges, "The End of the Job," *Fortune*, Sept. 19, 1994. See also Tim Davis, "Reengineering in Action," *Planning Review*, July 1993; Katzenbach and Smith *The Wisdom of Teams: Creating the High Performance Organization*, HarperCollins 1993; Tom Peters, *Liberation Management,*

Knopf 1992; Gifford and Elizabeth Pinchot, *The End of Bureaucracy and the Rise of the Intelligent Organization*, Berrett-Kohler, 1993.

4. Theodore B. Kinni, "Boundary-Busting Teamwork: Motorola Leaps Organizational Borders to Create the Infrastructure of Iridium," *Industry Week*, March 21, 1994.

Chapter 4

Meet the Players

P ROJECTS CANNOT BE ACCOMPLISHED BY just a project manager and team. The individuals "at the coal face" of a project cannot be held responsible for many of the potential obstacles to success—things like poor definition of the business case for a project, lack of alignment with strategic corporate objectives, inadequate funding, or refusal to cooperate cross-functionally among the departments. These types of obstacles must be cleared away at the executive level of the organization; that's why the project sponsor plays such a critical role in the successful management of an individual project.

When initiating an organizational change project on the scope of a project office, executive sponsorship is even more important. The level of authority required to drive this kind of change does not exist on the project team or even the departmental level. Only the company's executive staff has that authority and the responsibility to architect and oversee the implementation of change of this magnitude. The executive leadership of the enterprise must commit the organization to this new direction and exhibit the resolve necessary to see these changes through to completion. Many sources in the literature on successful reengineering and implementation of new processes agree that executive commitment is the first and most crucial piece in any drive to improve or change organizations.

Thus, in discussing the staffing of the Strategic Project Office, we will "take it from the top."

The Executive Role

The primary role of the executive staff is to provide the strong leadership, strategic vision, and program definitions necessary to implement the project office. A company can have a best-in-class project management process defined, but if the strategic vision that underpins that process is missing or ill-conceived, the process simply cannot make that company successful over the long term.

The executive staff must establish vision and direction for the project management initiative and allocate funding and resources to it. Such sponsorship from the members of the executive committee ensures a voice for programs and projects. Many organizations have strong support for project management at lower levels, but very little acceptance or interest at the top. Such an organization is not managing effectively by projects and is unlikely to derive the benefits that strategic project management has to offer, unless a cultural evolution takes place. It isn't necessary for executives to become project managers; it is necessary that they enthusiastically support, with words, actions, and funding, the aspirations of the project management community within their organizations.

Once the initiative is in place and the projects that fall under it are gearing up, the executive staff has minimal involvement in day-to-day project activities. However, even though the executive team is not performing the day-to-day detailed work, they must be involved as an executive oversight team. Ideally, management understands the strategic implications of the project office initiative and its impact on the company's bottom line in terms of more rapid new product development and the resulting increased return to shareholders.

Where Executives Fail

The dilemma that arises in most organizations is that the impetus toward improved project management begins at the middle management level. And because middle management tries to implement changes that are really beyond their scope of influence, the project management initiative usually receives inadequate funding. Middle management usually only receives enough support to cobble something together—*if* they don't get tied up with other things. Without executive management sponsoring/driving/overseeing project office development, project management initiatives do not deliver the promised value, not because the initiative itself is not a sound idea but because the implementation is half-hearted. Without the backing of executive management, project office resources typically find themselves implementing the project office initiative part-time, periodically pulled from deployment efforts to manage current "hot" projects, or juggling multiple priorities. Many times they are defocused to the point where the project office initiative loses its direction and momentum (see later section, "Two Cautionary Tales").

These are typical of the problems we see in companies that have tried and failed to implement better project management practice. Front-line or middle management may see the need for process improvement, but given their immediate pressures and responsibilities, it is almost impossible for them to rise above the tactical level to focus on the strategic. Make no mistake: deploying a corporate level PO is a strategic program. So executive management has a critical role to play.

How to Succeed

What are the critical elements of successful management participation in Strategic Project Office deployment? There are many, including the strategic decision-making that supports the project, protecting the resources in the SPO so that they can focus on what they need to do; supporting the budget, the plan, and the schedule; and providing conflict resolution when resistance to change arises within the departments most affected by the deployment. However, the keystone in the SPO deployment strategy is the executive sponsor. The executive sponsor paves the way for the SPO deployment by dealing with other executives as a peer when conflicts over resources arise.

Without an executive sponsor, the chances of successfully deploying a project office are very slim. The more influential the sponsor, the greater your likelihood of success.

Identifying the Executive Sponsor

SPO deployment is a project in itself, and therefore it is relevant to apply some of the techniques we use in managing other projects.

In identifying an executive sponsor for your SPO deployment project, it might be helpful to think about the usual role of the sponsor on the kind of individual projects with which you may be more familiar. The project sponsor is the executive in charge of the area in which most of the business functions connected with the project reside. He or she initiates the project and is a member of the oversight committee. The sponsor makes business decisions at the various project phases, communicates the larger vision of the project throughout the organization, and, from the customer's (the executive leadership team, in this case) point of view, is ultimately responsible for the project's completion. Project sponsorship is most effective when accountability resides with one person, a person high enough in the organization that he or she has enterprise-wide influence. There will of course be a project sponsor for every project undertaken by the company, but the sponsor chosen to spearhead the project office initiative will have a particularly important role in leading organizational change; thus the sponsor of the SPO initiative must be highly placed. The project sponsor for a critical technology development or deployment project might be the CIO, for example.

For an SPO deployment supporting the technology division, a CIO could also serve as an executive sponsor, depending upon the level of influence he or she wields within the organization. Some organizations have realized that IT is integral to overall corporate success, and their CIOs have won a seat at the strategy table. A CIO with this kind of organizational clout can be an appropriate executive sponsor; however, in most companies a higher-level executive will be more effective—in some cases this may even be the chief operations officer or even the CEO. However, in our experience, for a mid-sized organization or within a business unit of a larger organization, the executive sponsor would typically be at the vice-president level. As you move up into the Fortune 100, a junior vice-president or director-level executive may serve as the executive sponsor. A simple rule of thumb for choosing a person with sufficient authority is simply this: Does he or she have the authority to cancel the project?

Lack of an executive sponsor with sufficient authority is a major risk to the success of your initiative, and we recommend that work not proceed until you engage an effective project office sponsor. This step should take place early in the initiative to ensure the project will move forward. Securing buy-in across the executive positions in your organization significantly improves the probability of project office success, giving the project team the ability to resolve the kinds of issues, conflicts, and challenges that occur whenever you try to deploy an organization-wide system of this magnitude.

One example of the kind of issue that will come up early on in SPO execution is in the critical elements of collecting data relating to resources, budget, and schedule. An SPO must have access to statistical data to validate whether or not you are working in accordance with the plan. There must be a collection of time reporting, cost reporting, technical adherence to deliverables, and other data. Taking the example of time reporting, which may seem simple enough: the issues surrounding time reporting reach into the human resources function and into the financial function. Setting up appropriate time-reporting capabilities for a project-oriented organization will require implementation of improved methods of process controls, procedures, timesheets and so forth. In this case, IT must be involved so that project teams can track time electronically. Integration with Accounting/Finance must be accomplished to collect actual time and costs from the financial system. The results of this data compilation and reporting must be compiled, consolidated, and regenerated into the appropriate formats for executive reporting and integrated into the project controls system for project-level statusing, updating, and reporting. Integration of multiple financial systems, coordination among the various organizations, compilation of the resulting data, and generation of appropriately tailored reporting only begins to reflect the complexity of the challenges surrounding the myriad of changes that an SPO deployment entails. Multiply this example by the many other issues raised by by a developing project office—coordination of the project/program/organizational budgeting processes, procurement, inventory control, capital equipment funding and allocation, and suppliers and we find there is a tremendous amount of coordination and systems integration required for a fully functioning Strategic Project Office.

In order to expedite these integration issues, the executive sponsor must be a champion for the SPO, while serving as an effective organizational facilitator. Being seen as a proponent of this process change for the good of the organization as a whole allows the sponsor to pave the way to work through some of the sticky issues of turf, information sharing, and power.

It's tempting for executives to hand these kinds of sticky issues over to the project manager selected to lead the SPO initiative. But the project manager, as a middle management level manager, most likely will not have the influence, authority, or reputation to work through the toughest challenges of integration. While a designated project manager for SPO deployment tries to deal with these issues, it's likely he or she will run into a political roadblock, or the department they are negotiating with has other issues that they view as more of a crisis and the SPO integration problem is put on the back burner until "later." As a direct stakeholder in the success of the SPO, the project office project manager is likely to be viewed as someone who is "empire building" as he or she struggles to work out these integration issues. If integration unveils some areas of duplication or inefficiencies between departments—as is likely to happen—the project manager as the bearer of bad news is likely to be subjected to that time-honored management technique of "shooting the messenger."

The value of a higher-level executive sponsor is that he or she can help adjust priorities relevant to the priorities of the overall organization, cutting through some of the political challenges that a mid-level project office project manager would have extreme difficulty in achieving.

The bottom line: Choose a sponsor for the SPO who can communicate the plan and keep the organization's priorities straight. He or she must be a strong advocate for the changes involved and extremely knowledgeable about the benefits of project management, and have the ear and confidence of the powers that be. The old saying goes, "You're never a prophet in your own land." If senior management doesn't fully understand and support the project management approach, it may be time to bring in an external consultant who has dealt with a number of companies in your market segment to explain and execute the advantages of project management and the results achieved by others who have successfully implemented a project office.

Management Participation: The Project Office Steering Committee

As the liaison between senior corporate management and the SPO project team, the executive sponsor should be the chair of the project office steering committee (see Table 4.1). This committee is normally made up of the director of the SPO, the project sponsor, the heads of key functional organizations (members of business units affected by the project or projects being dealt with at any one time), and a senior corporate official, such as the CEO or COO. I recommend the project office steering committee comprise three to seven individuals total. This committee is formed to change the corporate project culture and is active on a continuing basis to select, prioritize, and evaluate the

Table 4.1 Meeting Guide: Project Office Steering Committee Training

Barrier to Executive Education
Executives are too busy to take time for training.

How to Overcome the Barrier
- Adapt to the reality that they *do* have incredibly hectic schedules.
- Deliver information in bite-sized components, say, two hours maximum length for any one session.

Barrier to Executive Education
"Executives will never use project management; that's for their direct reports."

How to Overcome the Barrier
- The goal is not to create experts, but to increase their awareness of the potential of project management, to enlighten them as to how it can help them achieve their personal and professional objectives.
- Do not focus on tools and techniques; instead, give them the information needed to interpret the various types of reports generated by project management professionals.
- Teach enough project management so that they can ask the right questions to get the right picture from the project data.
- They should be able to review projects at a high level and get a clear picture of the status of any project in their portfolio.
- They should understand the realities of managing projects to avoid unrealistic expectations. They should be able to connect the improvement in the management of projects with the company's business strategy.

Barrier to Executive Education
"Executive education must be delivered differently than the traditional classroom approach."

Table 4.1 continued

How to Overcome the Barrier

- Recognize that senior executives are not the typical class-room student.

- The material presented must deliver the big bang quickly and show relevance to their bottom line. Senior executives must be engaged in a dialogue of exchange rather than the classroom paradigm of "I teach, you learn." This dialogue allows the senior executive to learn from the exchange of questions and answers. Allow them to evaluate information in smaller groups and report out to the larger group.

- An executive session requires a much smaller audience, preferably 12–15 at most.

- In this small group, one can also more easily conduct an analysis of where the organization rates on the project management maturity scale, identify steps needed to move towards maturation, and assign action items to the members of the executive staff. This action-oriented approach sends a message to all attendees that they are expected to be active participants in the process— not just passive "students."

Adapted from: "Even Executives Sing the Blues," Jimmie West, *Project Management Best Practices Report,* June 2000.

entire corporate portfolio of projects. In addition, it acts specifically on very large projects having overall corporate impact, such as the SPO initiative. When major issues or problems with the project must be escalated, the project office steering committee provides a forum for problem resolution. This committee initiates the project in a management oversight role, and also continues to hold end-of-phase reviews throughout the duration of the deployment project, monitoring progress against the objectives to determine whether or not the SPO is meeting the objectives that were established at initiation. The project office steering committee may also discover the need to include technical and internal client representatives—senior staff from other business units that may be affected by the SPO deployment. If there are external customers who are critically affected, you may want to include them on this committee as well. This group is, in effect, the board of directors for the SPO and other mega-projects.

As a "board of directors," the project office steering committee has input into the strategic direction and will play a part in the review of the SPO charter. In some cases, members of the committee will need to sign off on key elements of the deployment plan (such as the project charter) since the charter defines the scope of the proposed SPO and its specific roles and responsibilities with respect to functional departments and business units. While the SPO project office director will write the initial draft of the charter for the project office steering committee meeting, he or she will ask committee members to sign the charter to verify that its provisions have been agreed to. If a conflict arises in the future, the members of the committee revisit originally agreed-upon terms of scope, priorities, and strategy prior to initiating change. The project office steering committee will also continue to revisit the goals and objectives of the SPO, as well as the critical deliverables, and continue to work within the organization to achieve executive buy-in to all those areas.

The project office steering committee is also involved in the commitment of all the various resources that the SPO deployment will require, from budget and personnel to space, equipment, and time.

In the early stages of an SPO deployment, the project office steering committee will be required to meet more frequently, perhaps as often as monthly. As the project begins to deploy, the committee will meet less often. As part of project planning, the project office steering committee may wish to identify key end-of-phase points when they will come together to review progress to date, determine whether the objectives of that phase have been achieved, whether the schedule has been maintained, whether proper cost controls have been put into place, and so forth. Another way executive management can make sure that project office steering committee representatives fully appreciate the importance of the project is to ensure that committee members devote sufficient time to committee proceedings, that they in fact attend meetings and provide meaningful input and feedback to senior executives on progress and problems. It may be necessary to conduct a session of executive-level training in project management before the SPO deployment project is launched to ensure the project office steering committee fully understands its role, responsibilities, commitments, and value.

Functional managers seldom have a sufficient grasp of the enterprise advantages of project management to fully appreciate "what all the fuss is about." The members of the project office steering committee must understand enough about the project management process and its value to be strong advocates; and they must also have a high-level understanding of the phases and processes of the discipline in order to provide leadership and guidance during project reviews. (For a brief description of training appropriate to the executive oversight committee, see the Table 4.1.)

Periodic progress reviews are a normal part of the "controlling" processes of project management. For the SPO deployment project, as for any other organizational project, executive participation will be necessary in these project reviews. These reviews will be scheduled into the implementation plan. One reason executive involvement is important in these reviews is that the project office steering committee must have the authority to both launch and cancel the project if necessary. Otherwise, the committee will not have sufficient authority to make other critical decisions necessary for the successful outcome of the project. Project control is all about identifying problems, risks, or issues early in the deployment initiative, and addressing them as a project moves through its life cycle of planning, deployment, and transition to ongoing operations.

Keep in mind, however, that the project office steering committee must be made aware of the highlights of the program only: a very high-level roll-up of all the project activity. The SPO project manager should also provide the committee with an agenda and a menu of decisions that must be made during the project office steering committee meetings. Some of the typical issues the committee will be asked to address include major changes to the direction of the Strategic Project Office deployment project or other significant change control items, budgetary impacts, resource conflicts, need for involvement from other organizations, or lack of support from a critical "power center" in the organization. A simple word from the CEO or COO to a recalcitrant player is sometimes all that is needed to get the project office deployment back on track. All the issues the project team itself is not able to resolve should be elevated to the project office steering committee so that the committee can use its influence or decision-making ability to redirect, correct, provide funding/resources, reprioritize, or take other action. And, as always, it is necessary to document committee decisions and incorporate them into an updated plan or issues log.

Lastly, one of the most important areas in which the project office steering committee plays a role is in the realm of culture change. As we discussed in Chapter 1, managing by projects is an entirely new way of doing business in many organizations and anyone attempting to align projects and strategy will impact not only those individuals doing project management, but also functional teams and managers and systems from HR to payroll to facilities to procurement to finance. Changes of this magnitude cannot take place without management support and advocacy, and this will be a primary role for the project office steering committee. It has been said that much of implementing project management is "missionary work" and the executives involved have to be the primary "missionaries" of this new business doctrine. (For a discussion of culture change, see Chapter 10.)

Staffing Requirements

How the Strategic Project Office is staffed is determined in large part by the role your organization expects it to play. If the PO is to play the central role in guiding project management in the organization (a Level 3 Strategic Project Office), staffing is complex. The project office director position within the organization should be equivalent to that of a high-level functional manager—even a vice-president, in some cases. The SPO director at this level is supported by large numbers of professional associates and administrative personnel.

Has the project office been established to serve a support and facilitation role? In this case, office staff may be composed of an experienced project office director, a few professional associates with project management skills, and a clerical specialist to handle office functions. The chief function of this simple configuration may be to operate in ad hoc fashion to address project management issues within the organization as they arise.

If the project office is equivalent to a project team, the project manager is also the project office leader, and full- or part-time team members form the office staff.

If the project office acts simply as a repository, or storehouse of methodology and lessons learned, project mentors, project management methodology experts, or a project librarian may be sufficient as dedicated staff. Typical project office sizes range from five to twenty; in very large organizations, there may be hundreds of project managers linked directly or indirectly to the project office.[1]

Some of the positions and titles we have seen within Strategic Project Offices include: project office director, project manager, project mentor, project controller, project planner, methodology expert, librarian/documentation specialist, relationship manager, administrative support coordinator, communications coordinator, issue resolution and change control coordinator, risk management coordinator, and software guru. For a summary of the responsibilities and skill requirements for several of these key roles, see Table 4.2. We have selected a few of the key roles for further discussion.

The Strategic Project Office Director

If your organization is prepared to make the SPO the central driving force behind the management of projects, you will want to consider establishing a director of project management who will sit at the director or vice-president level with other senior executives in the organization. This position, which we will call the SPO director, provides project oversight in virtually all areas of the organization, managing corporate level projects and overseeing corporate-wide resource distribution and allocation on all projects. Any project that crosses divisional boundaries, as well as some large projects performed within a department, would be under the auspices of this SPO director.

But the SPO director position is more complex than simply a glorified project manager. He or she will have several critical roles to fill. The SPO director must ensure that the project management process runs well while also seeking to continuously improve it. As the expert on project management, the SPO director also serves as an ad hoc consultant and advisor to project leaders and teams. The existence of a SPO director guarantees a focus on the consistent use of the project management process throughout the organization.

Michael Hammer wrote of the "two flavors" of manager: one a process manager who oversees a process end to end, with skills of performance management and work redesign, and one an employee

Table 4.2 Project Office Positions

STRATEGIC PROJECT OFFICE DIRECTOR

Responsibilities
- Resource prioritization
- Project review and analysis
- Business interface
- Liaison to executive and functional management
- Develop standards, policies, guidelines, procedures
- PM skills development
- Project oversight
- Budget

Skill Requirements
- Leadership
- Directing and managing programs
- Building organizations
- Identifying and developing new business
- Selecting and developing key personnel
- Multi-tiered management
- Strategic planning

PROJECT MANAGERS

Responsibilities
- Delivery of projects against schedule, cost, resource, scope, and quality baselines
- Interface management in product, project, client, and information flow
- Resource management in schedule, staffing, budget, equipment, facilities
- Planning/control management to increase performance efficiency, reduce risks, identify changes, identify alternative solutions
- Implementation of standard PM practices

Skill Requirements
- Team building
- Conflict resolution
- Entrepreneurship
- Planning and allocation of resources
- Focused vision
- Managing multidisciplinary tasks
- Leadership
- Technical expertise
- Administration

Table 4.2 continued

PROJECT MENTORS

Responsibilities
- Senior advisor
- Project visionary
- Planning direction
- Guidance to project teams
- Counselor
- Facilitator
- Support

Skill Requirements
- PM competency
- Leadership
- Conflict resolution
- Facilitation
- Team building
- Politics

PROJECT PLANNERS

Responsibilities
- Schedule development
- Resource forecasting
- Critical path diagramming
- Project budgeting
- Planning support
- Cost estimating
- Software tools support

Skill Requirements
- Risk analysis
- PM software
- Project software tools and methodologies
- Cost estimating
- Office software use (word processing, spreadsheet, database, presentation)
- Change control

PROJECT CONTROLLERS

Responsibilities
- Project prioritization
- Variance analysis
- Project integration
- Resource forecasting and integration
- Budgeting
- Project and program reporting
- Tools integration
- Reporting

Table 4.2 continued

Skill Requirements

- PM software
- Risk analysis
- Database development
- Project software tools and methodologies
- Office software use (word processing, spreadsheet, database, presentation)

- Cost estimating
- Change control
- Communication skills

METHODOLOGY EXPERTS

Responsibilities

- Develop repository standards
- Develop training requirements on methods and processes
- Develop performance guidelines
- Author, maintain, and update methods and processes
- Evaluate, select, and maintain process management tools

Skill Requirements

- Analytical
- Methodical
- Expert in methods and processes

- Logical
- Organization

LIBRARIAN/DOCUMENTATION SPECIALIST

Responsibilities

- Develop templates
- Manage and coordinate documentation revisions and releases
- Maintain repository standards
- Maintain and perform periodic archiving of project records

- Generate special reports

Skill Requirements

- Administrative
- Communications
- Data entry, word processing, and spreadsheet tools

- Organization

Table 4.2 continued

ADMINISTRATIVE SUPPORT COORDINATOR

Responsibilities

- Provide back-office support
- Perform scheduling and calendar functions
- Prepare travel itineraries
- Distribute project status reports
- Prepare project review presentations
- Maintain project office personnel contact list
- Maintain office supplies
- Maintain and report action items lists and status

Skill Requirements

- Administrative
- Organization
- Data entry, word processing, and spreadsheet tools

COMMUNICATIONS COORDINATOR

Responsibilities

- Help develop enterprise-wide and project communications plan
- Determine communication strategies and medium for information delivery
- Interface with internal and external organizations for information delivery
- Ensure timely delivery of all project statuses
- Determine audiences requiring communications

Skill Requirements

- Oral and written communications
- Interpersonal
- Organization
- Administrative
- Knowledge of communications delivery instruments

Table 4.2 continued

ISSUE RESOLUTION & CHANGE CONTROL COORDINATOR

Responsibilities
- Develop and maintain issue resolution and change control processes
- Establish standards
- Create and distribute open issues reports for all projects
- Develop, maintain, and update issues and change control database/log
- Facilitate issues and change control meetings
- Help project managers prioritize change requests

Skill Requirements
- Administrative
- Analytical
- Facilitation
- Knowledge of legal and regulatory requirements
- Organization
- Communications

RISK MANAGEMENT COORDINATOR

Responsibilities
- Identify project risk during project definition
- Qualify risk
- Quantify risk
- Identify impacts
- Respond through prevention, mitigation, and contingency planning
- Monitor schedule and cost variance

Skill Requirements
- Risk assessment
- Communications
- Alternative solutions/negotiations
- Knowledge of legal and regulatory requirements
- Analytical
- Facilitation

coach who supports and nurtures employees.[2] A good SPO director must be both: both the overseer and "owner" of project management methodology and a leading mentor to up-and-coming project talent within the organization.

The SPO director must possess enough stature and respect throughout the organization to champion projects from start to finish—and to recommend canceling projects whose objectives either can't be met or are no longer valid. He or she must have the demonstrable backing of senior management, especially critical early in the transition to the SPO structure. However, instituting an SPO director alone is not enough to bring the organization into a mode of "managing by projects." It is also necessary to alter the role of functional managers from resource owners to project resource suppliers—an equally significant change that organizations must make to fully realize the value of effective, cross-organizational project teams.

It's useful perhaps to think of the SPO director in a similar light as a "program manager." Those readers who have worked in government or major corporations will be familiar with this role. Like a program manager, the SPO director is responsible for the on-time delivery of projects that fall within the domain of the total program and is responsible for moving resources between and among projects as well as prioritizing projects within the program. While individually accountable for their own program (overall direction of the SPO in our case), they may also be measured and held accountable for the success of *all* projects within their domain. Thus the structure supports the natural desire to work closely with other program managers (or, in the case of the SPO director, with other division or department heads) on leveraging opportunities.

The following list includes just some of the many tasks required of a SPO director, depending upon the size and scope of the SPO:

- Managing elationships—working to smooth the interfaces with the business units and develop project requirements through consensus with customers[3]

- Communicating the mission, vision, scope and benefits of the SPO

- Interfacing with all aspects of the business to increase a level of awareness of the services provided by the SPO and the benefits of using those services

- Serving as a liaison to executive and functional management to ensure availability of the appropriate services and participate with them in setting direction for the SPO

- Developing the skills of the SPO staff and project managers throughout the organization

- Prioritizing the application of project office resources

- Providing corporate project oversight, checkpoints, and controls

- Reviewing and analyzing the process of project management throughout the organization

- Managing the project office budgets.

As "owner" of the project office methodologies, the director may also be in charge of the following areas, either by taking personal responsibility for these items, or by employing a methodology expert to fulfill the functions:

- Authoring, maintaining, and adapting the project management methods and processes

- Evaluating and selecting project management tools

- Contributing to definition of training requirements on corporate project management training, project management methods and processes

- Developing knowledge management standards and processes for archiving and disseminating project documents, lessons learned, and other intellectual capital derived from project activities

- Developing tools for measuring the level of usage and effectiveness of project management methods used by the organization

- Soliciting and incorporating feedback from project managers for the continuous improvement of the methods and processes

- Defining and conducting project audits.

He or she may also act as a professional development coordinator—or oversee such a position—in order to ensure that:

- Job descriptions are created, maintained, and refined for the project management career path

- Criteria are defined for interviewing, rating, and hiring for project management skills, as well as for identifying people in the organization who are currently acting as project managers and those who are interested in developing their skills in order to become project managers

- Each individual is assisted in identifying strengths and weaknesses in the project management discipline and opportunities for developing the appropriate skills and knowledge

- The internal training organization is aided in identifying project management training courses

- Management identities individuals or assignment opportunities in order to develop skills and project management experience.[4]

In short the SPO director is an integrator of process, a manager of staff, a coordinator of project resources (including project managers), the coordinator of standards and methods, as well as the developer and maintainer of tools expertise, a mentor, a training coordinator, and the point of interface between projects, programs, and the executive staff. A tall order—and one that must be filled with the same care that companies take in placing a CIO, a CFO … or a CEO. In fact, project management consultant and author Paul Dinsmore has called for the institutionalization of a role called the "Chief Project Officer," on a peer level with other executives in the organization.[5] The alternative—spreading the project-management-related responsibilities out among existing executives in the organization—is cumbersome. In fact, this arrangement has been tried before, under the title of "matrix organization" and, as we discussed in Chapter 2, the jury is in: it's too slow and bureaucratic a system to satisfy today's rigorous time-to-market needs.

The Project Manager

Normally, in a single-project environment, the project manager manages the day-to-day tasks necessary to move the project through all its phases, while keeping the project sponsor (for an individual project) apprised of progress and pertinent new information. As a member of a complex corporate SPO, a project manager carries the same responsibilities with regard to individual project performance, but is somewhat relieved of the duties involved in keeping executive staff informed, since the SPO Director serves as liaison between projects and the executive. The major exception to this general rule occurs when the project manager's project is in trouble. In a troubled project, the project manager is "invited" to discuss the project with the project office steering committee, including what went wrong, the projected impact on the baseline, and corrective action planned. Naturally, these opportunities for exposure are not always welcome.

Paradoxically, the simpler the project office, the more difficult it will be to find a project manager with the requisite skills. That's because the project manager of a Level 1 PO (the least complex level of project offices) must not only manage the project at hand competently, but also perform some of the more sophisticated organizational roles of a SPO director: communicate with the executive staff, understand strategy and business goals, negotiate for resources, and so on. Project managers within a Strategic Project Office are insulated to a degree from these tasks by the SPO director. While communication and facilitation skills are always important for any level of successful project management (with some of the higher-level communication heat taken off them) project managers, as part of the Strategic Project Office and working within the formal SPO infrastructure and corporate project management methodology, are relieved of process and methodology design to focus on the technical and leadership tasks associated with their individual project success, such as project planning, time and cost estimating, leading the project team, controlling variance to the baseline, and successfully transitioning the project to operations and support.

All project managers are not created equal. Many have knowledge, skills, and personalities ideally suited to the project environment, while others don't. One of the stumbling blocks for project management growth in organizations in the past has been the failure to recognize that technical excellence does not translate to successful project management. Project management is a profession—a *discipline* that requires specific knowledge and skills in order to succeed at bringing projects in on time, on budget, and within specifications. Team management, negotiation, financial and business acumen, an understanding of organizational politics—all these areas and many more are also required to demonstrate success in managing projects. The more competent the project manager is in these areas, the more capable he or she is to help the organization as a whole execute projects that are closely coupled to corporate and departmental strategic goals.

The Project Team

Team members on projects make it all happen by executing the tasks necessary to move a project through all its phases to a successful closure and delivery. Typically, the number of team members increases as the project progresses, and decreases as the project approaches delivery and closure. Full-time dedication to the team is also more prevalent during the execution stage.

Among the roles that will be filled by project team members in an SPO are:

- Administrative support: back-office tasks, report generation, software support, calendars

- Best practice or process experts: training, project oversight, quality assurance, methodology development

- Librarian: managing project records, standards, methods, and lessons learned, which must be stored in a project database. In a large organization, the maintenance of such a repository can develop to become a full-time job. Once envisioned as a clerical task, the SPO librarian is now evolving into a sophisticated knowledge-management function and will become a fruitful source of benefits and value to the entire organization for historical data, successful practices, and effective templates, with knowledge that was previously lost with changes in personnel.

- Resource manager: Most organizations contemplating a Strategic Project Office will want to maintain a resource library or resources database, an inventory of all available resources throughout the organization. To complicate matters, the specific individuals available for assignment to projects constantly change as people join and leave the organization, technical resource skills are added and developed, people are assigned to other projects, or individuals become otherwise unavailable. In organizations with significant project activity, the responsibility for resource management may become a full-time job. Individual project managers, rather than having to "beg, borrow, and steal" resources wherever they can find them, turn to the SPO resource manager for assistance. The resource manager prioritizes resource requests and works with the project office steering committee to manage the "fit" of resource skills to project requirements, and balance scarce technical resources, forecast and aid in planning for acquisition of resource shortfalls, and secure assignment of key resources to projects according to a project's relative rank on the organization's prioritized project list. Of course, all projects on the list are, by definition, linked to corporate strategy and each possesses some degree of importance. If not of importance to the organization, projects should be canceled or rescheduled for execution in the future.

Rewarding the Project Team

Individual performance objectives are generally arbitrary since they cannot account for the interdependence of the team's tasks. As we generally use them, individual performance goals are simply subgoals based on the functional process measures of more senior managers. What is surprising is that many companies are just beginning to realize that the ways performance is measured and compensated determine whether or not teams reach their full potential.

The most radical—yet most obvious—change is to base all performance appraisals and review systems on the team and make the team accountable for team results. For true teamwork to occur, people need common purposes, measurable goals, and a common fate. Thus moving toward a project-oriented organization means creating a team-oriented appraisal and reward system. Because the team is in the best position to control the task, the team should be the primary focus of any performance measurement. Functional expertise is very much a prerequisite to team participation, but it is appraising performance based on the team's results that encourages people to wear two hats.

By measuring performance in the context of the whole process, we can begin to overcome the functional silo mindset, which encourages people to focus on their function to the exclusion of the project customer. In the project-oriented company, all employees take responsibility for interpreting the voice of the customer and acting on that to feed new ideas back into the system.

Individual contributors to projects will ultimately benefit from the institution of an SPO, but there will also be changes and dislocations for them to adjust to as they give up certain tasks and take on responsibility and authority to meet customer needs, while gaining the required expertise in their function.

Glenn M. Parker, of human resource consulting and research giant Watson Wyatt, recommends reward structures that foster collaboration, in which individuals are acknowledged, but primarily for being strong team players—those who "help the crowd stand out, rather than standing out from the crowd."[6]

Other Team Members

The stakeholders in a project are those individuals and organizations who are involved in or may be affected by project activities. Key stakeholders, then, are the individuals (generally no more than eight to ten, and often only two to three) or organizations that are *most* affected by the project and may include external customers, vendors, or regulatory personnel, depending on the project and industry.

Studies of organizational dynamics have revealed that a core team should number no more than eight people, with five to seven being the ideal number. A study at 3M showed that team members should be located near each other; as little as 100 yards of separation severely hindered team interactions! Procter and Gamble, a company renowned for rapid product development practices, provides employees with desks on wheels to facilitate easy relocation of people when teams change.[7] That's because strong successful teams remain intact as much as possible. Keeping teams together is practical, especially given the time and effort needed to create a team from a new group of people—another argument for centralizing project personnel within an SPO.

It's an old project management axiom that "people do projects." In the old matrix-style organization, those people were fragmented and isolated, scattered across the organization and bedeviled by conflicting priorities. The centralization of project management talent, training, and execution under the auspices of a Strategic Project Office realizes benefits related to streamlining, eliminating duplication, and allowing project personnel to focus on their primary areas of expertise.

Two Cautionary Tales

Speeding Up Development Cycles

In the early 1990s, one company initiated a project office deployment program. As a forms company with clients in the automotive industry, they had evolved from simply printing paper forms to electronic media. With that transition, they found they needed to provide integrated documentation across the industry as a whole. Manufacturers, dealers, and repair shop operators needed to have standardized forms for things like parts ordering, repair work, and automobile purchases. In the past they would fill out a form, send it in, create an order for parts for repair; suddenly all these steps were automated. With the promulgation of the personal computer and the benefits derived from automation, the company now provides full solutions, including computer hardware and software with links back to the automobile dealers to simplify the process. Today, a body shop, for example, does an estimate that details all the parts; the estimation software creates a parts order list, which gets relayed to the distributor; and the parts are shipped. In this process, it is important to know whether or not parts are available, when they are going to be shipped, whether they need to look at alternative resources, what the pricing is, what the available quantity is, and so on. Our featured company realized that their development cycles were too long—product development cycles for new automated products were taking over 18 months. In 18 months, another generation of computer technology (or two) has been developed, making their new products obsolete at launch. Facing a loss of market share, this organization saw the need to significantly decrease product development cycle time in order to remain competitive in the marketplace. Company leaders saw the only way product development and information systems organizations could work together effectively was by using project management. As a result, a project management training program was established through their corporate university and centralized project controls were established under one project office. Despite having a few false starts, they were able to significantly reduce product development lead times.

The Half-Hearted Project Office

A major insurance company initiated a small project office effort from within their IT organization. After two years of primarily conducting research, they have not made much progress. The reason? No sooner had they gotten into the research than their management called them off the project office effort to troubleshoot individual projects. While they were able to improve performance on individual projects, they lost focus on deploying the project office, which would have had a far greater return. After two years, they have realized that in order to have a structured process in place, they would need some consulting advice. Deploying an SPO requires everything that any project requires: a project plan, a project charter, an implementation plan, and executive support. And just as any individual project needs dedicated personnel, so does a project office. Without treating a project office deployment like the important, strategic project that it is, years—in this case, two years—can be wasted.

Endnotes

1. M. Light and T. Berg, "The Project Office: Teams, Processes, and Tools," *Gartner Strategic Analysis Report*, Aug. 1, 2000.
2. Michael Hammer and James Champy, *Reengineering the Corporation*, HarperCollins, 1993.
3. M. Light and T. Berg, op. cit.
4. Carolyn M Hennings, "Proposing a Program Office for a Service Organization," *Proceedings of the 30th Annual Project Management Institute Seminars & Symposium*, PMI, 1999.
5. Paul Dinsmore, *Winning in Business with Enterprise Project Management*, Amacom, 1998.
6. Glenn M. Parker, *Cross-Functional Teams*, Jossey-Bass, 1994.
7. Brian Dumaine, "How Managers Can Succeed Through Speed," *Fortune*, 13 Feb. 1989.

Chapter 5

Project Office Planning, Preparation, and Strategy

ITH THIS CHAPTER, WE FIND ourselves at the threshold of the project office itself. Before stepping across that threshold, consider how well you have laid the organizational foundations. You will not need to study the steps and recommendations here if you have not already dealt with the broader issues raised in Chapters 1 through 4—if you have not made the business case for a project office, assessed your organization's readiness for a project office, designed a project office of the appropriate level of integration and sophistication for your particular organization, and received executive commitment for the sweeping organizational changes that will be necessary for·success. Without first tackling these critical issues, merely going through the ordinary project management steps for implementation that we are about to address will most likely be in vain. Introducing strategic, enterprise-wide project management via a project office cannot be done from the bottom up in an organization; it cannot be done piecemeal; and it is unfair to the discipline of project management (not to mention the individual project managers) to set your project office up for failure from the outset by not properly preparing the ground.

With that caveat, let's dive into managing the project of creating your project office. As with any project, we'll begin at the beginning: a project charter.

The Project Charter: Agreeing on a Destination

A project charter formally recognizes the existence of a project. It describes the project at a high level and explains the business need for the project. The charter is completed typically by the project office director or the PO project manager, and approved by the business executives who are affected by the project, beginning with the project's executive sponsor and other senior managers (members of the project office steering committee). The project charter authorizes the PO director to expend company resources in planning the project. With an approved charter, the project is added to the organizational budget. (For help in creating the project charter, see Table 5.1.)

The project sponsor, project office steering committee, and all stakeholders are identified in the project charter. The charter coordinated with all stakeholders, who initial the document to indicate their approval. The charter is then approved by the project sponsor and issued to the project manager.

Objectives and Milestones: The Map to Your Destination

As with any project, planning begins with the establishment of goals, objectives, and milestones. It's incredible how many businesses begin projects without a clear idea of the end, a map detailing how to get there, or a set of criteria to tell them how to know when they have arrived. When you don't define these things very early on in the planning process, your project is almost certain to end up somewhere unforeseen.

The objectives of your project office initiative should follow the old SMART guidelines: objectives to deploy a project office should be specific, measurable, agreed-upon, realistic, and time-constrained.

Specific

Whenever possible, the objective should be expressed in terms of defined deliverables. For example, for a project management methodology development project, a specific objective statement might read:

> *To achieve a PM HealthCheck average of 3 or better within a six-month period, through implementation of an organizational project office.*

Measurable

How will you know when you are done? Your objective should enable you to be clear about when the objective is completed by defin-

Table 5.1 Project Charter Template

PROJECT PARTICIPANTS

Project Name
Enter a brief name to describe the project. For a project with broad organizational impact, it is wise to choose a name that will generate some excitement about the project.

Project Sponsor
As discussed in Chapter 3, the sponsor for a project office deployment project must be of sufficiently high level in the organization to influence other senior managers to cooperate with the changes required by the project. This person will be responsible for budgeting the funds to undertake the project and will have final authority to approve project completion.

Project Office Director/Deployment Project Manager
The primary liaison with the project sponsor and project office teams. This person is responsible for carrying out all project-related activities.

Other Participants
In addition to the sponsoring business area, indicate other business groups that will have crucial responsibilities for the project.

PROJECT DESCRIPTION

Business Background
Give an overview of the business reasons for the project. This should include the business justification for the project office deployment project, value the organization can expect to achieve, why the initiative is being undertaken, and the span of influence of this initiative.

Project Scope (detail both what is *in* and *out* of scope)
Provide a general description of the project scope (provide details in the following sections). Indicate both what is *within* the anticipated scope and what is *outside* the scope. Consider these topics:

- Systems
- Communications
- Infrastructure
- Business locations

Table 5.1 continued

Objectives
List specific business objectives that the project is anticipated to achieve.

Deliverables
List the specific deliverables expected from the project and how these will fulfill the objectives. The deliverables should be as tangible as possible. See the discussion in this chapter on Phase II and Phase III for some examples of deliverables.

Constraints
List factors that will limit the project team's options. For example, a predefined budget range is a constraint that is very likely to limit the team's options regarding project scope and staffing levels.

Assumptions
List factors or situations you will assume for the purposes of planning the project. For example, if the availability date of a key resource is uncertain, the team should make a reasonable assumption about the date of availability and list this as an assumed or contingent factor in the plan.

We agree that this is a viable project. We authorize the beginning of the planning process.

Date:

PROJECT SPONSOR

Member of the Project Office Steering Committee:

Member of the Project Office Steering Committee:

Member of the Project Office Steering Committee:

ing a measure or set of measures. In the example above, the project will be finished in six months upon approval of the steering committee.

Agreed Upon

All the stakeholders should buy in to the project objective; in most cases, this means senior management across several divisions, but could include vendors, suppliers, and other industry partners.

Realistic

The objective should also be realistic in that it is obtainable with the time and resources allocated. Too many project office initiatives reflect an unreachable objective that isn't obtainable even with unlimited resources and unlimited time—or which, even if obtained, cannot be objectively measured. Referring to the our example, before the time and cost objectives were set, the project manager may have issued a request for information to several consulting companies to ensure the objective was realistic. and attainable.

Time-Constrained

Project management is all about meeting deadlines. In the case of a project office, the objectives should be staggered in phases to allow the project to both meet immediate project needs and address longer-term issues involved in changing the organizational culture to a project-based one. Notice in the example that part of the objective is a firm completion date in six months. The following interim milestones may also appear in the charter for this project:

- Gather current project management practices being used within the company in 1 month

- Kickoff meeting with outside consultant in six weeks

- Conduct "PM for Executives" workshop in two months

- Draft of "Initiating Section" in ten weeks

- Draft of "Planning Section" in three months

- Draft of "Executing Section" and "Control Section" in fourteen weeks

- Draft of "Closing Section" in four months

- PM Methodology workshop with cross-functional team for review and refinement in eighteen weeks

- Revisions completed in five months

- Project completed in six months.

Using Gap Analysis to Set Milestones

The project office charter will ultimately include the project objective statement. Results from the gap analysis are incorporated into the project objective statement, project milestones, and the detailed project plan (see Table 2.6 in Chapter 2, the sample gap analysis chart). Gaps identified are incorporated into the project plan as specific outcomes to be achieved. This book does not cover basic project planning, but suffice to say that the planning process is carried out in the same manner used for any project. Keep in mind the objective of this particular project is to deploy a project office; therefore, the project objective may be a little broader in scope than the typical project objective.

A note of caution: Many times companies skip this step and approach the project office design by merely looking over an organizational chart and identifying which functions they want to transfer into the project office. In our view, this approach merely skims the surface of the value-adding change that a project office, especially a Level 3 SPO, can bring. It is prudent to concern yourself with function identification, not just function transfer. Future needs, while perhaps beyond the scope of the initial deployment, should become long-term goals for the next three to five years.

A project office should be established based on an organization's needs, both short term and long term. Specific project objectives and milestones flow from those identified needs, and the staffing plan is determined based on those objectives.

Delivering Value with Specific Short- and Long-term Objectives

Where to start? The best way to win converts for the project office method of managing projects is by adding value and getting results as quickly as you possibly can. Even senior management executives who are receptive to implementing a project office have probably been involved far too many times with programs that took two to three years of implementation before any results were shown. Money is tight,

114

competition is fierce, and companies have raised the bar on expectations for major change initiatives. It's likely that your management will be looking for fairly immediate results out of a project office deployment. To satisfy those concerns, find a set of short-term objectives that provide immediate value, such as developing, deploying, and supporting a project management methodology that brings immediate improvement to one or two pilot projects. At the same time, continue to work toward longer-term objectives related to changing organizational culture and adapting the organization to a new way of doing business. If you don't add value quickly, you will lose momentum; but if the larger-scope organizational change agenda is not pressed, the organization won't derive the greatest benefits from the project. Again, the gap analysis should help bring to the surface the areas in which the problems with projects are most pressing.

Specific long-term objectives should focus the organization on achieving increasing levels of the Project Management Maturity Model (PMMM), enabling optimized project management performance as an end result. Long-term objectives might include:

- Achieve Level 2 of the PMMM in six months
- Achieve Level 3 of the PMMM in one year
- Achieve Level 4 of the PMMM in two years
- Achieve Level 5 of the PMMM in three years.

Implementation Strategy

The project office approach should take a tactical focus in the beginning considering immediate concerns, business necessities, and the minimum requirements necessary to jumpstart the change process. During this initial period, preliminary steps can be undertaken to lay the groundwork on broader, complex issues. Long-term solutions address permanent maturity efforts that result in long-term value to the organization and ensure that you achieve your time-to-market timeframe. To accomplish this, we have found that a four-phase approach works well (see Table 5.2).

Phase I—Establish the Foundation

In this phase, define the project office and determine your immediate concerns and long-term objectives. As appropriate, start with an

Table 5.2 Short- and Long-Term Objectives for the Project Office

Phase I—Establish the Foundation

- Establish the project office
- Identify and prioritize all projects
- Deploy project management methods
- Train core teams
- Successfully complete pilot projects
- Attain management oversight on pilot projects
- Establish time and cost collection by project

Phase II—Startup with Short-Term Initiatives

- Train all project teams
- Utilize project management methods on all projects
- Plan, track, and manage resources
- Collect and manage projects
- Establish the project management costs for all culture changes
- Integrate management oversight into all projects
- Implement project reviews and audits

PHASE III—Rollout with Long-Term Solutions

- Train all business teams
- Fully integrate PM throughout organization
- Integrate resource and cost management across the organization
- Keep management actively involved utilizing PO reporting and analysis.

PHASE IV—Support and Improvement

- Implement a continuous quality improvement program

assessment of your current capabilities, goals, and objectives. Baselining against the project management maturity model identifies the baseline positioning of project management within the organization and aids in planning future tasks and activities. A series of meetings is held with key stakeholders and subject matter experts to understand current capabilities, challenges, issues, and goals. Based upon the discussions, an assessment report is developed which captures the current state and future vision along with an improvement plan recommending short-term initiatives and long-term solutions.

After developing the top-level improvement plan, determine the project office functions and staffing, identify stakeholders (to include key management, mentor programs, and pilot projects), and prepare a communications strategy. This phase ends with issuance of the project charter, authorizing the project office project team to proceed with funding and fill immediate staffing needs. This phase's activities have been covered in detail in Chapters 2–4. The timeframe for this phase varies widely, depending on the organization. Some companies feel driven to ramp up their project office quickly and can lay this organizational groundwork in a matter of a few weeks. Others will spend a longer period on the assessment process.

Phase II—Startup with Short-Term Initiatives

In this phase we start up the project office, put in place short-term initiatives, and initiate the project mentoring effort. Project office startup includes staffing the office for near-term needs, initiating communication activities, and making the organization aware of the project office and its responsibilities.

Two efforts are initiated to demonstrate the immediate value of the project office within the organization: short-term initiatives and project mentoring. The short-term initiatives provide solutions to immediate concerns and take care of issues surfaced by key stakeholders, solutions that can be implemented quickly.

Examples of short-term initiatives are:

- Deployment of a project management methodology (see Chapter 6 for detailed information on methodology and standards)

- Building an inventory of your projects (new product development, information technology, business enhancements, etc.)

- Preparing an executive report, showing the status of all active projects

- Establishing summary project report structures and project success metrics

- Organizing "brown bag" training lunches: brief, informal training sessions that familiarize members of the organization not only with the project office initiative, but also delivering key project management concepts

- Establishing support for new projects and projects in need (see section titled: "Reining in Runaway Projects")

- Conducting project planning or project control workshops

- Identifying and deploying one or more pilot project initiatives

- Providing templates for recurring project activities (see Chapter 6 for a discussion of using templates to encourage adherence to project management standards).

In conjunction with these short-term initiatives, project mentoring can be kicked off almost immediately, either by using the experienced, previously successful project managers already on board or by soliciting the assistance of external consultants experienced in the mentoring process. Project mentoring is an excellent way to provide immediate project management value to projects that are in the initial startup phase or are in need of support without waiting for the implementation of formal training programs or process roll-outs. For more information, a discussion of mentoring is included in Chapter 9.

Phase II ends when the short-term initiatives are in place and the team is ready to focus exclusively on the longer-term solutions planned in Phase I. In addition to the initiatives discussed, Phase II may include

- Training the core teams—teams for the pilot projects and for projects associated with project office startup, such as methodology development

- Beginning to involve management through the oversight committee review meetings

- Beginning to collect time and cost information by project in order to do the project tracking that will validate benefits to the organization

- Implementing an active communication plan to secure the confidence of the organization that these projects are going well and also that they have control and oversight on the pilot initiatives by communicating quantifiable results on the pilot projects; this will gain positive recognition from the business units because they are used to seeing projects fail or struggle

- Developing and deploying processes and standards (see Chapter 6)

- Establishing a bench of project managers.

Phase III—Rollout with Long-Term Solutions

There are increasing benefits to an organization as its project management capabilities mature. Phase III focuses on improving/streamlining the processes, developing personnel, and putting in place the more permanent support structure necessary for project management to succeed. In this phase we develop the long-term solutions, continue the project mentoring effort, conduct additional pilot tests (as appropriate), and gradually roll out the fully functioning project office. Examples of critical success factors include

- Continuing development and tailoring of processes and methodology

- Development of a training curriculum

- Development of detailed reports and metrics

- Addressing resource management issues

- Tool deployment (see Chapter 8)

- Project portfolio management (see Chapter 9)

- Project manager career progression and certification (see Chapter 9)

- Organizational change management and transition planning (see Chapter 10).

All of these items take time to develop, and the deployment should be done incrementally starting with pilot tests on selected projects. The assessment and improvement plan done during Phase I provides the overall long-term goals and objectives for the project office, and this phase develops, pilot tests, and rolls out the methods, standards, training, and support activities to achieve those overall goals. Other Phase III activities not mentioned may include

- Training all the project teams

- Implementing the methods established in Phase II for planning, tracking, and control

- Integrating projects into programs

- Implementing reviews and audits

- Establishing competency standards for project managers.

We move to yet another level of maturity when we begin to integrate project management throughout the organization. By the end of Phase III, all project-related estimating, budgeting, scheduling, change control, variance analysis, time tracking, issues tracking, risk analysis, and project reporting should be carried out under the auspices of the project office.

Phase IV—Support and Improvement
In this phase, the project office is in full operation and is supporting the organization's projects both from a tactical and strategic perspective. The project office conducts day-to-day activities, refines project management activities, and expands the involvement of the project office where appropriate. Training and other initiatives continue under the direction of the project office. Key stakeholders provide feedback on the project office's efforts and activities are continually refined as part of a quality management program. Portfolio management becomes more sophisticated as more project metrics are collected. A lessons-learned library, benchmarking, collecting best practices, and other knowledge management activities are hallmarks of the mature Strategic Project Office in Phase IV.

From our consulting practice, we have gathered the following ten practical keys to the successful deployment of a project office.

A Project Office—or—a Project Management Culture?

Is it possible to effectively deploy a project office without changing the organization's culture to a project management way of doing business? I contend it is not. To be effective as a project office—if it is to enable significant improvements in the ways projects are managed—requires an organization to mold itself into projectized form. Effective project management must become the core of how all projects are conducted. The project office will be ineffective if its only role is generating timelines and reports without the cultural change in how projects are initiated, planned, executed, controlled, and closed out. Movement to a project management culture throughout the organization is critical to success in managing the company's projects.

Ten Keys to Success for Deploying the Project Management Culture in an Organization

1. Keep it simple. First and foremost, be realistic and work the basics. If your staff can't explain why they are doing a particular project and they can't identify their 60-day plan, focus on helping those areas first. Don't worry about a sophisticated estimating process yet; focus on simply understanding project goals and developing basic plans. Once you identify these basic needs, stay focused and don't do too much too soon. Employ the minimum project management essentials (such as a project charter, project management plans, project schedules, project metrics, and project reporting) and start up the office to help project teams. Don't try to optimize every aspect of project management.

2. Communicate. The best idea goes nowhere if you keep it to yourself, surprise everyone at the last minute, and expect it to be accepted and practiced. People don't like surprises, so explain what you are doing and why, frequently and in plain English. This is one of the keys to successfully creating a project culture, discussed further in Chapter 10. Let everyone know how the project office and the new business practices will help them. Package a "story" and spread it around. Say the same message over and over, tailoring it for the different levels of the organization. Communicate your goals and successes via different avenues—a project bulletin board, status review meetings, brown bag sessions, e-mail, or communiqués. Just get the word out. (See the section "Best Practice: Communication" later in the chapter.)

3. Make sure that expectations and goals are shared. Make sure the charter for the project office deployment project is endorsed by all stakeholders. Have a kickoff meeting—a big event—to share the elements of the charter, the goals and vision of the executive sponsor. Have the sponsor say a few words, focusing on the benefits to be achieved. Keep people informed as you create the project office. Make a big deal out of your successes.

4. Focus on value. Determine the organization's most pressing concern and fix it. Find what hurts the most and focus on it. Talk to key stakeholders at all levels within the organization. Try to fix one key concern for each level. Sometimes the immediate fix is an interim solution that is done inefficiently (such as manual reports)—but at least the report provides information and insight with some degree of confidence. Whatever you choose to do, link the goals of the project office to the organization's goals and explain how the pffice and project management practices help meet the organization's goals. Immediate results in selected areas are important to keep interest and excitement about the churning, as well as to prove to executive management that the PO isn't just business as usual. Be very clear in identifying the deliverables at select phases of the pilot project(s) to show that results are occurring.

5. Support project managers. Often someone who has been a wonderful technician or a proficient business analyst or engineer is placed into the role of project manager with no training, no assistance, no support; then we wonder why they struggle. A key to success is providing support, assistance, mentoring, and guidance to project managers. Project managers need support to help develop the plans, manage the schedules, monitor the costs, manage the resources, do the variance analyses, and generate the reports. When a project manager is expected to do all the specialized work on a major project, he or she cannot focus on the areas where project managers add the most value: the "art" of project management, which involves communication, facilitation, negotiation, creative problem solving, and other critical tasks.

6. Take time to understand the organizational problems from various points of view. Project managers don't just deal with the executive level or only with their project team members. In order to gain widespread acceptance of the project office throughout the organization, the PO director should take time to learn about the issues and challenges facing all the departments or business units that will be affected by the changes. In particular, the input of the technical staff should be included in the project plan, since this can be crucial to issues of change and risk, as well as configuration management. The PO director will be able to work much closer to the plan if the technical risks have been identified, assessed, and planned for.

7. **Conduct pilot tests.** No two organizations are the same. There are different organizational cultures, personalities, approaches, techniques, and technologies. This uniqueness requires us to begin implementing a project office by conducting pilot projects, deploying methodology and process against those pilots and then refining the processes and methodologies with lessons learned for subsequent deployment. Through pilot testing of the strategic project management approach, we are able to gain experience, adapt and reapply lessons learned, and be much more successful in the enterprise-wide deployment of the SPO.

8. **Establish incremental goals**. Research on project failure[1] tells us that in order to be successful, projects must be broken down into phases or periodic review stages. This applies to any project undertaken in the organization—not just the project of implementing a project office. At the end of each phase, we can look at where we are, look at where we have been, compare our progress to where we need to be going and revaluate our approach, redirect our efforts, reprioritize our initiatives, and reestablish our commitment for management that they projects are valid and critically important. At one time, midstream corrections of this type would have been frowned on in project management circles. Thankfully, however, the discipline has realized that it is foolhardy to hold fast to a course of action when the environment around you is changing.

9. **Involve the right people up front, starting with your executive sponsorship.** No matter what you do, without executive sponsorship, you will fail. Make sure you understand who cares, who will be impacted, and who makes decisions. Get the leadership team involved from the beginning. Find out their needs, expectations, and

goals. Identify their concerns and work to address them. Remember to keep it simple, focus on value, and plan. Understand the problems at different levels. Identify an executive "cheerleader" (or sponsor) and encourage as much "cheering" as possible. Plan regular status review meetings with the project office steering committee. But don't focus only on the executives: it's important to get the right people on the project teams as well. Don't choose these important pilot project teams strictly because they were available. Involve people who are most knowledgeable in the technology, the process, and the business area. By getting the right people involved in the initial planning stages, even if you have to delay the initiation of planning for the project, you can do a much more effective job of planning, identifying the issues, identifying the risks and planning for success for the future. The "right people," it should be noted, may also include stakeholders from outside of the immediate organization, such as clients or vendors. If implementing new technology is to play a major role in your project office initiative, it only makes sense to include a knowledgeable vendor, rather than relearn all those skills or make all the mistakes that a more experienced person might be able to foresee.

10. Plan. We've covered planning in considerable detail already, but it is one of the real keys to success. Although it is sometimes painful and may at times appear to be nonproductive, take the time to plan thoroughly up front. The plan will help set expectations and facilitate communications. Establish incremental goals to show progress and results to the organization. Identify specific short-term and long-term solutions and explain how, in some cases, an interim solution will set the stage for a long-term objective (for example a current report that is done manually may need to be automated). Make sure you plan enough time to conduct pilot tests and train individuals before setting in place the new process or tool. So many times we launch into a frenzied work effort because of the attention the project is receiving from management. We want to show results immediately, but often in doing so we begin working away at all the wrong things. It may not be necessary to plan the full project office project in detail. Rolling wave planning allows us to fully plan out the first phase of the project and then at a higher level plan out the remaining phases. This allows us to incorporate lessons learned from earlier phases into subsequent phases of the project.

Related to this item is *taking time to adequately train the project teams.* The great majority of teams are not prepared to embark on this new discipline. Many don't share a common terminology. Many don't understand the techniques. Many don't understand the business case, or the "soft" side of project management. And many don't appreciate the rigor that is necessary for effective planning. Most of the time, project teams are simply anxious just to get started doing the work. Unfortunately, although many project teams are absolutely convinced that they are on the right track, past rates of project failure tell us that it's likely project teams will hit a roadblock and find out that they were going down the wrong path all along—having wasted time, resources, and money along the way. Thanks to the research done by the Standish Group, the Gartner Group, and others, we now know that many project derailments can be avoided with appropriate planning, forethought, risk identification, risk analysis, and workaround considerations. Therefore, training to transfer knowledge of project management process is absolutely critical to get everybody working on the same wavelength, as well as to prevent resistance to the organizational changes wrought by the implementation of a project office.

... and Five Ways to Fail

Just as there are key activities that work in a project office implementation, there are factors that hinder progress. Avoid doing these things. At minimum, recognize what is happening which may require a change in behavior and approach. Your implementation will fail if you:

1. **Forget key stakeholders.** Earlier, we mentioned the importance of executive sponsorship. But executives are not the only key stakeholder or customer of the project office. Others include project managers, project teams, functional/resource managers, and line managers. Just like the executives, these stakeholders must be involved from the beginning. Determine their needs, expectations and goals. Understand the problems from the executive's point of view; otherwise, you may overlook a key concern. Even if buy in has been developed, and a blessing has been bestowed on the project charter, it's important not to let communication with stakeholders diminish as the project progresses.

2. Demand before providing. A project office must be viewed as an entity that helps, an entity that *provides* services to ease project management administration and to facilitate smart business practices. All of this results in an improved track record of project delivery. The project office should never be in a position of always demanding information and seldom providing services. You will not be successful by asking for too much too soon.

3. Do it all at once. There are three factors to a project office implementation: people, process, and tools. Obviously changing all three at once is a very complex undertaking. If possible, avoid doing this. Change the environment (tool) but keep the process the same; or change the process but use the same environment and tool. A phased approach makes this feasible. As project office director, don't do it all at once. You may not be able to deliver, and people will get confused. Don't allow overeagerness on the part of executive sponsors to push you into making promises you cannot keep or which will overextend the resources at your command. It's better to succeed incrementally than fail spectacularly.

4. Procrastinate. Once a decision has been made to implement a project office, move on it. Don't hesitate or partially support the idea. You will lose support and focus. The organization will stop believing in the concept. In addition, the longer it takes to implement, organizational changes and upheavals may occur to disrupt the project office initiative. Such adjustments may result in changes in executive sponsorship and other key stakeholders. Priorities may change and the effort may lose support and funding, resulting in a failed initiative. When implementation gets prolonged due to administrative issues or organizational restructuring, decisions are postponed on the budget, administrative support is not given until a crisis occurs, staff is pulled off to work on other projects, etc., and soon the project office initiative is moribund. Plan thoroughly—and hit the ground running.

5. Work in a vacuum. In a project office implementation, a team approach wins. The office is intended to serve multiple customers, each of whom have personal experiences and ideas to share. Incorporate other people's ideas and acknowledge them and give credit where due. Learn from others' experiences—don't re-invent the wheel. Find out individual requirements and needs, and design accordingly and appropriately. Leverage all the knowledge and experience at your disposal.

Measuring Success: How to Know When You've Arrived

As we've detailed, the key to deploying a project office is to make sure that there is added value to the organization, that the value accrues incrementally, and that the value is communicated to all stakeholders. Therefore two things need to be in place: metrics to define success at each stage of the deployment and a communication plan to get the good news out.

Metrics

"When performance is measured, performance improves. When performance is measured and reported back, the rate of improvement accelerates." So said Thomas S. Monson[2] in *Pathways to Perfection*. While project management metrics can be a confusing subject, when implementing a project office, you are fortunate to have the one thing that must be in place in order for measurement to be meaningful: a baseline.

The baseline in this case is provided by the assessment of organizational maturity done as a necessary first step (see Chapter 2). By reassessing the organization using the same assessment tool and maturity modeling approach that you started out with, organizational improvements in project management can easily be evaluated.

As for measuring progress on the project office deployment project itself, we can use the tried-and-true metrics we use for any project: variance analysis. Once the charter is issued, the team creates the work breakdown structure. Then, using the WBS, the project schedule is created and displayed either as a logic network (precedence diagram/critical path network) or a Gantt chart with relationships among tasks embedded. By conducting the usual periodic progress meetings and updating the Gantt chart, schedule variance can immediately be determined and acted upon. Cost variance is not difficult to measure in a project such as this for the simple reason that most of the expense is either in payroll of internal team members or contract costs for external consultants. Identify cost variance and take corrective action. Finally, technical variance and scope change must be addressed. Using the list of desired capabilities in the short, mid, and long term discussed earlier, create a requirements matrix to ensure that each desired capability is addressed by the WBS and project plan. Create milestones for each capability and track progress toward those goals. Identify variances and act promptly to keep technical progress on track.

One important step when measuring the success of the implementation is to re-visit the gap analysis and do a "reality check." Have you covered all the areas of weakness that were identified? Have the issues raised been addressed? And, finally, simple though it seems: is everybody happy? Simply surveying all the stakeholders to get their input on how they feel the new initiative is working can be extremely valuable.

Communications Planning

As part of the initial project planning effort for the project office initiative, a communications plan must be in place. First, there will be the need to communicate about the initiative to the overall organization. Then there will be specific planning for meetings related to assessment and deployment.

Early on in the pilot stage, there should be opportunities to generate success stories—rather than waiting to stumble over these opportunities, however, they need to be programmed into the deployment and integrated into the communication plan so that, as they are experienced, they are communicated back to the appropriate stakeholders, management.

The Meeting Guide (Table 5.4) describes a variety of forums that can be used to communicate throughout the organization and through all project phases. Keeping everyone informed, without swamping them with an overload of information, is key to creating a sense of "ownership" at all levels of the organization (see also Table 5.3).

Purpose

Communication among the various entities working on (or interested in) a project is absolutely essential. The purpose of a formal project communications plan is to ensure that all teams and interested parties who are involved in any way provide and receive appropriate communications.

The involvement of multiple teams and organizational units enlarges the web of necessary communications and increases the complexity of conveying the right message to the right audience at the right time.

Table 5.3 Communications Plan Template

Audience (who)	Message (what)	Intent (why)	Media (how)	When	Responsibilities

Table 5.3 continued

COMMUNICATIONS PLAN TEMPLATE DEFINITIONS

Audience (Who needs to know?)
Who is the audience for each communication? Check the project charter, statement of work, and other project documents to determine audiences. Some messages will go to audiences defined by function or group membership:

- Project (key project stakeholders, project personnel, project managers, project sponsors, business area project manager, consultants)
- Business area (business group participants not on the project team, cross-business groups, business group by business group notification)
- Corporate (executive committee, selected executive officers)
- Outside customers (customers who use the project)

Some audiences will be defined by project phase, milestones, and status:

- Introductory audience
- Audience for various phases and milestones
- Testing audience
- Implementation audience, by phase
- Conclusion audience for project review and sharing the success

Message (What?)
Describe the message that needs to go out to this audience:

- What does the project need to communicate to its audiences?
- Who is authoring, sponsoring, and/or standing behind the message?
- What's going to happen? What other needs or work is it related to?
- How far along are we? When is it going to happen?

Table 5.3 continued

- Where's it going to happen? Where's it *not* going to happen?
- How is it going to take place, in what steps or increments?
- How will the project team help you get through the change?
- What does the recipient need to do and by what date?
- When will there be further communications, second warnings, etc.?
- Where can they get more information, who should they call?

Intent (Why?)
Why is this communication taking place?

- What is the intended effect? What do we hope to achieve?
- What are the benefits?

Media (How?)
How to communicate will depend on the phase of the project, the audience, etc. It generally takes face-to-face communication to achieve buy-in, support, and to get someone to take action. At other times, you will use hard copy print and electronic media or combinations of media.

When
Consider the statement of work, the evolving project plan, and the advice of project leaders and key stakeholders to determine a communication approach and timing.

Responsibilities
For each message in the project communications plan:

- Who will prepare the message, develop the media, and coordinate the delivery?
- Who will author or sign the communication? (Who is the message from?)

Key reasons for project communications include

- Establishing (and maintaining) the support of those involved, including project sponsors, team members, and those who will use the project deliverables

- Educating decision makers on the "whats" and "whys" of the project

- Informing the ultimate beneficiaries and others who will be affected by the project and preparing them for what to expect.

In addition to the effect on those closest to the project, other impacts include

- Any phase of project implementation (testing, for example) may involve some change or even disruption in regular services to some or all users. These impacts need to be communicated in advance.

- Implementation also may involve changes in local procedures, new training for users, and other effects. All possible impacts need to be communicated in a timely manner.

Origination and Timing

The project manager completes the project communications plan in consultation with the business area project manager and other key project participants. Much of the requisite information for the communications plan will come from the statement of work (SOW); so it is suggested that the project communications plan be completed *after* laying the foundations in the SOW. Then, the project communications plan should be summarized in the body of the SOW and appended in its entirety to the SOW.

Inputs

- *Statement of Work.* Even if it is not 100% completed, the SOW is a reference for communications planning.

Outputs

- *Project Communications Plan.* Use the form to organize your plan. Changes and updates to the completed project communications plan should be stored in your central project files.

Other Outputs

- *Tasks*. As you prepare the project communications plan, you will identify additional tasks or task groups to include in later versions of the project plan.

- *Issues*. Issues that arise during preparation of the project communications plan should be logged in the project issues log.

Project Communications Plan Guidelines

Communication is not a single event—it is a composite, the result of several messages that build on one another. In your project communications plan,

- Strive for "no surprises." The objective is that everyone who needs information about any aspect or phase of the project gets the information they need in time to assimilate it and, if necessary, respond to it.

- Communicate "down the chain," that is, communicate with leadership first, then team members, and so on.

- Define your audiences carefully—both who needs to know and who does not. You will have different audiences for different aspects of the project.

- Anticipate the information needs of each audience and time your messages to coincide with project milestones and the audience's anticipated need to know.

- Target each audience with appropriate media—different audiences may require different approaches.

- Plan for multiple messages to the same audience, with repetition and reinforcement. Repetition will not necessarily upset the recipients—as long as you target them well and send the right message.

- Create a mechanism for anonymous feedback from your audiences.

A DECISION TO IMPLEMENT A PROJECT OFFICE does not need to be followed by a lengthy, drawn-out implementation. You can't afford it— there is little time, limited resources, competitive pressure, and the need to do business. The way to implement a project office is to first focus on immediate value and business necessities. You should design an implementation approach that takes care of these immediate concerns and, in parallel, lays the groundwork for longer-term solutions. The key is to keep the implementation simple, focused on value, and structured with a plan. Don't try to do it all at once. Build an office that provides services to ease administration and put in place smart business practices. The net result will be a structured, consistent method to manage projects and an understanding of project performance—resulting in overall better project performance.

Best Practice: Communications

During their project office deployment, a large insurance company had a wall outside the cafeteria where anyone with any concerns, issues, or questions about the Strategic Project Office deployment could just stick a Post-it Note up on the wall. Responses to questions and issues were also posted. As people were walking to and from the cafeteria, they would stop and see what the latest issues were, the latest concerns, the latest feedback. And many of those questions found their way into the regular newsletter that was published, and those in charge of the PO responded and addressed the issues there. In many cases, the CIO or one of the executive VPs would respond and, in responding, show their support and encouragement, show insight into why the PO project was valuable, and why everyone should support it.

How to Select a Project Office Steering Committee

The project office steering committee should be made up of three to five executives in the organization. The chair of the steering committee must be the executive who stands to gain (or lose) the most from a successful implementation of a project office. The remainder of the steering committee is represented by corporate leaders whose organizations maintain a vested interest in effective deployment of a project management culture. It is critical the project office steering committee possesses the authority to 1) approve the plan and budget for deploying a project office, 2) authorize changes to the project office deployment plan and budgets, 3) provide resources for the initiative, and 4) assist the project office deployment manager in building support for the project office, resolving conflicts, and successfully de-

Table 5.4 Meeting Guide: Communication that is Right for You

Description	Purpose	Audience	Media
One-on-One	Address "What's in it for me"	Sponsors/ management	Face-to-face
Kickoff meeting	Inform	Project managers and sponsors	One-to-many
General information	Information updates	Entire company	E-mail, internet etc.
Intranet BBS	Questions, comments	Entire company	Intranet
Newsletter articles	Information updates	Entire company	Electronic or paper (but more formal than e-mail or memos)
Team meetings	Status	Team	Face-to-face

ploying a project management culture. The capstone consideration for qualifications to participate as a member of the project office steering committee is that the steering committee must have the authority to cancel the project office deployment project should conditions warrant.

PO Value-Adding Strategy: Rein in Runaway Projects

According to Standish Group principal Jim Johnson, the improvements that have been made in project failure rates over the past few years are in large part due to organizations learning how to control, even to stop, projects that are in trouble.[3] Virtually every organization, no matter how mature and experienced, will occasionally be forced to deal with one or more failing projects. Rather than ignoring the problems, it's useful to view the struggling project as an opportunity to learn and reference for continuous process improvement. How do you know when a project is in trouble?

Early Warnings

Although it is customary to focus on schedule and budget overruns as red flags of troubled projects, these indicators come too late in a project to forestall problems. According to the Gartner Group, there are four early indicators of runaways which can often be identified as early as the planning stage so that potential problems can be nipped in the bud.[4]

- Inadequate project planning—Ambiguous milestones; failure to chart the interdependencies between tasks and establish a critical path; estimates not based on actual organizational history and experience (lessons learned); lack of attention to cross-project resource dependencies (in a multi-project setting). The Gartner Group has noted that as the number of projects in an organization increases, resource scheduling becomes more important because resource management errors, even on small projects, have a cascading impact on the crowded organizational resource calendar.[5]

- Poorly defined objectives and requirements—When the business objectives of a project are muddled, or when the customer (end user) has not been involved in defining the requirements for a project, the project is likely to go off track or to deliver an end product that is not satisfactory to the customer. Worse, a project may "succeed" in terms of meeting time and cost constraints, but be a failure because it does not answer the business needs of the organization.

- Technology disconnects—The project whose schedule depends on estimated productivity gains from the use of new technology or tools is likely to derail. The effort required to implement complex new tools cuts into productivity; in addition, the change management issues surrounding the introduction of new technology can create cultural upheavals with no quick and easy fix.

136

- Missing skills—Failure to assign or identify all the critical skills when doing resource allocation. Whether this problem is later addressed by seeking help from outside consultants or by acquiring new skills through training, the schedule and budget will be significantly impacted. "No project should be undertaken unless the required skills will be available on an as-needed basis," says Gartner.[6]

Another early warning signal is extreme project complexity. The Standish Group has found that breaking large, complex projects down into component projects—with smaller teams and shorter time-frames—is a key success factor.[7]

In-Progress Problem Indicators

- Schedule and budget overruns, caused by restarts and rework and scope creep—Schedule slippage of over 10% for any task, or a scope creep (the accretion of additional requirements once a project is planned and under way) of more than 5%, is generally a serious red flag. Restarts and rework are classic runaway symptoms. In 1994, the Standish Group found that for every 100 failed projects, there were 94 restarts. Each time significant rework or a restart occurs, the team must revalidate the project's scope and objectives, reestimate, reevaluate risks, and decide whether to proceed. Be on the lookout for faulty task management, leading to deliverables that are consistently late and abrupt scheduling changes.

- Poor communications—reports that are inadequate (or overwhelming), insufficient documentation, ineffective meetings.

- Team dysfunction—This can be demonstrated by low morale and high turnover, by team conflict, or by confusion and disorganization. Don't gloss over conflict by dismissing it as personality clashes—it can sometimes reflect deeper problems. Team members on a failing project may develop a "bunker mentality," treating anyone who points out problems as a troublemaker. When the team is constantly requesting more details or bogged down in meetings, intervention may be called for.

Pulling on the Reins

Where should the project office start once the runaway and failing projects have been identified? First, *focus only on the highest-priority projects*: these can be identified by examining the business case and identifying the tangible and intangible benefits to be derived from project completion. This is a process the organization must master in order to succeed at project portfolio management anyway, and the selection and prioritization of projects is a key function of SPOs. Once the highest-priority projects have been identified, initiate a project recovery program:

- Assess the problems—Identify the specific problem or problems that were the root cause or causes of the loss of control. Look especially hard at the "early warning signals" for clues.

- Develop an action plan to address them—Even if the project cannot be saved in its current form, it's likely that some components of it may be restructured into manageable phases. But don't restart without a strategy in place to prevent recurrence of the problem, on the current project as well as on future similar projects. For example, if missing skills were the cause, implement an appropriate training program.

- Get commitment to work the action plan from the stakeholders—team members, executive management, and other stakeholders, including suppliers and subcontractors. The inclusion of all stakeholders cannot be overstressed. A project cannot be successful within the context of an organization whose long-term business needs are not being met. Thus, stakeholders external to the project—subcontractors, users, government agencies, and the like—should have a significant interest in and focus on how projects are managed.

- Set project standards. *A Guide to the Project Management Body of Knowledge*[8] provides the most widely known standard for managing individual projects. Update project plan templates and methodology documentation to capture the results of the analysis phase and to ensure mistakes are not repeated on future projects.

- Provide coaching and mentoring to the project staff—According to a report in *Computerworld*,[9] training in the "soft skills"—

138

including leadership—is perhaps the most important factor in improving project performance.

• Be sure knowledge transfer is taking place during the recovery— Learn from your failures.

• Stay on top of it—Conduct reinforcement reviews.[10]

A Real-Life Experiences

"If Only We Knew This Before"

The airline was adding a new type of aircraft to their fleet. A new technology passenger convenience unit was planned as part of the rollout. With four years of development and production expected, a subcontractor was chosen to build the units. Five years after the contract, the subcontractor is asking for a delay in delivery and more money. The technology also is now two generations old. On reviewing the situation, we find performance and technical specifications were severely lacking from the start (especially the performance specifications). No requirement was levied to the subcontractor regarding the specific project reporting requirements and delivery milestones. Little (or no) accountability for schedule delays and cost overruns were included as part of the contract. What happened? During contract negotiations, the airline failed to include specifications with sufficient detail to include operating performance characteristics and requirements. No provision was established in the contract for the subcontractor to adequately plan and control the development project or to report ongoing status to the airline. Many delays, technical complications, and overlooked deliverables built up to create a project disaster. Lessons learned: The airline itself did not perform sufficient project planning nor did it require the same from one of its key stakeholders—the subcontractor. The airline delayed reaction until the damage was already done, then wanted to put project controls in place. In the end, no one was happy; a poor deliverable was produced, airplane delivery was delayed, costs were overrun, and protracted litigation ensued.

A Real-Life Experience—"Too Much Too Soon"

An information technology organization saw the need for standard project management practices and a central office to manage ongoing efforts. The project budget was expected to increase significantly and management recognized the need to smartly manage the resources. The organization was going from an informal project management environment to one with more structure in process and tools. Both process and tools were being changed at the same time and most project managers did not welcome the change. The project office effort progressed smoothly until the project managers were asked to change their tool environment and be more disciplined in drafting project management plans. The leadership was focused on other pressing issues and did not have time to support the project office initiative. There was rebellion on one side and lack of interest on the other. The initiative was pushed to the back burner and significantly decreased in scope and importance. Several factors contributed to the situation: organizational changes and upheaval, changes in priorities, doing it all at once, and lack of executive sponsorship. Lessons learned: 1) Keep things simple and focused on value to "preserve" the initiative during the organizational changes. 2) Put in place a strong communications program to obtain buy-in from all key stakeholders. 3) Introduce the tool environment and new processes in an incremental fashion. 4) Secure and repeatedly work to keep executive sponsorship.

"Executive Focus on Value"

A financial services company decided to deploy project management methodology in their information technology organization. The deployment plan focused on three key project office areas : 1) Deployment of a standard project management process and methodology, 2) project management tool development and deployment, and 3) training for the staff affected by the project management initiative. Regular meetings were established to communicate developments and expectations with two primary career groups: the project managers and the project planners. A standard approach to managing projects was developed, deployed, and taught to all project teams. Project brochures were distributed listing the Top 10 projects, their deliverables, milestones, and quality metrics. Entire project teams received performance bonuses based on delivery against the Top 10 goals. Directors and vice-presidents routinely participated in project reviews and led meetings to discuss the value of the divisional project management initiative. Actual improvements: Planning was sufficient for all stakeholders to understand expectations for the project. Most of the Top 10 projects were delivered on time and satisfied or exceeded the quality metric goals. Experience was developed to further enhance delivery quality for future projects. Lessons learned: Mentoring support was critical in the first phases of project office deployment due to severe lack of internal project management competency. Methodology efforts were started and redirected on three occasions; it is critical to deploy an effective methodology and integrate that tailored methodology into project management training initiatives.

"The Global Office and Time-to-Market Reductions"

A new product development organization wanted to decrease the time-to-market period for new products. The project office decided to modify their project management practices in an effort to reduce time-to-market. The project office put in place a mentoring program, project planning and estimating, project tracking and control, and additional project coordination/communications avenues. The project office ensured that the project management methodology was established and followed. The organization started planning and showing the impact to key milestones. Regular meetings were held to address issues. The project office enabled comprehensive resource capacity planning and project prioritization, resulting in better planning for resource demand. The attention and focus placed on project management caused project teams to pay closer attention to detail and employ better discipline in meeting deadlines. The net result was a reduction in the launch cycle of a particular product by two months, resulting in an increase of tens of millions in revenue. Lessons learned: 1) Project methodology buy-in at the business unit level is critical. Those buying in saw their time-to-market improve while others who didn't "pay for the service" languished and time-to-market even got worse. 2) Take small incremental steps and show results continuously (keep it simple and focus on value). 3) Get an executive sponsor high in the organization.

Endnotes

1. The Standish Group, *The Chaos Report*, 1999.
2. Thomas S. Monson, *Pathways to Perfection*, Deseret Book Company.
3. *PM Network*, Sept. 1998.
4. D. Brown and R. Hunter, "Putting the Shrapnel Back in the Grenade: Recapturing the Runaway RAD Project," The Gartner Group, July 5, 1996.

5. Brown and Hunter, ibid.
6. Brown and Hunter, ibid.
7. Jim Johnson, "Turning CHAOS into SUCCESS," *Software*, Dec. 1999.
8. PMI, 2000.
9. Julia King, "IS Reins in Runaway Projects: Users Fight Failures with Better Management." *Computerworld*, Feb. 24, 1997.
10. Richard W. Bailey II, "Six Steps to Project Recovery," *PM Network*, May 2000, 33-34,36; Paula Jacobs, "Recovering from Project Failure," *Infoworld*, Sept. 27, 1999; Lauren Gibbons Paul, "Turning Failure into Success: Maintain Momentum," *Network World*, Nov. 22, 1999; J. Roberts and J. Furlonger, "Successful IS Project Management," Gartner Group, April 18, 2000.

Chapter 6

Establishing a Project Management Methodology

ETHODOLOGY IS ONE OF THOSE fine-sounding words that many times is used in such a way that it delivers less than it promises. Even the *American Heritage Dictionary* notes that, in recent years, the word *methodology* has become merely a pretentious synonym for *method*. Since one of our editors has pointed out that imprecise use of words often stems from fuzzy thinking about the subjects they describe, it seems worthwhile to begin this chapter by defining our terms.

We have repeated throughout this book that one of the primary functions of a project office (and a source of almost immediate value) is the promulgation of a methodology—the establishment of methods, standards, and processes.[1] What do each of these words really mean, and how do they interrelate?

Defining Our Terms

A methodology is "a body of practices, procedures, and rules used by those who work in a discipline or engage in an inquiry; a set of working methods."[2] But it's also more than merely a collection of methods, it's a framework for making sense of them. As the dictionary goes on to say, there is "an important conceptual distinction between the tools of scientific investigation [methods] and the *principles* that determine how such tools are deployed and interpreted."

If this seems like hair-splitting, bear with us. In our experience, nothing produces more confusion than giving someone the grand-sounding task of establishing a methodology without being clear about what that entails. Like any project—and the establishment of a methodology is an important subproject in the deployment of a project office—the most critical step toward success is the first one: defining requirements.

What is required for a company to institute a project management methodology? A methodology standardizes the structure of managing projects, sequences the project phases, and describes best practices so that there is predictability, repeatability (of desired results across the organization), and more efficient utilization of resources. It also reduces the risk of cost and schedule overruns by promoting a deliverables-based program for every project. With a little research, many off-the-shelf methodologies can be readily tailored to your environment and practice, and then implemented.[3]

A glossary of project management and process improvement terms compiled by Boeing[4] defines "process" as a systematic series of actions directed to some end ... a series of progressive and interdependent steps by which an end is attained.

One elegantly simple definition of methodology was suggested by Tony Nish in *PM Network* in 1999: "When managing projects in a business context, methodology is how we do what we do to ensure high-quality, repeatable results."[5] One of the most immediate values of a standard methodology is that it serves as a common language among practitioners.

Despite this, many organizations lack discipline in the application of methodology. Nish suggests three possible reasons for this:

- They are using a methodology recommended by company edict but which experienced practitioners haven't bought into.
- They feel it is too high a level to be of any practical value.
- They have yet to see the direct positive impact of using one.

How do organizations without a methodology achieve project success? By heroic performance and hiring experienced project managers with a good track record. These "heroes" have long figured out that good methodology is useful and best used when it can be taken for granted. A good methodology is transparent in the hands of an experienced practitioner. It is most simply a non-content-specific guide for defining and sequencing phases, activities, and tasks. It is, essentially, "pure logic that an experienced practitioner applies to meet the needs of a particular business situation or problem." And that's fine for those rare superheroes of the project world, but what about the vast majority of us who are just trying to figure out a better way to manage our projects day in and day out? Imagine an organization with 100 to 1,000 project managers. Do you really want each one to use his or her "pure logic" to come up with a method for managing projects? So let's get into more detail on developing a methodology for the masses.

A methodology should include questions or prompts for all potential issues that might arise in the process of managing a project. This is why methodologies look high level to a non-practitioner. It is in the *application* of the methodology to the project at hand that the direct practical value emerges.

It is common to hear a project management software package described as a methodology when it is really simply a project management tool. The critical difference is that a project management methodology deals with all, or at least most, project management processes in an integrated, orderly way, while a software tool offers some project management functionality but does not cover all the processes necessary for success. An uninformed user may not be aware of what is missing. That's not to say that software cannot play a part: for example, some methodologies are integrated into a project planning tool. Since creating the project plan is a major (and very time-consuming) part of a project manager's responsibilities, using a schedule-creation template that is integrated into a project planning tool can be a useful method, but it does not comprise a methodology in and of itself.

"A project management methodology means documentation that incorporates project management processes; teams use a project management methodology as a reference for defining the methods to be used, as well as activities to be undertaken, during the conducting of a project," says Nish.[6]

Five Steps to Establishing a Methodology

While this might seem like a daunting task, the good news is that many of the elements of a methodology (see Figure 6.1) already exist in your organization. Thus the first challenges for a project office when tackling methodology development involve looking around to find

Figure 6.1. What is a Methodology?

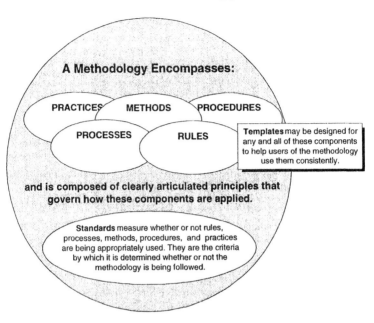

A Methodology Encompasses:

PRACTICES METHODS PROCEDURES

PROCESSES RULES

Templates may be designed for any and all of these components to help users of the methodology use them consistently.

and is composed of clearly articulated principles that govern how these components are applied.

Standards measure whether or not rules, processes, methods, procedures, and practices are being appropriately used. They are the criteria by which it is determined whether or not the methodology is being followed.

out what already is working well and where the gaps are between what you have and what is necessary.

1. **Map** what's already going on in terms of practices, procedures, methods, and processes. The assessment process described in Chapter 2 offers a road map for this step.

2. **Benchmark** how to manage the types of projects and activities that your company engages in. This is a little tougher and is somewhat outside the scope of this book. While we can discuss best practices in terms of generic project management, which are applicable across industries, there will always be practice standards and methods particular to industry sectors. See Chapter 7 for a discussion of benchmarking practices.

3. **Define the processes** that will bring improvements to your company's project management practice. Those processes can

then be standardized across all projects by means of rules, templates, and procedures. Establishing measurements (metrics) that reflect whether or not the processes are being properly implemented, and linking those to rewards, plays a major role in the cultural change to a project-based organization. This process audit function is discussed in more detail in the section "Quality and PM Methodology" later in this chapter.

4. **Document** all the processes and their component pieces—templates, procedures, metrics. The resulting compilation of principles, processes, and best-practice tools can properly be called your methodology.

5. **Reassess and refine** in an iterative process. Methodology components will (and should) be in a regular state of review, modification, upgrade, and change. It is a continual evolution as the organization matures in project management practice. A methodology should not be static—if it is, the actual processes that people use in their work will leave the documented processes behind. It is in human nature to tinker with things and try to change and improve them, so no methodology should be allowed to gather dust in a notebook on a shelf. Instead, it should be regarded as a "live" set of documents, describing a lively set of processes. One of the primary functions of the project office is to gather lessons learned and suggestions for improving the project management process from practitioners to continuously improve the methodology.

Now you begin to see why the chapter that follows is focused on knowledge management. The collection and dissemination of ideas and information is the backbone of establishing and refining your project management methodology.

What are the Elements of a Methodology?

Methodology can be likened to a road map that leads project teams from point A to point B during the course of a project. A collection of best practices and repeatable processes, it includes key pieces of information to help project teams succeed. These include:

- An overview of the entire project management process—initiating, planning, executing, controlling, and closing—tailored to your unique organizational environment and best practices. This includes project processes, activities, and tasks and the relationships between these elements.

- Checklists of the things that a project team needs to consider, with a description of what is required in each task.

- Key inputs and outputs associated with each of the activities and tasks. These should be accompanied by templates and examples for each of the outputs.

- Guidance on staffing the project team—how many people, and with what skills? Templates or decision trees can help identify these players.

- Guidelines for identifying and enlisting the support of the project sponsor.

- An approach for developing project requirements and specifications.

- Standard database structures—a project management information system—for collection, integration, and summary reporting of schedules, costs, and resource usage.

- Guidelines for identification and responsibilities of the project steering committee.

- Guidelines for project portfolio selection, prioritization, and management, including project cancellation procedures.

- Guidelines on application of the project management methodology to projects of various sizes and complexity.

An overview of a proprietary methodology (PM Solutions' *Project Management Guide*) is provided later in this chapter. The overview provides a top-level summary of the five project management process groups, activities within these processes, and some examples of detailed tasks within selected activities.

There are two qualities that are characteristic of successful methodologies: (1) they are based on recognized standards, and (2) they are flexible and customizable. Every organization is unique and needs to approach projects differently due to its internal processes; and different projects will require the methodology to be scalable. When an organization can add its own activities into a methodology and provide guidance to users on how much of the methodology to use for different sizes and types of projects, the ensuing sense of ownership will make it much more of a "live" document, and that will help an organization move to a higher level of capability.

Consistency/Repeatability

In the effort to develop a consistent approach to implementing project management, practitioners have found it easiest to begin with existing internationally recognized standards and models. While by no means the only possible foundations for building a project management methodology, the two that are most commonly referred to—and which we have used in the development of PM Solutions' proprietary maturity model (the PMMM) and methodology (the *PM Guide)*—are the SEI Capability Maturity Model (CMM) for Software Development and PMI's *PMBOK Guide.*

The CMM. In recent years, SEI's Capability Maturity Model has evolved to become globally recognized as the best practices standard for methodology development and measurement. Although the principles outlined in the CMM focus on the software development process, the CMM approach forms an outstanding framework for establishing a best practices methodology in project management. The Software Engineering Institute says that, "For most organizations, the ability to estimate and predict accurately the results of their product development activities from a viewpoint of cost, schedule, and quality is a fundamental business goal. Case studies … suggest that addressing issues of process management, measurement, and institutionalization [i.e., standardization across the enterprise] improve the organization's ability to meet its cost, quality, and schedule goals."[7] How can an organization know how good they are at addressing these issues? First, there must be a *standard* against which to measure. That was the concept behind SEI's Capability Maturity Model, which has become the de facto standard model for assessing and evaluating process maturity in the software industry.

On a broader scale, the organizational challenge of estimating and accurately predicting the outcomes of projects of any type or size, in any industry, must address these issues as specifically related to project management:

- **Process Management**—There must be a *repeatable*, quantifiable project management process in place throughout the organization.

- **Measurement**—There must be methods/systems for the measurement of scope, quality, schedule, and cost that are a natural part of running the project, and which are *consistently* applied so that all projects in the portfolio can be compared.

- **Institutionalization (Standardization)**—The processes must be precipitated by the organization's senior management, and *applied uniformly* throughout the organization.

Thus, taking the CMM as our guide, we can collect and document project management processes, assign metrics to determine whether those processes are being correctly carried out, and get management involved in making sure those processes and metrics are uniformly applied throughout the organization. Consequently, we have established a consistent and repeatable methodology for project management.

The *PMBOK Guide*. The other most commonly reference document in methodology development is *A Guide to the Project Management Body of Knowledge*.[8] While the SEI research established an intellectual framework for process improvement as related to projects, the *PMBOK Guide* fills in the details by examining what project managers need to know, and what they need to do, to actually manage a project. Many times companies having defined a process, or set of processes—such as those that are laid out in the project management body of knowledge document, the *PMBOK Guide*—feel they have established a methodology. In fact, according to many experts, they have stopped short of doing so.[9] As the seminal documentation of project management practice, the *PMBOK Guide* is often called upon to serve double duty and be more than it is. There has been some debate among project management practitioners as to whether or not it can properly be termed a methodology. As Tony Nish of IBM has written, "While the *PMBOK Guide* describes, at the process level, *what* project management is all about, it does not provide the explicit guidance and tools detailing exactly *how* to manage a project." This confusion between a guide and a methodology, he says, leads many companies to feel a false sense of security. If you have long-term ambitions for the success of project management as a discipline in the future success of your organization, merely establishing the *PMBOK Guide* as a standards document won't assure your success. You can manage individual projects very well here and there throughout the organization just by knowing the steps and processes laid out in PMI's document. In fact, giving everyone who works on project teams a copy of this document can go a long way towards moving an organization out of the ad hoc state of chaos described in Level 1 of the Project Management Maturity Model (See Appendix A). In large measure this is because it brings a new level of consistency to the vocabulary of people working on projects.

However, a methodology is larger than these foundational elements. A methodology states the standards for processes and knowledge areas; but it also provides, as noted in the section on the CMM, metrics for judging performance, a system whereby those processes may be consistently applied across an organization, and an overall method—the maturity model—for evaluating the effectiveness of the methodology once it is in place.

A Word About Discipline. The other piece of having a consistent and repeatable methodology is, of course, sticking with it. This may prove challenging when you have an organization full of people who are used to doing things their own way. Tying rewards and performance measurement to application of the methodology is one way to gain compliance. For example, on the positive side, a project manager's performance report could state that he or she enthusiastically applied the new methodology and achieved success; while on the negative side comments in the performance report might show that the individual was slow to adopt the best practices embodied in the methodology, leading to project problems, fragmented team effort, or other indicators.

While rewards/sanctions are an effective way to gain *compliance* after a new methodology is deployed, getting *buy-in* during development is better. Two tips toward gaining buy-in:

- Get representatives from throughout the organization to act as a steering committee for developing the methodology. Get the

151

Table 6.1 Roles in Methodology Development

ROLES AND RESPONSIBILITIES

Project Office Director
- Oversee PM methodology development
- Champion PM methodology implementation

Project Office Staff
- Develop content (e.g., templates, forms, etc.)
- Document methodology

Company Project Managers
- Provide subject matter expertise and guidance
- Implement PM methodology

Source: Adapted from *Imaginary Obstacles: Getting Over PMI Myths,* by Tim Jaques, www.gantthead.com/articles.

most vocal, highest performing representatives you can find. Even critics of the initiative may soon realize their contributions to the methodology are being incorporated and become converts. Table 6.1 shows some of ways in which various positions in the organization can participate in methodology development.

- Second, use the standard methodology as a conflict resolution tool. A formal system that can be invoked when people have complaints or criticisms can help separate out the serious issues from the mere complaints, if it is used consistently. When faced with a complaint, suggest, "Why don't you file a risk statement for that?" or "Submit that to the change control board."[10]

Scalability to Projects of Varying Size and Complexity

If this is sounding very complicated, relax. One of the primary concerns most organizations have with establishing a methodology is that, while they know they need a comprehensive approach to managing projects, they also worry about getting into "analysis paraly-

Table 6.2 How Much Methodology Do You Need?

FIRST TIER EVALUATION	Project Size		
	Small	*Medium*	*Large*
Effort hours	40–200	200–1000	> 1000
Elapsed time	< 3 months	3–6 months	> 6 months
# Project team members	1–6	6–12	> 12
SECOND TIER EVALUATION			
Technical complexity	Level of integration, skill sets, done before?		
Business complexity	Number of business units, level of business process changes		

sis." They wonder whether on the many smaller, less complex projects that make up their portfolio, the focus on planning, the project board, the project reviews, risk analysis, change management, extensive reporting, resource allocation, resource control, schedule variance analysis, cost variance analysis, and knowledge management will actually hold up project completion, rather than facilitate it.

This is a commonly voiced concern, but the truth is that any good methodology is scalable. It can be used in an extremely rigorous fashion to make large, complex projects a success, but it should also be flexible enough that smaller projects can be carried out under a simpler set of rules. To assist managers of small projects in achieving a viable balance between overmanaging projects and running unreasonable risks from undermanaging them, we developed some simple tools and checklists to aid the project manager in scaling the methodology to the project.

Use Table 6.2 to help determine the size of your project. First evaluate your project per the First Tier Evaluation. Then think through your project in light of the Second Tier Evaluation. This Second Tier Evaluation may cause you to move your project *up* (e.g.: from small to medium), but almost never *down*. The numbers can be adjusted up or down, depending on what kind of projects are most common in your organization: however, always keep in mind the Standish Group's findings: small, short-term projects have a far higher rate of success than large or long-term ones.[11]

All project management deliverables (i.e. project charter, statement of work, etc.) need to be produced in some form, even for small projects. The important thing is that some thought has been given to how much of the methodology should be used for smaller projects. The actual amount of information documented for a small project will normally be much less than for a medium or large project. The *minimum requirements* for small projects, whether internal or external, are:

- Clearly defined and justified business needs

- Tightly defined scope and key deliverables

- A documented project plan

- An organized set of resources

- Appropriate control procedures.

With small projects there is a strong temptation to "just do it" without worrying about managing it properly, as called for in the methodology. This approach often leads to project failure due to major mid-project scope/deliverable changes and course corrections or, worse yet, production of the wrong, unusable, or unsupportable deliverable.

All projects, regardless of size and scope, need the fundamental processes of project management applied. On smaller projects, risk is lower, the cost impacts are lower, and the impacts of the technology on the delivery of the project may be lower, so the need to engage in rigorous analysis may be lessened. However, risk must still be assessed and costs determined before a decision can be made to move to a more compact set of guidelines.

For example, all projects need to be chartered. All projects should have a project manager assigned, even if part-time. All projects need a project plan, including scope, WBS, schedule, budget, risk analysis, and control processes put in place. And a project manager on a small project still should understand the enterprise-wide implications of every project, be trained in managing projects, and have access to a

Figure 6.2 Interrelationship of Organizational Elements

Process + Knowledge = SUCCESS

SUCCESS = Stakeholder Satisfaction

comprehensive methodology. He or she may choose (or be required) to apply only limited segments of the methodology that are relevant to challenges faced on a specific project, but in order to choose the methodology must be available, commonly practiced, and must include a matrix or table categorizing projects and listing the portions of the methodology that must be applied to projects of various sizes and complexity.

Finally, this scalable feature of methodology means that the project office has a rapid and relatively low-cost way to add value. With a series of templates and a methodological approach to planning and managing projects, a small PO staff can quickly open shop and begin to show results. Many companies can maximize the expertise and existing technologies to offer a core set of services that can be of great value to the organization. As the organization phases in the full Strategic Project Office, capabilities increase to match the organizational needs.[12]

Overview of a Sample Methodolgy

As we noted earlier, PM Solutions' methodology documentation, the *Project Management Guide*, a portion of which we offer here as an example, is based on experience in the field, on process definitions developed by the Project Management Institute, and on principles of process improvement laid down by the Software Engineering Institute. We chose these standards documents as foundational material because they incorporate process and methodology standards known to be successful in the initiating, planning, executing, controlling and closing of successful project management initiatives worldwide, as well as knowledge from many seasoned project managers.

Figure 6.3 Project Management Processes

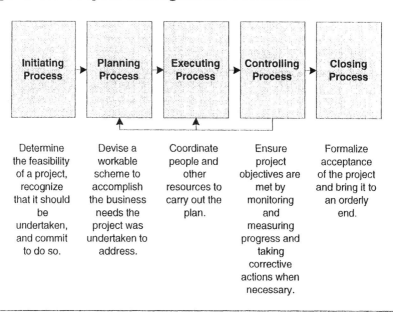

Determine the feasibility of a project, recognize that it should be undertaken, and commit to do so.

Devise a workable scheme to accomplish the business needs the project was undertaken to address.

Coordinate people and other resources to carry out the plan.

Ensure project objectives are met by monitoring and measuring progress and taking corrective actions when necessary.

Formalize acceptance of the project and bring it to an orderly end.

The Processes

The Project Management Institute defines project management as "the art of directing and coordinating human and material resources throughout the life of a project by using modern management techniques to achieve pre-determined objectives."

It is a truism that an organization's success is dependent upon documenting and understanding (i.e., knowledge of) the best practices (processes) in which that organization is involved. It is also axiomatic that the success of any project can be defined by how "satisfied" the stakeholder (or customer) is at the end. Figure 6.2 is a graphic representation of how these elements interrelate.

We set out with the intent to provide all the processes and tips necessary for a project manager to manage any project, regardless of size. In order to do that, we must first define those processes. The overall process of project management can be viewed as five separate but related processes, as shown in Figure 6.3.

Notice that one process feeds the next. Also notice that there is a high degree of interaction between planning, executing, and control-

Figure 6.4 Initiating Process

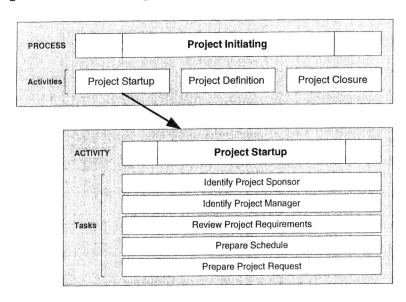

ling. Not only are these processes interactive, they also *overlap* as the information (results/deliverables) flows from one to the other.

The project management processes are not individual, one-time events. Rather, they are overlapping processes that occur at various levels throughout the project:

The initiating process happens first in a project. Project initiating is the process of formally recognizing that a new project opportunity exists and establishing a project charter. This process involves verification of a business case to establish the validity of a project, recognizing that a project should be undertaken, and committing to do so. Output from project initiating should include a project charter that formally recognizes the existence of a project, an identified project sponsor, a project manager (for at least the next phase of the project), benefits and success metrics, and high-level constraints and assumptions such as predefined budgets and schedule dates. It feeds information into the planning process. See Figure 6.4 for an overview of the initiating process from PM Solutions' *PM Guide*. This figure, and each of the figures supporting the five process groups, contains an

Figure 6.5 Planning Process

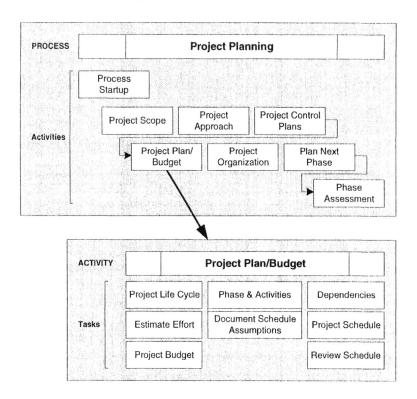

overview chart and a detailed chart showing one of the activities within the process.

The planning process happens concurrently with the initiating process, although it starts somewhat later. The objective of the project planning process is to take the information from the project initiating process, specifically the project charter, and convert it into a formal, planned, resourced, and funded project. It should be accomplished in a manner that clearly and explicitly defines the objectives and scope of the project, develops a high-level schedule of activities and required resources to carry out the whole project, develops a detailed schedule of activities and resources required to carry out the individual phases of the project, and defines a project organizational structure that will

Figure 6.6 Executing Process

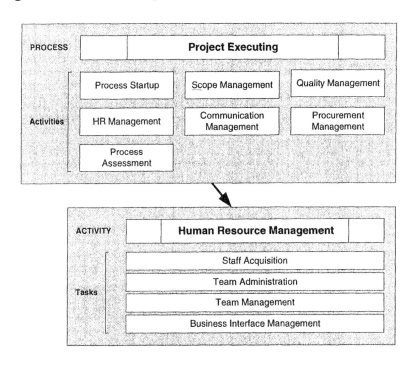

effectively manage and carry out the work. It is where much of the information for the remainder of the project is gathered, created, and documented. It feeds the executing process and receives feedback from the controlling process. See Figure 6.5 for a top-level view of the sub-processes in the planning process.

The executing process creates the "product" of the project (the programs, the system, the services, the building, the event, etc.). The overall objective of project execution is to manage the project work and the project team performance to ensure the successful completion of the project. It should be accomplished in a manner that manages the scope of the work being done, builds quality into the project deliverables, manages the human resources working on the project, manages the vendors and contractors working on the project and administers the associated contracts, and manages the communication

Figure 6.7 Controlling Process

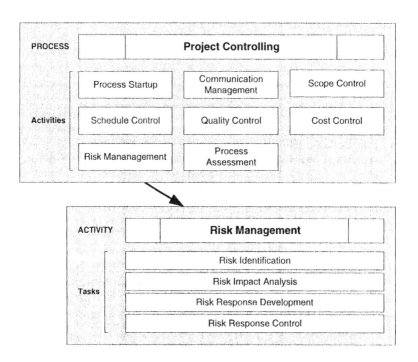

of the ongoing status of the project. This process feeds the controlling process. See Figure 6.6 for an overview of the executing process.

The controlling process goes on throughout the project. It monitors the plans, reports status, features corrective action to control variances, controls changes to the project scope and plan, and feeds information back to the planning process. Controlling and executing are tightly linked. See Figure 6.7 for an overview of the controlling process.

The closing process completes the project when the executing/controlling process is drawing to a conclusion. The objective of project closing is to formally close the project. It should be accomplished in a manner that identifies recommendations that can be applied to future projects, establishes mechanisms for the continued development or improvement of future projects, sustains the project management process, and updates the metrics used for the project to ensure value. The overview of the closing process is shown in Figure 6.8.

Figure 6.8 Closing Process

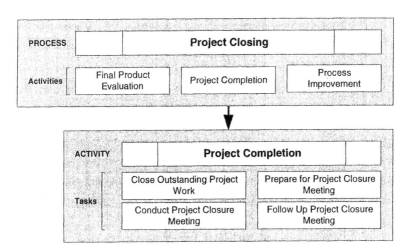

Since project executing and controlling are the processes where most of the actual management of the project takes place, let's look at them in detail. The following list provides some factors and guidelines to help you determine how much (and what kind of) ongoing monitoring, control, and adjustment will be required for successfully managing your project.

- **Size and Complexity of the Project.** Small projects may only require a subset of the control procedures. Large projects will most likely require rigorous control procedures in all areas. If the project has a *large scope* and it is being delivered in a relatively *short period of time,* a lot of project management will be required.

- **Risk of the Project.** Risky projects typically require tighter control in those areas of risk that affect the project the most. A thorough risk analysis will identify these areas.

- **Deviation from Standards in the Project.** Projects with tight tolerances in any one of the in any of the "triple constraint" areas—scope and quality/schedule/resources—require tighter control to ensure that the tolerances are met.

Figure 6.9 Relationship of Project Management Processes and Knowledge Areas

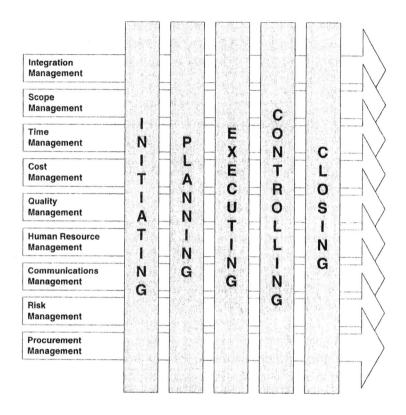

- **Critical Nature of the Project.** Projects that are delivering functions critical to the business (whether the customer is external or internal) must be controlled tightly, specifically around scope and quality, to ensure that the critical requirements and success criteria are being met.

- **New Techniques or Technology Used in the Project.** If the project will be working with new techniques or technologies, there will be more uncertainty and risk associated with the project. This will require more project management specifically in the areas of risk and quality management.

Table 6.3 Typical Project Management Templates and Checklists by Process Group

Initiating
- Business Case Instructions
- Project Determination Checklist
- Scope Statement Checklist
- Project Charter and Template Instructions
- Project Binder Contents Checklist

Planning
- Project Logistics Checklist
- Kickoff Meeting Agenda
- Project Risk Log Instructions
- Issues Log
- Issues Log Instructions
- Project Planning Process Checklist

Executing
- Project Status Report Template
- Customer Sign-Off Checklist

Controlling
- Scope Change Request/ Impact Template
- Change Log
- Project Control Checklist

Closeout
- Project Closeout Checklist
- Project Closeout Report Template
- Project Sign-Off Form

- **Specific End Date to the Project.** Pre-determined deadlines affect how a project is managed and the level of monitoring and control required. If the project has a specific end date that must be met (for business or legal reasons), tight monitoring and control needs to be employed to ensure that the date(s) is met.

- **Regulatory Requirements.** Federal, state, and local regulations often require that projects produce specific deliverables and provide evidence that control procedures were in place during the project's life cycle.

Finally, project closing processes ensure that all necessary project work is completed and that all valuable experience and feedback is captured for future use. A general rule of thumb is that project closing should take no more than 2% of the total effort required for the project;

Table 6.4 Additional Project Management Templates and Checklists by Process Group

Initiating
- Roles and Responsibilities Checklists: Sponsor, Project Steering Committee, Project Manager, Key Stakeholders
- Project Manager Assignment Letter
- Project Organization Chart and Guidelines
- Project Requirements Matrix
- Statement of Work Template/Instructions
- Project Initiation Process Checklist

Planning
- Customer Requirements Checklist
- Work Breakdown Structure Template
- WBS Dictionary Template
- Cost Estimating Guidelines
- Logic Network (PERT Chart) Template
- Resource Responsibility Matrix
- Project Communication Plan Template
- Project Schedule Review Checklist

- Project Budget Review Checklist
- Project Quality Plan Template
- Customer Relations Plan
- Test and Acceptance Plan

Executing
- Project Staff Acquisition Procedures
- Supplier, Vendor, and Subcontractor Payment Certification

Controlling
- Cost and Schedule Control Procedures
- Vendor/Subcontractor Management Procedures
- Project Steering Committee Status Report Format

Closeout
- Final Product Evaluation Checklist
- Post-Project Review Template
- Project Management Process Assessment

however, project closing should not be minimized, as is often the case—particularly the activities involving lessons learned. There is far too much knowledge and experience that is lost to future projects and project managers by not giving this process proper attention and having a knowledge management system to capture the knowledge for future use by all resources (see Chapter 7). Proper capture of lessons learned can be of particular usefulness to the ongoing improvement of your methodology.

In addition to the five major process groups, the *PMBOK Guide* defines nine areas in which it is very important for the project manager to be proficient (see Chapter 2 for a list). Managing the interplay of these areas is much of the "art" of project management. These knowledge areas thread their way through all the project management processes, as shown in Figure 6.9.

The Templates

Tables 6.3 and 6.4 give an overview of some of the templates included in the methodology; this list is scalable and adaptable to your organization's business and size: not every organization will need every template listed, and not every project within that organization will make use of all of these. Note: Templates included in Table 6.3, which are representative examples of those normally included in a project management methodology, can be found in Appendix C. Many additional templates and checklists are typically tailored and included in an organization's methodology. While the scope of this book prohibits us from including examples of each one, a list of these additional templates is included in Table 6.4.

Quality and PM Methodology

Why discuss quality when talking about project management methodology? Because it is such an integral part of project management that it must be covered, in considerable detail, in a project management methodology. After all, organizations implement a methodology primarily as a way to ensure better quality of deliverables. In this section we present an overview of just what we mean when we say "quality." In practice, we find considerable confusion when discussing the topic.

The overall objective of any project is to satisfy the customer—this is the real meaning of *quality*. Yet this apparently simple concept is often misunderstood. Quality in project management has a very specific goal: to ensure that the customer's requirements are being met and that the project team is adding value to the project by adhering closely to the project management process defined in the organization's project management methodology.

The project team is responsible for project quality. By using established project management techniques and exercising an appropriate level of technical oversight, the project manager and project team can make quality a regular, essential part of day-to-day project planning and execution. To assure or control quality, the project team must monitor quality on two dimensions. Let's take a close look at this often-misunderstood concept of quality in both of these dimensions.

To begin, we'll pose two questions:

- If a project manager follows the project management process to the letter—does everything exactly as defined by the organization's project management methodology— does that constitute project quality?

- Looking at it from another angle, if the project manager totally ignores the methodology—doesn't have a kickoff meeting, doesn't build a WBS, doesn't keep others informed of progress— yet produces a deliverable that completely delights the customer, is *that* project quality?

Let's face it, the latter event does sometimes happen. What we are interested in, when we develop a methodology, is to capture the best practices employed by those heroic individuals to whom project management comes naturally. While they may not label their activities the same as we might, chances are good that they are, indeed, adhering to a project management process each time they manage a project. And to the extent that a formal project management methodology captures the best practices of all those heroic practitioners, the correlation between following the methodology and ultimate project quality—as measured by customer satisfaction—is also high.

Can we measure or assess project quality defined in terms of both the quality of deliverables and adherence to the process? Yes. To measure the quality of deliverables, we perform a "test and evaluation" process of the technical work. To measure the quality of the project management process, we perform quality process audits. We'll discuss each in turn, providing practical guidelines you can use to assess both elements of quality on your project.

Quality of Deliverables—The Product

The goal of any project is to produce a product or service that satisfies the customer's expectations, be it a customer internal to the organization or an external customer. Implied in this statement is the understanding that we actually understand what the customer wants. That is frequently not the case. In fact, meeting the customer's true requirements is not easy, and even satisfying the stated requirement is, in many cases, not sufficient for the following reasons:

- Customers may not completely understand their needs; therefore they cannot clearly state what those needs are.

- There may be opportunities for additional value to be added through performance of the project; therefore the requirements may change during the project.

- There may be a disparity between the stated needs and current capabilities.

Obviously to have any chance of meeting the customer's expectations, the supplier and customer must agree on the customer's needs and expectations before launching the project. Since it is so difficult to satisfy a customer's emerging requirements, we should modify our definition of quality to "conformance to mutually agreed-upon customer specifications." The only way to obtain this agreement is through a detailed joint examination of the customer's requirements, a discussion of the supplier's ability to meet those requirements, and documentation of the agreed-upon requirements. Then to ensure that the project team continues to satisfy the requirement, it must practice rigorous change control throughout the project life cycle. Adequately examining, evaluating, and defining customer requirements are essential to successful project implementation and form the basis for assessing quality as it pertains to project deliverables. How should the project team proceed?

The project team should not force its vision of the requirement on the customer. A better approach is to follow these guidelines:

- Strive to understand the customer's requirements as stated by the customer.

- Determine whether those requirements are achievable in the current environment.

- Identify potential solutions to the customer's requirements.

- Strive to understand the business needs that drive the requirements.

- Identify alternative approaches that may address the customer's business needs.

- Identify the organization's own capabilities that must be expanded to meet the customer's requirements.

Once the project requirements are understood and the customer and project team mutually agree upon and document expectations, project planning, execution, and control may proceed. After the project plan is put together, control of product quality during the execution phase becomes our priority. Monitoring and controlling project implementation is, in many ways, the same as monitoring and controlling project quality.

Earlier, we defined quality as satisfying or conforming to mutually agreed-upon customer specifications. These specifications comprise four main attributes:

- **Business requirements:** What business purpose the initiative must satisfy and how its value is determined.

- **Technical requirements**: What the product or service must do, how it must appear, and what performance criteria must be met.

- **Schedule**: When the project must be completed.

- **Cost**: What the completed project will cost.

Through customary project control mechanisms, the project manager controls project implementation and, ultimately, its quality. Each of the usual project control mechanisms is also a means of controlling project quality. With an emphasis on controlling the project's schedule and costs, and with continual evaluation of technical progress, the project manager ensures that appropriate work is being accomplished on schedule, within the established budget.

The project manager must establish a routine of evaluating progress and monitoring quality based on reviewing reports from project team members and evaluating the information they contain. For example, using an earned value methodology helps the project manager understand quickly whether a project is meeting schedule and cost requirements (two of the four attributes of quality). The project manager assesses the third and fourth attributes, technical and business performance, through ongoing assessment of performance and through a comprehensive testing process.

Quality of the Project Management Process

When an organization creates and deploys a project management methodology, it does so in the belief that those who follow the methodology will achieve better results—on-time delivery, within budget, and according to specifications (defined as product quality). This will lead to satisfied customers and long-term health of the enterprise. Performing project management quality assessments is a way to provide senior managers and project managers with an indication of the health and strength of the project management practices being applied within their organizations.

Project management quality assessments, or audits, can be applied in two ways. The first way is simply to assess whether the organization is following the published, mandatory project management methodology. This is done by developing checklists to determine if the steps in the project management process are being followed as required, and if the project management artifacts being produced (an artifact is a PM deliverable such as a project plan, critical path schedule, etc.) are being prepared properly. The audit process requires an auditor, typically from the project office, to conduct interviews with selected project managers and team members to review the project management artifacts against the guidelines in the methodology and to score the project against objective criteria contained in the checklists. Audit results are provided to senior management independently for information and corrective action.

Typical project management artifacts include the following:

- Project Charter. A document, issued by senior management, that authorizes the project manager to use corporate resources to fulfill the purpose of the project.

- Statement of Work. A document describing the expected outcome of the project, including the deliverables to be produced and what will/will not be included as part of the project.

- Success Criteria. A document describing the factors by which project success will be measured. These could include schedule and budget performance, ROIs to be achieved when developed product is deployed, and a measure of user satisfaction.

- Project Organization Chart. A pictorial representation of the project team structure. It should include position titles and names of individuals assigned to those positions. It should also identify all user and support personnel.

- Corporate Organization Chart. A pictorial representation of the corporate structure. It should include position titles and names of individuals assigned to those positions. We should be able to identify the project sponsor and project manager within this organization chart.

- Responsibility Matrix. A matrix indicating who on the project team is responsible for what. We should be able to readily identify the project's requirements manager, quality control staff, configuration manager, status reporter, schedule manager, etc. Many times these are additional duties assigned to development staff.

- Job Descriptions. Specific job descriptions for each position on the project team.

- Work Breakdown Structure. A hierarchical representation of all work to be performed as part of the project. We should be able to associate each WBS element to a scheduled activity and to a statement within the project's statement of work. The document should also include the WBS dictionary, with a definition of each work element.

- Product Breakdown Structure. A hierarchical representation of the products to be produced by the project. We should be able to associate each PBS element to the WBS elements and to a statement within the project's statement of work.

- Estimating Standards. The estimating guidelines and actual data used by the project management team to estimate the level of effort needed to complete the project. The standards should identify the type of estimation performed (i.e., lines of code, function point analysis, size of documentation) and any tools used in the estimation process.

- Project Schedule, Including Baselines. The documentation that informs all concerned parties when various project activities will begin and end. The schedule should identify who is doing what work and the dependencies within the activities.

- Weekly Project Status Reports. Any reports produced for distribution internally within the project team that communicate project status

- Project Plan, Including Cost and Schedule Management Plans. The documents that identify how the project will be managed and what the final product developed will be. This document is usually developed during the project planning activities.

- Project Review and Approval Process. A description of who will be selected to perform the role of project sponsor and project steering committee members. This documentation will include roles and responsibilities, duties, approval process, and frequency of project steering committee meetings for the project.

- Deliverables Sign-Off Process. This describes how the project will be closed down upon completion of all deliverables or upon cancellation. The document is a management document, not a technical document.

- Risk Identification and Mitigation Plan. The document that describes the project risks, their probabilities, and the strategies that will be used to mitigate those risks. It should also describe how risks are identified and quantified on the project.

- Requirements Management Plan. The document that describes how requirements will be defined and managed throughout the project's life cycle. We should be able to identify the project's requirements manager and the requirements control mechanism within the plan.

- Quality Assurance Plan. The document that describes how the organization will evaluate the project's performance to ensure that the project will meet quality standards. The quality assurance manager should be identified.

- Change Control Plan. The document that describes how changes to the project's scope will be managed. The make-up of the change control board, including how often it convenes, should be discussed in the plan. Note that the CCB can be the same as the project steering committee.

- Change Requests and Log. The documents used in the project's change control process.

- Action Items Tracking Documents. The documents used to track action items for the project.

- Project Office Charter. The document that describes the roles and contributions of the project office.

- Sub-Contractor Contracts. The legally binding document describing the statement of work, including terms and conditions, applicable to sub-contractors used on the project.

- Lessons Learned Reports. Any postmortems that have been performed on the project to date.

- Miscellaneous Project Documentation. This umbrella category includes the following artifacts: project status meeting agenda, project meeting minutes, kick-off meeting agenda and minutes.

- Visibility (War) Room and Procedures. Any documentation supporting the project's visibility room if one exists. Today, it may exist only in cyberspace; this increases, rather than lessens, the need for thorough documentation of procedures for creating, accessing, changing, editing, and storing content.

Figure 6.10 PM HealthCheck Assessment Results

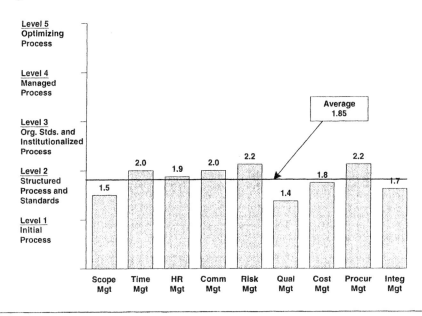

Each of these artifacts will be identified in the project management methodology, including its purpose, when it should be prepared, instructions for preparing the product, and an example of a completed artifact. The auditor compares what was produced against the standard in the methodology and assigns a rating.

The second form of evaluating project management quality is to use a project management maturity model against which project management practices are compared. Rather than use the organization's project management methodology as the standard, checklists are developed which measure the maturity of the process against the maturity model for each of its sections. Comprehensive interviews are conducted with project managers, team members, customers, other stakeholders, and senior management to assess the overall quality of the project management process and to identify areas in need of improvement. As in the first approach, project management artifacts are examined to complement the information gained in the interviews.

Using the PM Solutions PMMM as a model, a typical assessment report shows scores for each of the nine PMMM knowledge areas, with narrative to support the scores assigned. A project management improvement plan is also a feature of this method. Appendix B shows an example of such an improvement plan. Figure 6.10 shows a typical maturity graphic using PM Solutions' PM HealthCheck assessment process. The organization being evaluated obviously has a long way to go before achieving project management excellence.

Where does the project office fit in with respect to either product or project management process quality? That depends on whether the organization has a separate quality assurance office. If it does, the QA representatives will work with project managers to help them assure the quality of deliverables. When it comes to assessing project management process quality, however, it is more often the project office which performs the process audits, reports results to senior management, and works with project managers to improve the quality of their project management efforts. The QA representative advises and assists the project office as necessary.

To briefly summarize the topic of quality, the purpose of developing a methodology is to improve the quality of results that an organization achieves through projects. Process improvement, in a nutshell:

- Defines the gap between stakeholder needs, organizational objectives, and operational outcomes (see the assessment process outlined in Chapter 2).

- Conceptualizes, with input from project knowledge workers, the operational changes that need to take place in how work is done and how value is delivered in order to resolve the defined gaps (see "Gap Analysis," Chapter 2).

- Quantifies the value added that will be realized once the new processes have been implemented. This subject—the ROI of project management—has been hotly debated and researched over the past five years. It's a topic that's beyond the scope of this book; please consult the bibliography for references to research on this topic, including the *Value of Project Management* survey conducted in 2000 by the Center for Business Practices.

- Designs new work processes and procedures that embrace the changes identified. Chapters 3–10 of this book will assist your organization in doing exactly this.

- Quantifies the time, cost, and plan for implementing the improvements. These steps will form the planning stage of your project office deployment project.[13]

How Good Is Your Methodology?

In the research project on the quality of project management methodologies proposed by Nish,[14] quality of a methodology can be evaluated on four dimensions:

Breadth is a measure of how comprehensive the methodology is. That is, how useful it is at all stages of a project and how transferable and generic it is across industries and types of projects. *Test Question:* Can the methodology be applied across different project types?

Depth is a measure of how much detail is provided in each stage or phase of the methodology. Too much depth can be a negative in usefulness for a specific type of project, while too little doesn't provide the practitioner with sufficient explanation to apply the concept. *Test question:* Does the methodology support the development of detailed workplans, controlling cost and managing resources, and all other *PMBOK Guide* elements, for a particular project type?

Clarity is a measure of how easy the methodology is to use and explain to someone just learning it, either a new project manager or project team member. A high percentage of users of the methodology are satisfied they understand and can explain the methodology if called upon to do so. Words and phrases used in the methodology are readily translatable into words and phrases more commonly used in the industry. *Test question:* Is the methodology understandable and easy to use?

Since other criteria don't mean much without results, the fourth dimension is *Impact*. *Test question:* Does the use of the methodology contribute to better (more timely, cost effective, and/or higher quality) results on projects?[15]

This framework for evaluation is one that can easily be used to take a look at a given methodology once it has been in place for a time or to assess an off-the-shelf product. As it has not been fully tested, we don't endorse it, but refer the reader to it as a technique of interest.

Conclusion

A good strategy for implementing the methodology is to run a pilot project using it within one functional area of the company—IT or production, for example. This provides a venue to test and refine the methodology for a given set of project deliverables, while offering an excellent training opportunity for the managers. Managers would do well to choose an area that they know with authority and adopt a well-known methodological approach that can be tailored to meet the specifics of the environment. After a success, the methodology and the project office staff can move to another functional area of the organization and modify the approach yet again. This course of action complements the low-cost, scalable approach, and is in keeping with the process improvement spirit of methodology development.[16]

One concern that project managers have sometimes voiced is that, by standardizing processes via rules, procedures, and templates, we are promoting method at the expense of creativity—standardizing the life out of the "art of project management." This is certainly a concern, particularly in organizations where new product development and other creative endeavors form the bulk of the projects being managed. It should be remembered that the purpose is to improve organizational outcomes. The old saying about rules applies to methodologies here: "It's not knowing when to obey them; it's knowing when to break them." Be willing to bend methodologies when that makes sense for the project or the organization.

Endnotes

1. The purpose of this chapter is not so much to present our own methodology—although we will draw our examples and templates from it—but to discuss methodology, processes, and standards as general topics, and how the PO supports and offers these. We are striving to be more descriptive than prescriptive.

2. *The American Heritage Dictionary of the English Language, Third Edition.* Houghton Mifflin Company, 1992.

3. Tim Jaques, "Imaginary Obstacles: Getting Over PMO Myths," www.gantthead.com/articles.

4. Jaques, op. cit.

5. Tony Nish and Jeannette Cabanis, "The Consulting Methodology Survey," *PM Network*, PMI, August 1999.

6. Nish and Cabanis, op. cit.

7. Software Engineering Institute. "Capability Maturity Model, Systems Engineering Improvement," pp. 2-27, 1995.

8. PMI Standards Committee, Project Management Institute, 1996.

9. Nish, op. cit.
10. John Sullivan, "Hidden Roles of a PSO," *PM Network*, February 2000.
11. The Standish Group, *The Chaos Report*, 1999. See also *Best Practices Report Executive Briefing*, Center for Business Practices, Summer 2000.
12. Jaques, op. cit.
13. Michael Wood, "What Is a Process Improvement Methodology Anyway?" www.gantthead.com/articles.
14. Nish, op. cit.
15. Nish, op. cit.
16. Jaques, op. cit.

Chapter 7

Knowledge Management and the Project Office

THE PROJECT OFFICE IS THE place where project management and knowledge management intersect. In fact, despite the recent flurry of excitement, software releases and books about it, managing knowledge has *always* been an integral element of good project management. The processes for project closure, especially the capturing of lessons learned, are in effect knowledge management processes. However, going over what went well and what did not at the end of a single project does not necessarily harness that experience for the future good of the company. Knowledge management allows the enterprise as a whole to learn from the successes and failures of individual projects. To do this requires some central clearinghouse for those learnings—and the project office is perfect for this role.

Knowledge Management: The Short Course

It may be helpful to begin this chapter by stripping some of the buzzword aura away from the term *knowledge management* (KM). As with many terms enjoying popularity in business circles, the definition can depend on whom you are asking—a software vendor, for example, will tend to give you a software-based answer. And sometimes knowledge management may go under another name, such as data mining or best practices sharing.

However, KM is both more and less than software. KM authority Wally Bock[1] suggests the following definition: "Knowledge management is the way that organizations create, capture and re-use knowledge to achieve organizational objectives." He goes on to define KM as a four-part process that is iterative (see Figure 7.1).

Figure 7.1 The Knowledge Management Process

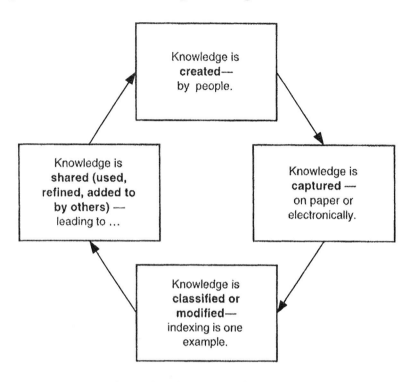

In the first step, people process data and information into knowledge. ("Knowledge is information combined with experience, context, interpretation, and reflection. It is a high-value form of information that is ready to apply to decisions and actions."[2])

In the second step, that knowledge is captured on paper or in a computer, or it may simply be remembered by the creators for reuse. In the third step, the knowledge is classified and modified, by indexing for example, or by the addition of keywords. This modification often adds context that makes the knowledge easier to reuse later. You can tell how well this step is being carried out by how easily people in the organization are able to find and use the knowledge when they need it. Finally, as knowledge is shared with others, it is refined, added to, and otherwise modified. This step merges into a fresh round of the cycle, as the new developments are captured, modified, and so on.

Companies initiate knowledge management projects to find ways to capture, interpret, organize, disseminate, and capitalize on what they've learned; when these learnings take place on projects, project management and KM can merge and reinforce one another. A recent article in *PM Network*[3] called knowledge management and project management "two revolutionary disciplines" that not only coexist but produce added value when they are married to each other.

Knowledge Repositories

Where and how is knowledge stored in your organization? There are three basic kinds of knowledge repositories, according to Bock. *Structured repositories* are databases, expert systems, and other storage that is searchable via indexes, keywords, controlled vocabulary, and so on. *Unstructured repositories* include things like project reports, sales call notes, and other sources. These are searchable by free text means. Those two kinds of repositories are for *explicit knowledge* (knowledge that's been captured and stored for future usage). However, *tacit knowledge*, which resides in the minds of people, is the most valuable. We all know and use the tools that are available to access this "repository"— company directories, resource libraries, and other lists that show us who knows what.

Key Success Factors in Knowledge Management

Not surprisingly, a big part of knowledge transfer and management is communications planning, a skill that should be familiar to project managers. Here are some pointers offered by Bock and others:[4]

1. Limit your efforts to those things most likely to make a difference. This is simply another way of saying, focus on core competencies. What areas of project management might be most improved by better knowledge transfer in your organization? Some obvious areas might be in bringing new team members up to speed or in stockpiling budget and actual figures so as to produce more realistic estimates.

2. Communicate, communicate, communicate. Give project personnel the widest possible array of information and knowledge: access to customer records, presentations, technical manuals, and other company, industry, and professional background and documentation—anything and everything they might need. The Web is the ideal tool for connecting people to information. You can give experienced people access to helpful tools and bring new personnel up to speed at

a relatively low cost online. And, you can enlist them in improving what you put online to prevent it from becoming static: Encourage them to collect customer and technical lore and add it to the database that is available to help customer service and tech support solve problems quickly.

3. Give project personnel access to each other (see the section "The Project Office as a Community of Practice" in this chapter for more details). Again, the Internet is an ideal tool: listservs, chatrooms, and discussion boards allow people dispersed across the company or the globe to share tips and experience. Personal contact is also important; we'll discuss the many opportunities for project review meetings later in this chapter.

4. Identify the knowledge drains and gaps. Bock suggests surfacing key knowledge by asking: "What do we lose when key people leave?" or "What do we have to teach every new person?"

5. Facilitate exchanges among technical experts who have vast company knowledge stored in their heads; encourage them to become leaders in the project management "community of practice" within the organization to spread that knowledge around.

6. Use the resource library capabilities of project management software to catalogue the competencies of employees to help match them up to the project teams that can best use their expertise; then expand these libraries beyond project management to encompass skills from other segments of the enterprise.

7. Encourage best-practice sharing between projects, between departments, and between project managers within and outside of your organization. Bock calls best-practice sharing "the most powerful knowledge management practice." It is also one of the simplest knowledge management tools; people who share an interest or a goal do it naturally. Companies can capitalize on this by providing infrastructure to spread the sharing around—networks, collaborative software, databases, libraries, and so on. However, the most important success factor in best-practice sharing doesn't involve technology. It involves strong leadership, with attention to culture and change. The application of technology can make a good process better, but will not substitute for organizational leadership that models an interest in knowledge management and process improvement.[5] Table 7.1 offers a quick KM practices assessment tool for your organization.

Table 7.1 The Knowledge Management Assessment

Leadership. Does your organization have a knowledge man- **Score**
agement strategy that is actively supported by the executive
level and which clearly articulates how KM contributes to
achieving organizational objectives?   _____

Measures. Does your organization measure and manage its
intellectual capital in a systematic way?   _____

Processes. Does your organization have systematic processes
for gathering, organizing, exploiting, and protecting key knowledge assets, including those from external sources?   _____

Explicit Knowledge. Is there a rigorously maintained knowledge inventory, with a structured thesaurus or knowledge tree,
and clear ownership of knowledge entities that is readily accessible across the organization?   _____

Tacit Knowledge. Do you know who your best experts are
for different domains of key knowledge, and do you have in
place mechanisms to codify their tacit knowledge into an explicit format?   _____

Culture/Structure
Is knowledge sharing across departmental boundaries actively
encouraged and rewarded? Do workplace settings and format
of meetings encourage informal knowledge exchange?   _____

Knowledge Centers
Are there librarians or information management staff that coordinate knowledge repositories and act as focal points for
provision of information to support key decision-making?   _____

Exploitation. Are your knowledge and knowledge management capabilities packaged into products and services and
promoted in your organization's external marketing?   _____

People/Skills. Have specific knowledge roles been identified
and assigned, and are all senior managers and professionals
trained in knowledge management techniques?   _____

Technical Infrastructure. Can all important information be
quickly found by new users on your intranet (or similar network) within three mouse clicks?   _____

Scoring Key: Rate your organization (either the project office or the organization as a whole) on a score 0 to 10: 0 = doing nothing at all; 10 = world-class KM.
Scores will be more accurate if several people complete the assessment and average their scores.

Adapted from: Knowledge Networking: Building the Collaborative Enterprise, David
Skyrme, Butterworth-Heinemann (1999).

Barriers to Knowledge Management Success

The biggest barrier most organizations face in implementing effective knowledge management is a culture that rewards information hoarding. As noted, software won't solve this problem; only a management culture that rewards knowledge-sharing will solve it.

In a recent survey, Ernst & Young asked 431 U.S. and European firms about their knowledge management practices.[6] While 87% of respondents said that knowledge was critical to their competitiveness, 44% reported that they were poor or very poor at transferring knowledge within their organization. Respondents reported that the chief barriers were top management failure to express the importance of knowledge management (32%); lack of shared understanding of strategy or business model (30%); and poor organization structure (30%). These research results were recently echoed by a study co-produced by International Data Corporation (IDC) and *Knowledge Management* magazine. Their findings indicated that an organization's main KM implementation challenge stems from the absence of a "sharing" culture in the organization and employees' lack of understanding of what knowledge management is and what benefits it offers. To address these challenges, companies must make training, change management and process redesign primary components of their KM initiatives.[7]

Before discussing how to address some of these barriers, let's examine what existing project management practice has to offer in the way of KM.

Capturing Lessons Learned—and Beyond

In the spirit of "limiting your efforts to those things likely to make a big difference," the best place to begin focusing on the KM potential of a Strategic Project Office is in that area of project management where process and technical information is gathered: the lessons-learned processes inherent to project management. The SPO oversees the end-of-phase/end-of-process reviews of individual projects and guides project managers and the teams through the review process. In its role as manager of project management knowledge, the SPO is responsible for documenting the results and conclusions from each end-of-phase review for developing an action plan and for preparing follow-up analysis to find if the things that were identified in the end-of-phase review are actually being implemented. On a macro-level, the SPO should also be in charge of capturing the knowledge created by every completed project and program and organizing it in such a way that this knowledge is readily available for future use.

A critical element of process management is continual improvement. This step can be incorporated within each of the project management processes (initiating, planning, executing, controlling, and closing) to ensure feedback on lessons learned and input of recommendations to improve the overall understanding, value, effectiveness and efficiency of the organization's project management methodology.

Here's a quick overview of the processes for capturing knowledge that should be a part of any project management methodology put in place by the project office.

First, there are two things about which we want to capture lessons learned:

1. The product of the project

2. The processes of the project.

Product evaluation objectives should include comparing the final project against the original quality objectives, identifying problem areas, and determining how to address them. While it may seem logical to carry out a product evaluation when the product is complete (see later section on "Final Product Evaluation"), many problems with quality can be avoided by including product evaluation elements in each end-of-phase review. (See Chapter 6 for a discussion of quality assessment.)

Process evaluation follows a similar evaluation procedure. A process/phase end assessment (as part of a phase-end review) should be held as each of the phases in the project draws to a close, when the project manager and project team report their progress to the project steering committee and gain its approval to proceed with the next phase of the project. An assessment should normally be held at the end of every phase and every process in the project. This assessment reviews the overall progress of the project and the plan for continuing the project (see Figure 7.2).

The objective of the process/phase end assessment is to document the status and results of the current phase, prepare for the next process, and review the current phase results with management. Just as important, however, is to provide a summary of the work that was

Figure 7.2 Process Assessment

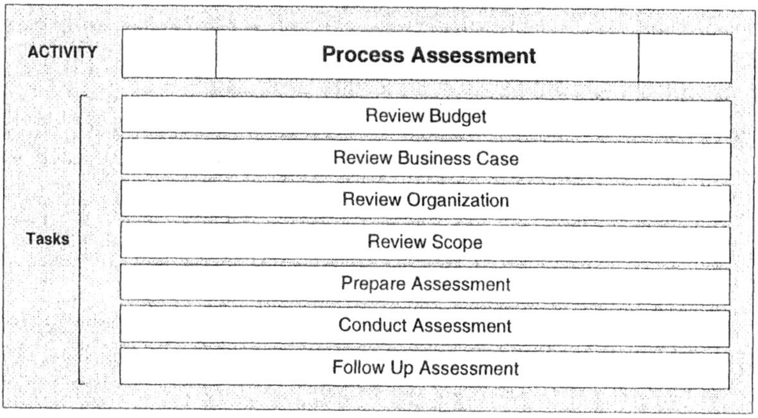

ACTIVITY		Process Assessment	
		Review Budget	
		Review Business Case	
		Review Organization	
Tasks		Review Scope	
		Prepare Assessment	
		Conduct Assessment	
		Follow Up Assessment	

carried out in the phase and a record of the project and phase plans for use in managing and controlling not only the current project, but any future project similar in nature. It also serves as a forum for issues identification and a nexus of communication with the project steering committee.

Suggested steps for each process/phase end assessment are:

- Review the overall project budget and make changes based on the latest adjustments.

- Review project business case.

- Update the business case to reflect any changes in costs, benefits, and risks for the project.

- Review the resource requirements from the phase schedule and update the project organization accordingly.

- Review the latest statement of project scope and ensure that it still accurately reflects the current status and plans for the project.

- Refine the project plan for the next phase/process by adjusting the phase schedule and verifying that the criteria for success and completion of that phase/process are still valid.

- Decide who should attend the process/phase end assessment in addition to the project steering committee and arrange a meeting to present the results of the assessment. At the meeting, request permission to proceed on to the next process/phase of the project or to stop the project if appropriate.

- Update the project and phase plan based on the decisions made by the project steering committee.

- Distribute minutes of the meeting to attendees and a summary to the project team. Document lessons learned from the phase process and provide process improvement recommendations to the project office.

An additional step is that the project management process as a whole—the methodology—may need to be updated in order to capture learning from process evaluations. This type of process assessment overview is best carried out as an integral part of the post-project review.

Project Closeout: The Knowledge Goldmine

All projects end at some point—that's the nature of project work. And though the project closing processes might seem like an afterthought, it is here that the organization can gain the maximum benefit from the work that was done.

All members of the project team and sponsoring committee will have valuable experience and feedback to be captured for future use. A large quantity of information is generated during a project, and this will have been stored with varying degrees of formality by the members of the team. This information needs to be filed away for possible future use. At one time, project information of this type would have gathered dust in binders on a shelf or in file cabinets. Now, however, thanks to knowledge management technology, these documents can remain live and readily accessible to the entire organization.

Project closure information is actually captured throughout the life of the project. It is important to capture information while it is still fresh in the minds of the participant. Consider what may be lost to the organization when people are transferred off the project before it ends, without having captured their key learnings from their participation.

In the same way, subcontractors whose work only extends for a portion of the entire project timeline have input that can be valuable if processes are in place to record it.

Projects should use lists and tracking mechanisms, such as change request logs, issues logs, and other tools and templates that are part of project management methodology (discussed in Chapter 6). These need to be closed to ensure all necessary work has been completed.

For smaller projects, the final project evaluation and post-project review steps can be very informal. The objective is to capture key learning and customer feedback.

Closing the project must take place in such a way that recommendations are identified that can be applied to future projects, that mechanisms can be established for the continued development or improvement of the final project or product, that standard processes and metrics (methodology) for this type of project can be improved, and that project management resources can be redeployed in the most beneficial way for their continued growth and for the company's best interests. Figure 7.3 illustrates the steps executed during project closure.

Final Product Evaluation

By this time in the project, all project work should have been completed. The deliverable(s) of the project should have been inspected and accepted by the customer and key points resulting from these reviews should have been captured. It is possible that the final deliverables do not fully meet the original objectives and quality requirements.

Before the project is completely finished, any deficiency in the deliverable(s) should be identified and evaluated. If it is decided that the deficiency needs to be corrected, it will be necessary to establish a corrective mechanism. This may be a new project or incorporated into this project (possibly as another phase).

Final product evaluation may take the form of a meeting with key members of the project organization, quality review of the final product, and/or a questionnaire directed to the customer(s). In any case, the final product evaluation should include an evaluation against the business success criteria defined in the project initiating and planning processes, an evaluation against the business objectives, and an evaluation against the defined quality objectives and measures. Briefly, you

Figure 7.3 Project Closing

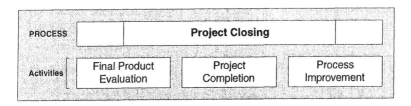

may wish to evaluate the product against a set of criteria which might include

- Fitness for use—The final product is capable of being used efficiently and reliably.

- Fitness for purpose—The final product provides the required business functionality identified in the project objective.

- Conformance to requirements—The project and its final product meet the requirements that were agreed to by the customer(s). These requirements include policies, business objectives, cost constraints, time constraints, and technological requirements.

- Customer satisfaction—The final product must meet the customer's expectations and provide value.

If the final product does not meet all the quality objectives and measures, identify and document the shortcomings. If product evaluation reveals that there are unresolved issues with the product, a follow-on project may be defined to address these.

Post-Project Review

Process improvement is the final step—and overall goal—of any quality process. This step evaluates the overall project management process itself and identifies any lessons learned from the project. If these lessons learned are likely to apply to future projects, they are provided to the project office to be incorporated as revisions to the project management process. Be sure to focus on what worked well as well as what could have been improved.

Figure 7.4 Process Improvement

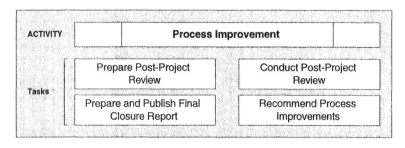

Figure 7.4 illustrates the tasks executed during the process improvement activity of the project closing process. The objective of process improvement is to review the process and provide input to improve it. This needs to be accomplished in a manner that involves both technical and business staff; covers the process used, the tools/ techniques, deliverables, standards, and the organization; identifies things that were not necessary and additional phases, activities, and tasks that need to be added; and improves the quality and efficiency (time and cost) of future projects. Only then can the organization learn from this project and ensure improved performance in future projects.

Post-project review may take the form of a meeting, a facilitated workshop, a questionnaire, or a combination of these. The review should involve all parts of the project organization and may also involve other staff personnel and key customer and supplier personnel. The post-project review collects all the data required for the project closure report and any additional data required by the project (see Table 7.2).

To identify process improvements, review notes captured during the various process steps. Survey all team members, solicit their input, and thoroughly document each recommendation for process improvement, including the rationale for the suggested change/addition and the benefit to the company. Focus on improving process efficiency and effectiveness. Classify the urgency of each change in order that the process steward can effectively prioritize improvements. Pro-

Table 7.2 Post-Project Review Template

REVIEW INFORMATION

PROJECT NAME:	REVIEW DATE:

PROJECT SPONSOR:

BUSINESS UNIT(S):

BUSINESS AREA PROJECT MANAGER:

IT PROJECT MANAGER:

REVIEW PARTICIPANTS:

PROJECT HISTORY

ACTUAL START DATE:	PLANNED START DATE:
ACTUAL COMPLETION DATE:	PLANNED COMPLETION DATE:
ACTUAL NUMBER OF HOURS:	BUDGETED NUMBER OF HOURS:
ACTUAL EXPENSES:	BUDGETED EXPENSES:

How well were the overall objectives of the project met, and did the project achieve the anticipated benefits?

How well was the scope of the project managed?

Were the specifications achieved?

What key lessons were learned?

TOPIC	SUCCESSES	AREAS FOR IMPROVEMENT
Project Planning	•	•
Project Control, Tracking, and Issues Resolution	•	•
Project Staffing and Resource Utilization (IT and Business Resources)	•	•

Table 7.2 continued

TOPIC	SUCCESSES	AREAS FOR IMPROVEMENT
Project Communication	•	•
Management of Project Team (IT and Business), Schedule, and Deliverables	•	•
Management of Business Group Expectations	•	•
Requirements Definition	•	•
Design of Deliverables (Interfaces, Screens, Reports, Documentation)	•	•
Development	•	•
Testing	•	•
Implementation	•	•
Documentation	•	•
Training	•	•
Technical Performance	•	•
Vendor and Contract Management	•	•
Quality of Application/Product	•	•

vide improvement recommendations to the process steward, and maintain a record of the recommendations as an audit trail.

Prior to the review session, conduct the team member questionnaire (see Appendix D), and then complete the review information and project history based on the project documentation. Provide for detailed note-taking during the proceedings. For the various topics, record the names of the commentators and the IT or business group they represent. After the session, complete the post-project review form by summarizing the responses of the attendees. Consider having a member of project office or another third party facilitate the session. Suggested steps:

- Prepare and distribute material as appropriate to the personnel involved in the review.

- Record all data required for the project closure report and any recommended changes to the processes, metrics, tools, techniques, standards, etc.

- Document the results of the post-project review into a single project closure report.

- Distribute the report to appropriate team members of the project organization.

- Recommend process improvement steps.

- Assess each suggested change to decide if it is likely to apply to future projects.

- Prioritize all suggestions and recommendations.

- Submit the recommended changes to the organization's project office.

Remember, the purpose of the post-project review is to communicate and document the experiences of a project in order to better plan and manage future projects. Before finalizing the post-project review summary, offer those who contributed a review draft of the proceedings so that they can correct their comments. (If appropriate, names may be withheld from the final summary.)

Why Are We So Bad at This?

All this sounds very well in theory, but research carried out by project management researchers Lynn Crawford of the University of Technology at Sydney (Australia) and Terry Cooke-Davies of Human Systems, Ltd., in 1994[8] found that while most project management groups are good at capturing lessons learned and storing them in some way, the step where KM fails for most project-oriented companies is

Figure 7.5. The Knowledge Gap in Project Management

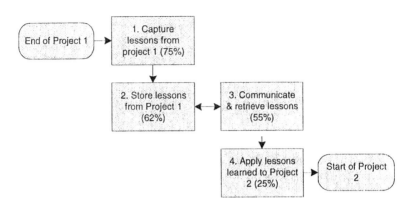

Source: Lynn Crawford and Terry Cooke-Davies, "Managing Projects—Managing Knowledge: Sharing A Journey Towards Performance Improvement," paper presented at the International Project Management Association Conference, 2000.

in the *transfer* of that knowledge to future projects and project teams (see Figure 7.5).

In Crawford's words, in terms of transferring lessons from one project to another, "a faultline runs down the center of the process." Lessons learned are captured toward the end of a particular project and are the responsibility of an "outgoing" project team, whereas knowledge generation and transfer occur toward the beginning of a project and are the responsibility of an "incoming" project team.

Some of the problem lies in the way project managers have traditionally thought of projects: as unique endeavors. "Unique" is even a part of the standard definition of project work. That being the case, it is tempting to dismiss the experiences of project A as being due to specific circumstances that don't apply in the circumstances of Project B.

Another condition of project work is a sense of rivalry between teams: the Project B team has a degree of disdain for those who worked on Project A; they may be less than anxious to learn what that team has discovered. Crawford notes that respect and sharing is much more likely if both project teams see themselves as members of a higher-level community, with accountability to all members of the community, rather than as separate entities in competition.

In addition, project managers tend to place the highest importance on aspects of the project other than knowledge transfer. The UTS researchers asked participants to rank the importance of project management practices relating to initiating and planning, monitoring and controlling, and closing and capturing lessons learned, and found that study participants ranked monitoring and controlling most highly, closely followed by planning, with closing and capturing lessons learned coming in a distant third.

Finally, in terms of personality characteristics, project personnel in the UTS study tended to be more task-oriented than people-oriented; in other words they did not readily take time to share their knowledge with others.

The project office, as the central repository of project information, keeper of project management methodology, administrator of project management infrastructure, and trainer of project personnel, is in a unique position to maximize an organization's ability to learn from its own experiences. Software, discussed in Chapter 8, provides a partial answer to the resolution of the loss of knowledge over time, but "humanware," Lynn Crawford suggests, can be even more effective. Crawford's work with international networks of project management practitioners has led her to adopt the community of practice as a model way to nurture project management competence.

The Project Office as a Community of Practice

MANAGEMENT IN A HIGH-TECH MANUFACTURING organization performed an audit and discovered that design teams were repeating common mistakes, resulting in tens of millions of dollars in rework and repair costs. A simple solution was formulated: create communities of practice (CoPs) across design groups to enable project personnel to more easily capture and share valuable knowledge, information, and best practices. Using existing collaborative software tools and databases, the CoPs focus on linking product engineers together so that they can collaborate and get assistance in real time from experts across the organization. The CoPs filled the gap that sophisticated information systems could not: they allowed the engineers to ask each other: "What do I know that you need to know?" and "What do you know that I need to know?" These simple dialogues have resulted in significant savings and increased team satisfaction and innovation.

—from *Embedding KM: Creating a Value Proposition,*
www.apqc.org, May 2001

"Any methodology worth its salt," says process improvement expert Michael Wood,[9] "seeks to harvest the wealth of knowledge that exists within the minds of those who actually do the work." How is this "harvest" best carried out? Wood contends that knowledge workers who are organized into cross-functional groups representing the end-to-end processes that actually deliver value to stakeholders can readily define and resolve the value-gaps in the process.

The cross-functional group he describes is an apt description of the teams that accomplish project and program work in most organizations. Thus, an organization in which most work is accomplished by teams is already in a position to engage in continuous improvement of its own methodology and processes. All the project office needs to do is learn how to nurture those cross-functional groups and provide them with the infrastructure to put up their "harvest" for safekeeping and future use. What organizational structures are best suited for making the most of that harvest?

Lynn Crawford has suggested project management communities of practice can be invaluable in facilitating knowledge creation, transfer, and learning between individuals and across organizational boundaries.[10] Table 7.3 shows the qualities and functionalities that characterize a community of practice.

Communities of practice are not new, but the term has acquired new significance in the era of the knowledge worker and intellectual capital.[11] Communities of practice are groups of people informally bound together by shared interest and shared expertise—a simple enough definition and one which might apply to most voluntary groups in our society.

Yet the importance of the community of practice to the development of technical and business knowledge began to be truly appreciated thanks to the Institute of Research on Learning (IRL), in Palo Alto, founded in 1987 and associated with Xerox's Palo Alto Research Center, and to the work of social learning theorist Etienne Wenger.[12] A key finding of the IRL's work was that learning is social. In this context, communities of practice have become associated with the concepts of the learning organization and knowledge management.

The primary reason to implement a project office is to improve project performance across the organization. Standardizing on best practices is one way to accomplish that goal. Thus, the encourage-

Table 7.3 Communities of Practice: Characteristics

- **Common language:** Group has a professional language of its own (jargon, terminology)

- **Shared background:** Members have shared background or knowledge

- **Common purpose:** The group has a common purpose which gives it an internal impetus

- **Creation of new knowledge:** The work of the group and the interaction of the members creates new knowledge for those members

- **Dynamism:** Social distribution of knowledge takes place in the group

- **Evolution:** Group develops beyond mere social interaction

- **Unofficial:** Group evolves rather than being created

- **Voluntary:** Membership is generally voluntary

- **Narration:** Swapping war stories is a key way in which members share domain knowledge

- **Informal:** Group is often informal—there is no hierarchy

- **Fluidity:** Newcomers arrive and old-timers leave

- **Similar jobs:** Group members have similar jobs

- **Self perpetuating:** As groups generate knowledge, they reinforce and renew themselves

- **Self-managing:** Groups benefit from cultivation but not from control

Source: Paul Hildreth, Communities of Practice, 2000. Available at http://www-users.cs.york.ac.uk/~pmh/work.html#Communities.

ment of best-practice sharing among all segments of the organization is thus a natural role for the project office to take. By recognizing the shared interests and goals of project management practitioners throughout the organization, the project office can play an important part in supporting, facilitating, and networking the informal communities that are "people repositories" of project knowledge around the enterprise.

Organizations such as Boeing, NASA, NCR, and Ericsson have provided support for project management communities of practice along these lines, even rewarding active participation in corporate communities of practice. Further, the development of communities of project management practice between organizations has led to initiatives that benchmark project management practices.[13]

Since it is a truism that informal channels of communication are faster than formal ones, and since a "firm's competitive advantage depends more than anything on its knowledge ... *on what it knows, how it uses* what it knows, and *how fast* it can know something new,"[14] the project office's facilitation of project management communities of practice can contribute not only to the capture and growth of project management knowledge, but to the speed of innovation and change in the organization as a whole.

In addition, the community of practice, like a distributed computing network, links and expands the "repository" of project management knowledge that is stored in practitioner's minds—the tacit knowledge that is otherwise so difficult to manage.

What do the experts tell us about building and maintaining communities of practice? In "Knowing in Community," knowledge management expert Richard McDermott[15] listed a number of critical success factors for communities of practice:

1. Focus on knowledge important to both the business and the people. This echoes Wally Bock's advice to limit the focus of your KM efforts to areas where you can make a difference. The topics addressed by the community need to be ones people feel personally passionate about.

2. Find a well-respected community member to act as coordinator, to keep people and to create opportunities for people to share ideas. A coordinator need not be a leading expert, but must be someone who connects well with people.

3. Make sure people have time and encouragement to participate. Some companies specifically allocate a certain amount of project time to community activities to insure that the time and energy people invested in the community would count in their performance appraisal.

4. Involve thought leaders who either have an important specialized knowledge or who are well connected and influential members of the project management community. These people legitimate the community and draw in other members.

5. Make opportunities for contact. While documented reports, templates, tips, analyses, proposals, and so on are helpful to most community members, face-to-face contact is key to building a sense of commonality, enthusiasm, and trust.

6. Allow people to participate at their own comfort level. Even lurkers often get great value from a community where they can drop in quietly to find out who is working on what or learn about the field and make contact later.

7. Encourage real dialogue about real problems and cutting edge issues by building a trustful and mutually helpful environment.

One of the things that these communities can do to add value in an organization is not only share but benchmark best practices, both internally and against other organizations.

Benchmarking

In Chapter 6 we discussed the important role that benchmarking best practices plays in continuous improvement of process and methodology. It's in the project office's own interest to see that benchmarking takes place, both on a project level against other projects of that kind as well as against other organizations that manage similar projects. How else can the project office offer proof that its policies are improving project results internally? How else can the organization determine if its project management practices are helping it to pull ahead of competitors?

The term *benchmarking* was scarcely known to the business world a decade ago, but today it's almost a buzzword. Textbooks define benchmarking as "the comparison of similar process across different organizations, companies, and industries to identify best practice." But another way to think of benchmarking is as a snapshot of a company, which can be compared to snapshots of other companies.

Benchmarking provides an objective starting point for organizational improvements. It answers the question, "Where do we stand versus others?" and points toward new practices and new metrics; convinces middle managers of the need for change; identifies opportunities for improvement; and justifies the investments needed to realize those opportunities. As a tool for process improvement, it works best if it is iterative—part of an ongoing program.[16] The cyclical nature of projects provides a perfect organizational context for benchmarking efforts to remain dynamic and effective. Benchmarking process phases are described in Table 7.4.

High-performing organizations employ benchmarks and best practices as management tools to support strategic thinking and planning. They integrate benchmarking into the management of everyday processes and use networking and technology to expedite and optimize benchmarking. As project management knowledge collection and dissemination becomes more and more of an organizational priority, all levels of project personnel can learn to become receptive learners and skillful benchmarkers who actively practice innovative adaptation and who recognize benchmarking as an essential skill.[17]

Benchmarking allows organizations a tool for gathering information and understanding the best practices external to their organization, as well as those that are internal. This information can allow organizations to improve profits/effectiveness, accelerate and manage change, achieve breakthroughs/innovations, and understand world-class performance, according to the American Productivity & Quality Center, which offers a benchmarking methodology to members. Some of the principles of APQC's methodology include:

- Make sure that the project is truly supported.

- Ensure that the scope of a benchmarking effort is specifically targeted to only the few key issues facing your organization or group.

- Make full use of the Internet—but make sure to verify all of the information found there.

- Examine your internal processes before starting a benchmarking project. Go through a true process mapping exercise with your internal peers.[18]

Table 7.4 Benchmarking Best Practices

BENCHMARKING PROCESS PHASES	BENCHMARKING CRITICAL SUCCESS FACTORS
Planning • Identify benchmark subject • Identify benchmark partner • Determine data collection method • Collect data	**Planning** • Active management commitment to benchmarking • Focus on benchmarking first on industry best practices and second on performance metrics
Analysis • Determine competitive gap • Project future performance	**Analysis** • Clear, comprehensive understanding of internal processes as a basis for comparison to industry best practices • Concentration of other recognized leaders against which to benchmark
Integration • Communicate results • Establish functional goals	**Integration** • Realization that competition is constantly changing; future needs must be anticipated • Openness to new ideas; creativity and innovativeness in their application to existing processes
Action • Develop action plans • Implement plans • Monitor results • Recalibrate benchmarks	**Action** • Willingness to share information with benchmark partners • Continuous, institutionalized commitment to benchmarking best practices

Adapted from: Business Process Benchmarking. Robert C. Camp, ASQC Quality Press, 1995.

Table 7.5 Benchmarking Guidelines

- Have basic knowledge of benchmarking and follow a benchmarking process.
- Determine what to benchmark, identify key performance variables to study, recognize superior performing companies, and complete a rigorous self-assessment—all *before* initiating contact with potential benchmarking partners.
- Have a questionnaire and interview guide developed, and share these in advance if requested.
- Possess the authority to share and be willing to share information with benchmarking partners.
- Work through a specified host and mutually agreed-upon scheduling and meeting arrangements.

In addition, when the benchmarking process proceeds to a face-to-face site visit, exhibit the following behaviors:

- Provide meeting agenda in advance.
- Be professional, honest, courteous, and prompt.
- Introduce all attendees and explain why they are present.
- Adhere to the agenda.
- Use language that is universal, not insider jargon.
- Be sure that neither party is sharing proprietary information unless prior approval has been obtained from the proper authority.
- Share information about your own process, and, if asked, consider sharing study results.
- Offer to facilitate a future reciprocal visit.
- Conclude meetings and visits on schedule.
- Thank your benchmarking partner for sharing their process

Adapted from: "Benchmarking and Its Myths," Robert J. Kennedy, *Competitive Intelligence Magazine*, 3:28-33, 2000.

Once you have decided what features of your project management process to benchmark, you must first learn how the process under study works within your own company. The benchmarking team then learns how the process can be improved by visiting other companies, reading literature, and talking to employees. Employees who have been performing the process for many years are often the best sources for ideas.

The next step is to develop recommendations based on other companies' best practices and present them to management staff. Management buy-in will be crucial to the implementation campaign. Staff should also know the recommendations so that they can effectively participate.

Table 7.5 offers guidelines for successful benchmarkers, based on the APQC research and recommendations.

ALL COMPANIES COMPETE based on knowledge. We leverage knowledge to improve processes, serve customers, update operations, and bring products to market. Many companies mistakenly believe that investments in technology are the primary route to success, while ignoring the deep well of knowledge and expertise that exists within the organization's members. Knowledge management techniques, when used to capture and link the experiences of project personnel, can offer a way to maximize resources. And further improving processes through benchmarking raises the bar another level. Research has shown that benchmarking results in more efficient processes which can generate substantial cost savings—as much as from 15 to 45%, according to some experts.[19] By combining the principles of knowledge management and project management, the organization can make the most of what it knows, learn more from its projects, and leverage knowledge gathered about competitors and industry.

Endnotes

1. Wally Bock, Knowledge Management 101, Intranet Journal, http://idm..internet.com/articles. (Article orginally appeared in Bock's Briefing Memo newsletter at www.bockinfo.com.)
2. Davenport, De Long, and Beers, "Successful Knowledge Management Projects," *Sloan Management Review*, Winter 1998.
3. N. Olonoff, "Knowledge Management and Project Management," *PM Network* 14 (2):61-64, 2000.

4. Cinda Voegtli, Know-All 10, archived on www.gantthead.com.

5. Wally Bock, op. cit., and Cinda Voegtli, op. cit.

6. Dave Webb, "Corporate Culture Blocks Better Use of Knowledge," *Computing Canada*, Sept. 1, 1998.

7. "State of Knowledge Management," *Knowledge Management*, May 2001.

8. Lynn Crawford and Terry Cooke-Davies, "Enhancing Corporate Performance through Sustainable Project Management Communities," *Proceedings of the 30th Annual Project Management Institute Seminars & Symposium*, PMI, 1999.

9. Michael Wood, "What Is a Process Improvement Methodology Anyway?" www.gantthead.com/articles

10. Lynn Crawford and Terry Cooke-Davies, "Managing Projects—Managing Knowledge: Sharing A Journey Towards Performance Improvement," paper presented at the International Project Management Association Conference, 2000.

11. T.A. Stewart, "Intellectual Capital: The New Wealth of Organizations," New York: Doubleday, 1999.

12. Etienne C. Wenger, *Communities of Practice*, Harvard Business School Press, 1991; E.C. Wenger and W.M. Snyder, "Communities of Practice: The Organizational Frontier, *Harvard Business Review* 78 (1):139-146, 2000.

13. Crawford, ibid.; Frank Toney and Ray Powers, *Best Practices of Project Management Groups in Large Functional Organizations*, PMI, 1997.

14. L. Prusak, *Knowledge in Organizations*, Boston:Butterworth-Heinemann, p. ix, 1997.

15. Richard Mcdermott, "Knowing in Community: Ten Critical Success Factors in Building Communities of Practice," *Knowledge Management Review*, May/June 2000.

16. Jeffery C. Egan, "Benchmarking as a Change Agent at IBM," *Supply Chain Management Review*, Winter 2000.

17. Christopher E. Bogan and Michael J. English, *Benchmarking for Best Practices*, McGraw Hill, 1994.

18. "Embedding KM: Creating a Value Proposition, American Productivity and Quality Council," accessed at www.apqc.org, May 2001.

19. Kimberly Lopez, "How to Measure the Value of Knowledge Management," *Knowledge Management Review*, March/April 2001.

Chapter 8

The Technical Infrastructure

T HIS IS A CHAPTER ABOUT tools that doesn't really talk about the tools themselves, but about the human and organizational structure in which they are embedded. In today's volatile software marketplace, there would be little point in the author of a book attempting to discuss the attributes of specific software products when those products may be upgraded or obsolete by the time the book hits the shelves. That's one reason you won't find any software recommendations in this book. But the other reason is that what software you use is far less critical to your success than how you use it, who uses it, and how you select it.

A project office needs three key elements to operate smoothly: people, process, and tools. Without the proper emphasis on each element, an organization will have difficulty making changes and improving the way it operates. You may have the best people, but without the right tools on hand productivity will suffer. You may have the best tools, but without the right process all you have done is automate an otherwise bad situation and your people will become even more frustrated. You may have the most comprehensive process, but without the buy-in of the people in the organization, that process isn't going anywhere except a dusty bookshelf. The point is, you need all three elements to make changes and, in particular, changes and improvements in project management.

That said, let's focus briefly on software tools. We'll explore some key questions: Why do you need software for your project office? What kinds of functionalities are important for the various levels of project offices? What are the best practices for selection? After you've selected your software tool, how should you roll out the software within the organization? The objective of this chapter is not to tell you what kind of software to use; that is a complex question that can only be determined through a rigorous selection process. Instead, we will raise issues and questions that are important for any company implementing a project office to consider.

Why You Need Project Office Software?

This question may seem obvious. It's just common sense to buy a packaged tool to jumpstart the project office—isn't it? Maybe, but many companies jump into the tool-buying stage without proper consideration of their specific needs and requirements. We recommend you think through your requirements before talking with software vendors. To help you in this process, here are some thoughts on why you need software. Select the ones that fit your situation and put them in priority order. This will help you to ultimately select the right package.

Project management software for the project office must:

- *Support integration for a total enterprise perspective.* In many cases, organizations are looking for software that will depict the big picture. You need the ability to summarize and capture the most pertinent information for an executive perspective. As things change in the supporting details, you want the top-level information to reflect the impacts and the new status. Not only do you want to see this for the enterprise schedule, but you want to see it for all your resources and project funding, too. Having the ability to efficiently integrate the details and provide a total enterprise perspective for schedule, resources, and cost is a capability of most sophisticated tools, but not of all tools. If this is a priority of yours, make it one in your selection.

- *Provide different capabilities and levels of information for diverse stakeholders who work at different levels.* Executives are important, but we can't forget about the project managers and their teams. The software tool needs to be sophisticated enough to provide the enterprise integration capabilities, but it should be simple enough to use on an individual project. Don't buy a software package that is overly complex and not intuitive. Make sure it is user-friendly and easy to work through (get your experts to test it and tell you). Some software vendors have an integrated set of software tools targeted at the different levels and needs of the software users. As an organization, you would get the simplicity for the single focus of a project team and the complexity for the enterprise focus of the organization—all easily integrated within one software suite. Make sure you think through the needs of all users.

- *Support dynamic, changing environments and priorities.* Doesn't that describe almost every organization? Most entities are dependent upon external influencing factors. Priorities shift. Perhaps the R&D department made a major breakthrough and project funding is realigned to pay for the startup project. Or, perhaps another project is in dire straits and resources are pulled from three other projects to help. That's why you need a software package that is flexible and can easily adapt to changes across the board. You don't want to manually reconcile different databases every time there is a fluctuation. Get a tool that makes it easy to make changes, not more difficult. (See comments on friction later in this chapter.)

- *Make a good process more efficient with software.* We have seen good status reporting processes that took forever to complete each month because most of the consolidating was done manually. Assuming your project teams plan and track progress within the software tool, it is much more efficient to have the tool summarize and provide total information for you to analyze. In this case, a good process definitely becomes more efficient with software automation. Select a tool that supports or enhances your processes. Identify the ones that are important and understand how the software can support them.

- *Support geographically separated, virtual teams.* Nowadays, virtual project teams and project offices are accepted as the norm. Today's technology makes it feasible to build project teams and project offices with experts from across the company. This virtuality in an organization adds another layer of complexity to communications management. E-mail, the external Web, corporate intranets, and the good old-fashioned telephone are communication instruments that support virtual teams. If your structure is virtual (or your technology architecture is heading that way), you need to select a software package that will operate in such an environment and be accessible by all parties regardless of their physical location.

- *Provide a historical database to gather company-specific information for future planning and estimating.* This is definitely a planner's dream. Can you imagine actually having historical information to estimate how long a task will take and how many resources you need to accomplish it? Imagine having access to how much it cost on similar projects to get the same effort done. A software tool in the project office can be a central repository of information and collect actuals on projects as they move through the life cycle. If this is important to you, understand how this is accomplished and maintained within the software you are selecting.

- *Reduce the administrative burdens.* Let project managers spend more time managing and analyzing rather than consolidating and summarizing those infamous status reports. Take a hard look at the software's capability to produce reports, and in particular the ease to tailor and/or develop your own reports. You want to minimize the time spent by project managers in consolidating and summarizing information. You want to maximize the time they spend on managing the project and interpreting the resulting information. Make sure the software maintains and provides the information you need to see.

- *Support the establishment of standards and consistency across projects.* In large part, software tools will support standardization and consistency. By their very nature, they are oriented in this direction with common database fields and nomenclature. In many instances, the software is simply a shell for you to populate as it best fits your organization. Ask about the software's capability to support such things as templates and tutorials.

- *Provide a central place for written communications and project exchanges.* Most folks like to keep things simple and are creatures of habit. It is convenient to have one place, a central place, to find things. It is a good idea to centrally locate project management guidance and new "things happening in the field." Individuals will then know where information is located and can access elements that will help their current activities. Ask the software vendor if its package provides a central location (or repository) to organize your information.

Software Functionality and Project Office Complexity

We can think about what type of software products the project office needs in two ways: by a project management approach and by the level of the project office in the organization (project office levels were discussed in detail in Chapter 3).

Project Management Approach

There are two basic approaches to project management that are reflected in software products:

- *Task management.* The project is seen largely as a collection of tasks to be accomplished. Organizations using the task management approach assume that the resources will be available when needed to accomplish the specified tasks. This assumption may be valid when resources are plentiful and the number of projects is low, lessening the chance for interproject conflicts. Desktop tools—even spreadsheet software—can be used to manage projects under this approach. Task management tools suitable for this type of project management are easy to implement and are relatively inexpensive. Unfortunately, few organizations today have a light workload of this type. Tools based on this paradigm generally constrict a project officer's ability to plan, organize, and control multiple complex projects in an enterprise portfolio. Scheduling tools are "necessary but not sufficient" for managing a portfolio of projects. A multi-project view of work is required, with facilities to ease collaboration, automate skill and resource management, facilitate issue management, and assist with metrics collection and organizational learning

- *Resource management.* Organizations assume that the primary constraint on successful completion of *projects* is availability of key resources. This approach requires more sophisticated methods and tools to gather information about project status and to reconcile resource requirements across projects; without sufficient investment in these methods and tools, little improvement in capability will be possible. Higher-end tools support multi-

Figure 8.1 Tools in the Evolving Organization

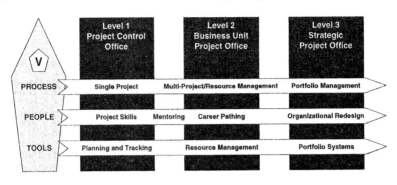

project management via resource sharing and leveling functionalities. These tools are typically are priced at more than $2,000 per seat.

Since most organizations are complex enough to have both simple and complex project activities in the works, Gartner Group studies show that most enterprises require various classes of project management tools to support business requirements—along with the training to use them appropriately.[1]

Project Office Level

We've discussed the three levels of complexity in a project office, ranging from single-project endeavors to the Strategic Project Office. In considering what kind of software is needed, the complexity of the project office is a starting point. Figure 8.1 shows how the need for software functionality co-evolves with the project management practice in an organization.

A *Level 1 project office* may not need high-end tools, although this has been a common pitfall that companies trip into—the "more is better" line of thinking, which can be summarized as "believing that you can lead cultural and organizational change simply by installing a tool with enterprise capabilities." Too often, the result is far from positive. Figure 8.2 illustrates the risks associated with the introduction of new technology.[2] So start simply. Some Level 1 project offices only need the ability to do individual project scheduling and tracking. Software

Figure 8.2 Risks Associated with the Introduction of New Technology

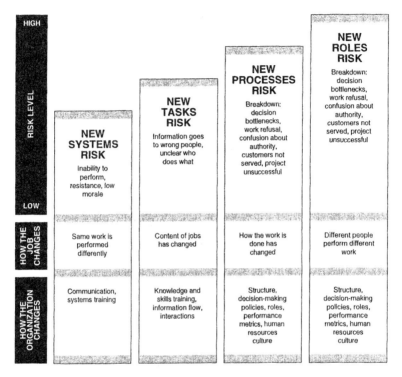

Adapted from: Patricia Averett, "The Do's and Don'ts of Systems Implementation," Employee Benefit News: 45-48, Feb. 2001.

is required when you need more than a to-do list and a calendar; you need to manage resources and control cost.

The next level of complexity is using software for planning and managing dependencies between project tasks. Software can help identify what work can be done in parallel and what needs to be sequenced by work process. The catch is that most people sequence tasks based on logical workflow—and do not take resource availability into consideration. As mentioned previously, this is where the basic project software tools can fail.

As complexity grows, resource assignment becomes crucial. Many times, in order to get resources allocated or committed to the task, a project manager has to engage in significant discussions concerning resource availability and allocation. Frequently the project starts moving forward before the resources are fully committed to the project. This is a time-consuming, error-prone and risky process in project management—one of the primary causes of project failure.

Many people are good enough at project management that if the project isn't too large, they can manage without project management software, using spreadsheets, whiteboards, checklists, and the like. But as you move to higher levels of complexity, you have to deal with resource constraints that aren't obvious and dependencies that require additional analysis to become clear. And with each added level of complexity, you need a higher level of sophistication in the product.

The *Level 2 project office*, as discussed in Chapter 3, oversees departmental or divisional groups of projects. Within this type of PO, the two main components of complexity that are added are:

- *Interproject dependencies.* Now software needs the ability to communicate an understanding what's going on in another project. At a minimum that means the ability to summarize reporting across project phases. Succeeding at this begins not with the software but with a thought process in place: How similarly are we going to manage our projects so we can compare apples to apples? What are our common methodologies, templates, and processes ? What are our common terminologies? What are the actual relationships between the people doing the projects? How integrated are the projects? What's the minimal amount of standardization of procedures needed to accomplish the organizational objectives? As always, when you standardize on a process, you must weigh the benefits to the organization against the handicap to the team.

- *Resource allocation.* Generally speaking, at this point you form a resource library (or resource pool) in order to track resource availability and utilization. If you want to do this within a departmental, at a minimum you must track time at the task level, not at a project level.

Two key factors exist in resource management: resource availability and resource allocation (the requirements of what/when the resource is to be utilized). To plan resource utilization in an organization, a resource "library" must be established. The resource library identifies all resources available for project assignment, their availability, and the timing of their availability. At the project task level, resources are assigned to accomplish the work required by the specific project task.

Human resource libraries can be designed using one of three resource management strategies:

- Individual resource assignment. Individual resource assignment specifies the planned utilization of Bob, Mary, or Harry to specific tasks. This style of resource library development assumes the planners in the organization fully understand the skills, capabilities, and performance of each individual in the company.

- Job-based resource assignment. Using a job-based system, the resource library consists of resources like; programmer, systems analyst, mechanical engineer, electrical engineer, and so on. Large organizations with significant staff who must allocate, spread, and level resources across projects may utilize job-based resource assignment.

- Skills-based resource assignment. Skills-based assignment takes the job-based system one step further and correlates individual skill within job category. Skills-based systems account for level of competency, degree of experience, and relativity of previous experience to the current task. Advanced skills-based resource libraries will account for skills level by individual to correlate individual assignment to task planning.

In a large organization, or one that is geographically disperse, where people don't know who Harry, Mary, or Bob are or what they do, you may need a comprehensive skills-based resource pool just to know who is available, their skill level, and the individual's competency/experience for the task under consideration. An enormous amount of information regarding resources must be catalogued and entered in that system in order to make effective decisions about resource allocation.

Resource management, it should be noted, can refer not just to people but to "stuff"—whatever you need to get the project done: equipment, materials, and supplies. Some industries think of resources as materials, while for others they are labor, and many industries need resource management that can accommodate both.

You need people to manage a system this complex. How much staff is required depends on how you will use the system. When interproject dependencies become so numerous and subtle that the project managers can't stay on top of them, a project controller is required; and maybe a project planner or two if it is a skills-based resource pool.

At the Level 3 project office (Strategic Project Office), you ratchet up the complexity and interaction within the system because you are taking projects across departments that don't even think alike: IT, manufacturing, warehousing, marketing, etc. You have to repeat the thought process described earlier, but on a corporate level.

At the corporate level, project management software must 1) provide sufficient capacity and capability to effectively manage large, multi-project initiatives, 2) enable interface with related corporate systems, and 3) support effective data collection, communications, and reporting through corporate intranets and the Internet.

Managing Large, Multi-Project Initiatives

For large organizations, strategic project management software capacity must be capable of managing data associated with hundreds of projects, thousands of resources, and hundreds of thousands of project tasks. I have been associated with large, individual projects which reflected 30,000-40,000 tasks utilizing over 200 resources. Some well-known project management software programs just will not perform at this high level of capacity. Data and computational accuracy has been known to falter when subjected to the sophisticated calculations required by critical path calculations, constraints between multiple projects, and resource leveling. At the enterprise level, the tool you select must be capable of accurate data collection and computation.

Interface with Corporate Systems

Level 3 project offices find the necessity to create and manage complex interfaces between the project management system and existing corporate collection and reporting systems. Financial systems require special attention in how they integrate with project management software with the two-way flow of information required from time collection and reporting systems, payroll systems, budgeting systems, and cost control systems. When materials and supplies are a significant element of the project execution, interfaces with the procurement, warehousing, and transportation systems may be important to plan the acquisition and delivery of critical components—the timing of which may have a direct impact on the successful attainment of a key project milestone. Direct interface with human resources systems may involve resource library integration with skills, training, performance measurement, and personnel databases. Many other corporate data systems may be affected by the introduction of strategic project management software. A few more to consider: change control, risk management, quality control, and communications interfaces.

Dynamic Communications and Reporting

The ability to collect data, rapidly analyze results, and accurately report status in a variety of fashions is critical to the success of an effective strategic project management system. In today's environment, that means full integration with your corporate intranet and for virtual project teams, the Internet. Strategic project management software should be expected to provide access to corporate project management methodology, project, procedures and templates to assist the project team in planning, executing, and controlling their projects. It should be capable of collecting data on individual project status, supporting the analysis of the data, and reporting project status, program status, and summarizing data in a variety of forms to include departmental, divisional, and enterprise rollups. Enterprise software must also have the ability to assemble resource requirements data by task for each project and accurately forecast resource utilization forecasts by job category. Integrated project management software begins to truly prove its value when it generates accurate project/program status, timely resource estimation and planning, and portfolio data for decision-making based on integrated corporate project schedules.

Portfolio Management Software Issues

At the enterprise level, we encounter true portfolio management issues: selection and prioritization issues that only the newer generations of software begin to handle. Even today, most project portfolio systems simply report on the "thought project" that has to go on at the executive level: What is our strategy? Which projects serve that strategy best? How are they doing? Where are our resources best allocated for overall corporate success?

There are decision support tools on the market that can be used in facilitating an executive team through evaluating a proposed project business case against current goals, an exercise that should result in committed and executed projects. This is a very effective process for identifying and prioritizing new projects as well as regular reevaluation of ongoing initiatives. But, often until you have some data from individual and departmental projects to roll up you cannot make that decision because you don't know what the projects cost or where they stand.

The software requirements at this level are evolutionary. If you don't have individual projects managed well, and that consolidating or coordinating function at the departmental level is not going well, you can't evaluate projects at the enterprise level. So good portfolio management is built on two things:

- Solid data from the bottom of the pyramid

- A structured decision-making process that ties corporate strategy to the projects, supported by that data.

The capabilities typically offered by project portfolio management tools include:

- What-if modeling: The ability to model the effects of newly added projects and changes to available resources or project schedules.

- Project views: Allowing executives, project managers, end users, and workers to view the project information tailored to their information needs. The project "dashboard," which offers at-a-glance high-level project information distilled down to the metrics needed to answer the question "Where do high-priority projects stand?" allows managers to manage by exception—that is, to take action when an agreed upon tolerance range has been exceeded.

- Project time reporting: Easy-to-report status changes in tasks or projects, and the ability to record time against them.

- Project information and status: Task and sub-task information, Gantt chart building, project searching, and the ability to drill down in a project or task from the retrieved information.

- Resource allocation: Resource profiling by skill, geography, business or organizational unit for more appropriate allocation.

- Internet or intranet enablement: Support for Web browsers to enable project and task review, as well as the ability to change status or record time against projects or tasks.

- E-mail notification: E-mail notification of project deadlines, tasks, and events to individuals or groups.

- Reporting: Standard and custom reports should have an HTML option for publishing as static Web pages.

- Database support: SQL databases typically are preferred.

- Security: Access to system features and functions based on username and password security. Other security protections may also be required, depending on the organization.[3]

A note of caution: If the organization isn't committed to engaging the thought project necessary to align strategy to projects, you shouldn't spend significant time on portfolio management software. In organizations that don't perform this alignment, projects are launched based on preference, whim, and sometimes just because it is a "pet project," and once launched they are hard to kill. There are tools that can help prioritize projects, but the bottom line is that portfolio management is 80% thinking and 20% mechanics.

So, if you take a long-term perspective in looking at the project management capability in the organization, as illustrated in Figure 8.1, tools and processes need to be able to grow together. Begin building project management capability on the individual project—and individual team member—level and invest in tools that give the organization room to grow. Somewhere between Level 1 and 2, commit to a tool you can use for the long haul. As advised by researchers at the Meta Group, when standardizing on tools, organizations must first establish consistent use of the low end of the tool spectrum (and this can be pre-software, including consistent use of tools such as templates and checklists). The focus at this stage is consistent, repeatable, effective delivery of individual projects—more of a focus on repeatable process. At the same time, the organization should be planning ahead for scalability of tools to a future state of project management capability and staying abreast of emerging technology to leverage developments in the field.[4]

Additional Software Concerns

Gartner Group research indicates that with the shorter duration of many IT and IS projects, knowledge professionals now move on to new projects, often in new organizational units, every two to eight months. The ability to orchestrate these workers, who are increasingly external to the enterprise, is critical. As a workforce becomes a more diverse mix of employees, free agents, long-term consultants, and others, the difficulty of resource coordination and project administration is driving the development of a new kind of tool, generally known as *professional service automation* or *administration tools (PSAs)*, which support electronic collaborative practices extending beyond the enterprise.

These tools offer features that extend project management to support project accounting, online analytical processing, management dashboards, Web schedule publishing, Web collaboration, project document support (knowledge management), estimating, and so on. PSA features may include the ability to track prospective customers, handle customer information, RFPs, and contracts; and track time and expenses for invoicing, billing, or chargeback.

Collaborative tools: promise and frustration. There is so much good technology for collaborating and sharing information that it is tempting to focus on the functionality of products. But the real challenge is to design the social side of information technology. And there is only one rule for good "social design" of collaborative technology, according to community of practice guru Richard McDermott: *Make it easy to connect, contribute to, and access the community.*

Software should make it easy for community members to connect with each other and to use information from the community's knowledge base. This is more a matter of how seamlessly the software integrates with people's daily work patterns, with the kind of knowledge they need to share, and with the way they envision their community's domain and navigate within it than with specific technical features of the software. For example, when saving documents for the team or posting for the community involve the same number of steps in a familiar software product, the friction involved in collaboration is reduced. *Friction* is a useful way to think about barriers to communication or collaboration within a community. How difficult is it to connect, contribute, or find help? Does it require going into a new program, accessing a separate area of a network, learning new computer skills? Is the collaborative software intuitive? The more special effort it takes to connect, the more friction is created. The greater the friction, the less likely people will take the time to connect.

This is why face-to-face communities have an edge over global ones: if you run into members of the community at lunch, the friction involved in sharing is minimal. The community "space"—websites, databases, libraries—should be organized according to some principles or taxonomy, preferably one that reflects the natural way community members think about their field or topic. McDermott gives the example of a community of geologists who preferred their knowledge bank to be visualized like a map, a kind of document they used in their work and were comfortable with. A well-designed knowledge community offers a bank of information that is easily navigated: users can intuitively find familiar "landmarks," use standard ways to get to key information, and browse for related items.[5]

There are a number of tools commonly thought of as "knowledge management" software. This list was developed by Dataware Technologies:

- Intranets

- Document management systems

- Information retrieval engines

- Relational and object databases

- Electronic publishing systems

- Groupware and workflow systems

- Push technologies and agents

- Help-desk applications

- Brainstorming applications

- Data warehousing and data mining tools.

The problem with this list is that it addresses *explicit knowledge* but ignores the human repositories of *tacit knowledge*. Such approaches to knowledge management display the technologist's fantasy that a system will do all the work. But in project management and knowledge management, as KM writer and consultant Wally Bock has written, "Thinking at all stages is mandatory."[6] While software tools can help to save and organize information, the social design of a project office/ project management community will be, ultimately, as crucial to success as the purchase of the sophisticated project management tools.

What are the Best Practices for Selection?

Most new software products claim to support project office functions. Of course, just because it doesn't say "project office" on the box doesn't mean it isn't useful to the PO. Most of the enterprise suites tools have jumped on the bandwagon offering strategic project management and portfolio management features. For more information and, in many cases, demos for each product, visit the company website. Extensive linked lists of project management software tools are available at www.pmforum.org, www.allpm.com, www.projectconnections.com, and other project management portals and organization sites.

Make selection a systematic and carefully thought-through project. The most experienced software selectors recommend at least three stages of analysis when selecting software:

- *User analysis.* How skilled are the personnel who will be using it? A third-party, objective assessment is best to determine this;

- *Needs analysis.* What are *they* going to do with it? What kind of reports are needed? What needs to be tracked? What problem are you trying to solve? Be specific.

- *Vendor analysis.* Are they financially stable, with a good support track record with other clients.[7]

One of the best processes for software selection we've seen was offered in the preface to a 1999 survey of project management software products. It laid out the following eight steps:[8]

1. *State the business problem driving the selection project.* Does the infrastructure need upgrading? Do needs exceed the capacity of the current system? Or is project performance below expectations? The

first two problems are more easily addressed: you document what data is not available, how it will be used when it *is* available, and how that information will help meet strategic objectives. Define the information required in detail in order to generate requirements for the software. The third problem is more intractable: If the process is flawed, new software won't fix it. Analyze the reasons behind poor project performance before launching the selection project.

2. *State improvement objectives early in order to define requirements in terms of the features that will actually be used.* This means documenting the current state of things, quantifying the improvements, and, finally, defining the information required to support the improvements. Document what information is not available from the current system. Treat this as a visioning exercise, using subject matter experts or consultants as appropriate. State the high-level goals of the project management environment (such as *Reduce time to market of new products by 10%* or *reduce project effort by 8% in 18 months*). Why can't these goals be met with the current system? Document how the software should help meet these goals.

3. *Document or re-engineer the project management process.* If the current process is inappropriate for solving the business problem, meeting the improvement objectives, and meeting the goals of the project management environment, document a new process before continuing with software evaluation.

4. *Map the project management process to the appropriate category of software.* This is the most labor intensive step. Schedule a series of detailed sessions to walk through each step in the process. Make detailed notes describing the inputs, outputs, and processing required to support the process. Involve subject matter experts, management, the current system, and IT staff. Produce a detailed document explaining how the system will support the process for each step. Capture the data elements required. There are many ways to achieve an information objective, so identify *what* is required, not *how* the software should make it happen.

5. *Generate a requirements list.* Most critical requirements will be uncovered during the mapping process. Articulate these and the short list will identify the best possible matches to the requirements.

6. *Select the short list.* A short list of two products is ideal—more products shows that requirement definition has not surfaced a differentiating feature, and almost any product will do. A detailed set of

requirements based on a sound process should always result in identification of a need that can only be met by one or two vendors.

7. *Test products yourself.* Invite vendors to introduce you to their software. Testing them with data that actually represents the business problem facing you will demonstrate which products handle the requirements in the way you expect. Use experienced people to evaluate the results. They should have an understanding of what results are expected, can articulate the pros and cons of the differences between how the packages perform, and can comprehend the potential benefits of differentiators between products.

8. *Decide on/judge the vendors.* Software evaluation efforts can take as little as two days or as long as four months. There is no one best product—seek not "the best" but one that meets the improvement objectives of your investment. One important element in selection should be careful consideration of the vendor's strengths and weaknesses. You should assess their reputation (years in business, customer base, financial condition, proven track record, alliances with other vendors, long-term strategy). Judge how they deliver software and support: Do they use partners and service providers? Who will deliver and implement the software? Do they have/need a local presence? Are there performance guarantees? Is there adequate training and documentation? Finally, what technology decisions have they made and how do those impact their future plans? If for example you choose a vendor that has "hung his hat" on a resource-management approach to project management, as discussed above, will you be limiting your company's future ability to evolve into a more sophisticated project management practice?[9]

To this we might add that at a certain point, there is a diminishing return on the time invested in evaluating software. *Computerworld* has pointed out that most of the leading software offerings will meet most business requirements, and fewer than 50% of the planned features actually end up in implemented systems, regardless of the upfront analysis. The most successful software selection efforts, they argue, strive for speed and results by setting a firm schedule, avoiding requests for proposals (since a written response to a list is of limited value, instead prototype requirements on a vendor's system), narrowing the field quickly, and getting all the costs on the table. [10] Our advise is to focus on the key elements important to successful deployment of an strategic project management system, test the software thoroughly using knowledgeable experts, and select the vendor/partner that is most likely to provide software support through a successful deployment of the toolset.

Finally, some of the most common pitfalls: focusing too much on price and getting locked in to a product that doesn't really meet your company's current and projected needs; not understanding the knowledge level of the staff and presenting them with a product that is either far too difficult or insultingly basic; failing to get senior management buy-in so that software is investigated but never purchased, or installed but ignored by users; buying software that doesn't easily integrate with existing architecture; and thinking the tool is the solution, when in fact training, communication, process improvement, and organizational culture drive project management success.[11] Don't fall into the trap of thinking that software is the keystone of a project management improvement initiative. People do projects—the tools are secondary.

Rollout: Putting the Tools to Work

Now that you've made the decision, how should you roll out the software? Everyone will want to touch, feel, and use the new software immediately. It's like a new toy and sometimes it is treated that way. That's okay as long as you use logic, reason, and patience in putting it together and introducing it to the organization. To do this, we suggest the following:

1. Proceed slowly and incrementally. Don't promise too much too soon. Phase in the capabilities of the tool in a building-block approach. Perhaps work on basic scheduling elements first, then resource management, and then full cost estimating. Phase in the tool *throughout* the organization. Don't roll it out to everyone all at once. Before you do anything, think through your project management requirements and build a logic structure in the database that supports your business needs. Don't curtail this part of the effort. The more upfront focus you put on thinking through the database configuration, the happier you will be in the long run.

2. Pilot test using select projects and portions of the organization to show successes and get supporters. This almost speaks for itself. The benefits of pilot testing are more than "working through the bugs"

they give you the opportunity to have successes (which you can brag about) and earn supporters throughout the company. It is always helpful to have strong advocates that openly support and willingly talk (positively) about the new software tool.

3. If needed, fix the process first and teach your people the new principles. Then adapt the software to the new business rules. There is an added complication if you plan to introduce new processes along with a new tool. If you can, it is best to keep the process somewhat similar and introduce the new tool using the existing process. In this situation, folks will learn and apply one new element versus two. In some cases, it is entirely unavoidable and you have introduce new processes and a new tool concurrently (e.g., perhaps your current method doesn't work or a process doesn't exist). In such situations, make sure your people understand and accept the new principles of the process before you expose them to the new software environment that will make it efficient.

4. Keep the software environment and database structure simple, especially at first; don't get too detailed or complex. I've learned this one first-hand. In one job I managed, we were overly exuberant and built a new system that met everyone's wishes and did everything imaginable. It took awhile to deliver and once it was delivered it was "too much." Keep it simple. Keep it straightforward. Satisfy basic needs then add enhancements to the database as necessary and you will be successful. Don't put too many details in the core structure of the database. It you need more, add the expanded capabilities in future increments.

5. Implement software components to focus on the most pressing needs of the organization (e.g., planning and time entry features should precede cost estimating templates). This ties back to one of the earlier comments of proceeding slowly and incrementally. Your incremental implementation should start by addressing the most pressing needs of the organization. This may be project scheduling or resource tracking. In the implementation, the best thing to do up front is to take care of the organization's most important needs. Identify what those are and structure a rollout plan accordingly.

6. Train, train, train, and mentor, mentor, mentor. People will make it happen, but you need to make sure they understand what to do and how to do it. Conduct multiple short training sessions. Make sure you

emphasize in the training sessions why the organization is implementing the tool (and process). Don't assume people know how to use the tool or that they understand the new process. (To ensure participant understanding of project management theory and philosophy, the PM College uses an industry standard core set of classes: Project Management Essentials, Project Cost & Schedule Management, Leadership in a Project Environment, Project Risk Management, Managing Multiple Projects, and a capstone, experiential course called PM Practicum.) Offer training using multiple avenues—classroom, intranet, handouts, one-on-one, handbooks. Focus heavily on training. You need to make sure everyone understands the basics; don't assume the word is relayed through management. Show your continued support after training by having a formal or informal mentoring program to help when they encounter specific problems afterward.

7. Plan the implementation and communicate the objectives to everyone and do it again, again, and again. Make it very clear why you are implementing the new software and explain the benefit to everyone. This should be done way up front and accomplished over and over again. Plan the implementation so the objectives are clearly laid out. If you are planning the implementation in phases, make sure there are clear objectives, benefits, success criteria, and identified risks for each phase. Whenever there is change in an organization, people respond better if you can explain the benefit and outline specific accomplishments. Then they understand what to expect.

8. Get senior level sponsorship and support; you need more than just the words, you need expectations. In other words, the senior staff won't help you with simple lip service. They need to believe in the reasons behind the new software implementation and tell you what they expect. The senior staff needs to personally tell the employees in the organization their expectations and that they stand behind the new implementation. Obviously, it is up to you to make sure the senior staff understands the whats, whys, whens, and what fors. Saying it once won't be enough; you will need to repeat the same reasons every chance you get.

IN SUMMARY, SOFTWARE TOOLS are a good complement and serve as a good foundation for project offices. Relatively speaking, the hard part starts after tool selection as you roll out the new tool environment within the company. Make sure you plan the implementation, attain senior-level support, communicate the plan, and proceed at a reasonable pace with reasonable expectations.[12]

Endnotes

1. M. Light, T. Berg, "The Project Office: Teams, Processes and Tools," Gartner Group, Aug. 2000.
2. Patricia Averett, "The Do's and Don'ts of Systems Implementation," *Employee Benefit News*: 45-48, Feb. 2001.
3. M. Light and T. Berg, op.cit.
4. _____, "Application Delivery Strategies," *1999 Trend Teleconference Transcript*, META Group, www.metagroup.com, 1999.
5. Richard Mcdermott, "Knowing in Community: Ten Critical Success Factors in Building Communities of Practice," *Knowledge Management Review*, May/June 2000.
6. Wally Bock, "Knowledge Management 101," *Intranet Journal*, http://idm..internet.com/articles. (Article orginally appeared in *Briefing Memo* at www.bockinfo.com.)
7. Max Feierstein, LDS Group, interviewed in *PM Network*, Sept. 1996.
8. *Project Management Software Survey*, PMI, 1999.
9. David Golan, *Call Center Solutions*, Aug. 1999.
10. Michael W. McLaughlin, *Computerworld*, June 19, 1995.
11. Max Feierstein, op.cit.
12. Dianne Bridges, "Software to Support the Project Office," *Project Management Best Practices Report*, March 2000.

Chapter 9

The Stategic Project Office

As PROJECT MANAGEMENT HAS GAINED in popularity, corporate executives have struggled to find a way to link strategic business objectives with the individual projects they have been
asked to authorize. Too often, projects are chartered that have little or
no connection to the corporate strategy formulated by top management. The reason for this is simply the lack of an organizational entity
with responsibility to map strategy to projects, and to monitor projects
and portfolios to ensure they continue to address strategic initiatives,
even as these initiatives change over time. Enter the Strategic Project
Office. The SPO not only provides all the services discussed in earlier
chapters to individual projects and department-level project offices, it
serves as the critical link between executive vision and the work of the
enterprise. Let's explore how this is done and just what a Strategic
Project Office can do for your organization.

Strategic Project Office Overview

We have previously seen that a project office brings project management expertise to bear on any project-related problem or opportunity, wherever and whenever needed. This could include any of the
six project office functions or services covered in Chapter 3:

- Project support
- Project management software tools
- Processes, standards, and methodologies
- Training
- Consulting and mentoring
- Project managers.

The Strategic Project Office goes beyond these traditional categories due to its expanded role of linking strategic objectives to individual projects and portfolios. Several of these additional areas of project control and coordination are discussed elsewhere in the book:

- Project office steering committee. The director of the SPO should chair the steering committee that will select, prioritize, and terminate projects, make resource allocation decisions, and provide guidance to project managers (covered in Chapter 4).

- Project management maturity. As the owner of the project management process, the SPO assesses project management maturity and takes action to improve the practice of project management across the organization (covered in Chapter 2).

- Creation of a project culture. The SPO, working with the HR department, takes the lead in creating the project management culture so necessary for many of the advanced topics covered in this book to be possible at the enterprise level (covered in Chapter 10).

- Process and system interfaces. It is vital that various systems within the enterprise share information. The SPO, working with IT, takes the lead in this effort to integrate project management software with the accounting, HR, and other systems. While the specifics of this subject are outside the scope of this book, some project office software issues are covered in Chapter 8.

- Project quality management. An enterprise-level standard and process for quality must be established. This usually falls to the quality assurance organization; however, if a separate QA organization does not exist, the SPO is responsible for ensuring that project management process quality is maintained and that project managers take necessary action to ensure the quality of product and service deliverables to customers (covered in Chapter 6).

- Resource management across projects and portfolios. Perhaps the most difficult job of a project office is to ensure that resources are assigned to projects according to their position on the prioritized list. This can be done in a number of ways, from having a resource manager within the SPO who takes requests from project managers and negotiates for resources with functional managers to forming a strong liaison with the HR department, which performs the same service for the project office. Regardless of the mechanism and procedure devised, the SPO is responsible for ensuring that key projects are not delayed due to resource shortages. Note that it is not the role of the project office to lead project teams. That job belongs to the project manager. Software aspects of resource management are discussed in Chapter 8.

In this chapter, we will discuss those responsibilities and functions of the SPO that specifically relate to its integrative and strategic role in the organization:

- Linking corporate strategy to programs and projects. The SPO provides the organizational home for taking the strategy document produced by senior management and converting it into the projects that carry out that strategy.

- Portfolio management. The interdependencies between and among projects can only be seen from the perspective of the SPO. This topic area includes:

- Project selection and prioritization. Most project managers complain that they don't know where their project stands in the "pecking order." The SPO selects and prioritizes projects on a continuing basis.

Finally, the SPO has a critical role in project manager competency and professional development. In an organization with an SPO, the SPO assumes responsibility for the professional development of project managers assigned full time to the project office. That entails developing a career path, position descriptions, training plans, and other elements of a professional development program for project managers. The SPO works with HR to these elements. In addition, the SPO is responsible for competency assessment. What makes a good project manager? Most managers would like to know that the probability of success is high before assigning an important project to a project manager. The SPO can assess project manager knowledge, skill, and even personality to help ensure a better fit between projects and those assigned to manage them. The SPO both mentors project managers and provides project managers as mentors to other areas of the organization.

As you can see from this extensive list, the role of the SPO is itself integrated with the roles and responsibilities of other staff organizations within the corporation. The relationship between the SPO and both line and staff organizations within the corporation must be worked out as part of the change to a project culture, discussed in the next chapter. In the meantime, those working to integrate the SPO will be faced with that old organizational demon: politics.

Organizational Politics, Roles, and Responsibilities

The Strategic Project Office must manage the politics of being a new player at the corporate level. There will be those who are not enthralled with the idea of sharing power with an organization whose very purpose is to execute corporate strategy through projects, instead of through functional departments. The director of the SPO must be adept at building strategic relationships, and make it clear to others at his or her level that the SPO exists to help the entire organization achieve its goals. By helping accomplish that, everyone will share in the rewards. Robert Block suggests the following when dealing with the politics of projects:

- Assess the environment. Identify the key players and sources of power in the organization; get to know them as individuals.

- Identify the goals of the key players. What are their overt goals, their covert goals. How can you help them achieve their goals?

- Assess your own capabilities. How are you at developing and nurturing personal relationships? What are your own personal values and how do they match up with those of other key players? Is there a conflict between the two? How good a communicator are you? (Communication skill is a prerequisite for the position of director of the SPO.)

Once this assessment is completed, Block says to continue with resolving key issues using the following familiar process:

- Identify the underlying problem to be solved or issue to be resolved

- Develop alternative solutions for discussion with key players

- Test and iterate solutions until final resolution is achieved.[1]

Figure 9.1 From Strategy to Projects: Strategic Project Office Influence

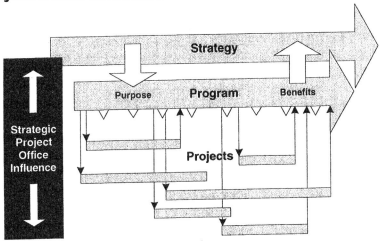

The Link Between Strategy and Projects

The SPO has two primary missions: to improve the organization's project management maturity (a process discussed in detail in Chapter 2) and to "link the organization's projects to its strategic plans."[2] Figure 9.1 shows that link.

The latter of these two—linking strategy to projects—is revolutionary thinking in some organizations. On a consulting engagement to help an organization improve its project management practices, the author had been speaking to a group of senior managers about the connection between what they set as corporate strategy and what was happening "in the trenches" with their real projects. After about an hour, a group manager tentatively raised his hand and asked, "So there's supposed to be a direct linkage between strategy and projects?"

The sad fact is that the concept of having someone in the organization (other than the marketing department) look at the strategic objectives with respect to ongoing projects is still new in many organizations. The good news is that the realization is dawning simultaneously on a large number of corporate executives, who are now establishing Strategic Project Offices to correct this oversight.

Tying the corporate strategic objectives directly to the activities designed to achieve them plays directly into the development of project management maturity as well. It speaks to the need, identified by the Software Engineering Institute, to "institutionalize" good project management practices throughout an organization. If project management processes are not supported by the upper management of the organization, they will not be applied uniformly throughout.[3] Recognizing the SPO as the organizational entity chartered to carry out this mission is one way that executive management can act to institutionalize best practices.

It is a source of constant amazement that corporations pay hundreds of thousands of dollars developing and deploying a project management methodology, then make its use discretionary. Human nature is such that most of us, given a choice to adopt a new process or continue with one that "works for us," will opt for continuing in our old ways. In the next chapter we will discuss how to overcome the natural resistance to change by stressing the advantages of adopting a new way of doing things.

Unfortunately, it is outside the scope of this book to discuss all the ways in which corporations can identify and establish strategic objectives, because it is in this step that the seeds of successful projects are planted. Ideally, project activities should be at the bottom of a "waterfall" in which corporate strategy is expressed as a set of long-term and short-term goals, and each of these goals is operationalized as a project or projects designed to carry out the strategic rationale. Furthermore, the setting of organizational priorities is expressed, on the project level, as a set of metrics by which executives can determine if the project activities are in fact moving the company toward the desired goal. These metrics, feeding into the project prioritization system and into the reward system for project team members complete the feedback loop, making the organization coherent: Project team members are rewarded for behaviors that make projects serve the overarching goals; company strategy becomes everyone's business instead of the yearly intellectual playground of a top few.

By contrast, in the past projects were insulated by many layers of management from the strategic rationale, with the result that work was undertaken on a departmental level which either failed to advance key strategic initiatives or, in some cases, was actually detrimental. Project managers are familiar with the frustrating case of the project which is delivered on time, on budget, and to specifications, but which is a failure in the larger organizational sense because it is irrelevant to the corporate mission or to the competitive stance of the company. Linking strategy directly to the projects that are organized to carry it out eliminates this frustration—and saves a good deal of time and money as well.

One program for establishing this link—although by no means the only one—is the Balanced Scorecard. As Randall Russell, director of research for the Balanced Scorecard Collaborative, noted in a recent interview,[4] 85% of strategies are never effectively implemented, mainly because no one has integrated the people who have to make strategy happen—the workforce. The traditional approach was to share as little information as possible, so organizations have to make some progress in their thinking before they even contemplate implementing a strategy-based approach that requires them to "make strategy everyone's job"—one of the principles of the Balanced Scorecard.[5]

The Balanced Scorecard helps companies clarify what their strategy is and ask the right questions (and take the right measurements) to determine if it's being implemented. Portfolio management and strategic project management are attempts to eliminate that disconnect between strategy and projects, while the Balanced Scorecard provides a structured framework for that purpose.

The scorecard includes four steps that flow into one another in a logical progression (see Figure 9.2): strategic objectives—for example, "Deliver successful IT projects consistently"—which are associated with measures (such as number of projects completed); then targets that will represent success (let's say 10 projects per year); and finally the initiatives that will be used to accomplish this—such as "train everyone in project management."

When a project is couched within a Balanced Scorecard framework you are able to fit the outcome within the strategic framework; it has context. If a project isn't linked to strategy, it becomes a "special project," which translates, says Russell, as *Who cares?*

Portfolio Management

The first order of business is to define portfolio management. The following four definitions explain the four different types of aggregations of projects:

Figure 9.2 The Balanced Scorecard

FINANCIAL
"To succeed financially, how should we appear to our shareholders?"
- Objectives
- Measures
- Targets
- Initiatives

CUSTOMER
"To achieve our vision, how should we appear to our customers?"
- Objectives
- Measures
- Targets
- Initiatives

The Balanced Scorecard provides a framework for translating strategy into action. "Initiatives" are in most cases, analogous to "projects." Scorecard developers recommend tracking 23-25 measures, with 80% of those in the non-financial areas of the scorecard.

INTERNAL BUSINESS PROCESS
"To satisfy our stakeholders, what business processes must we excel at?"
- Objectives
- Measures
- Targets
- Initiatives

LEARNING AND GROWTH
"To achieve our vision, how will we sustain our ability to change and improve?"
- Objectives
- Measures
- Targets
- Initiatives

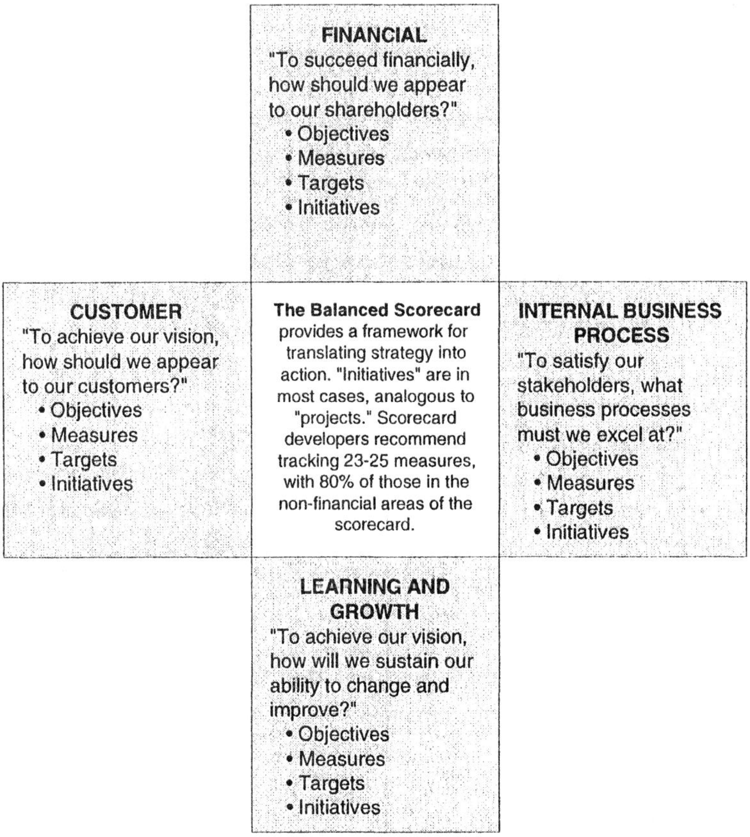

Source: Adapted from *The Balanced Scorecard*, Robert S. Kaplan and David P. Norton, Harvard Business School Press, 1996.

- *Portfolio management:* The SPO manages a collection of projects from potentially every unit within the organization, many of which are connected only because all projects within any organization should support the strategic plan.

- *Program management:* Interrelated projects which all contribute toward the same longer-term objective.

- *Many projects managed by the same individual:* This is the most common type of multiple project management. It could be a "basket" project office that handles a lot of small, short-term projects, which may or may not be closely enough related to be classified as a program.

- *Multitask management:* Many individuals do not actually manage the entire project, but instead manage some of its components and thus become engaged in multitask management.

What level of involvement does the SPO have with each type of multiple-project scenario? In some cases, all four, but primarily with true portfolios and programs. Of course, when an individual project manager with more than one project or the project manager managing an element of a larger project needs help from the project office, the project office provides necessary support, training, process, software, and other basic services.

According to Dye and Pennypacker, project portfolio management provides a consistent way to evaluate, select, prioritize, budget for, and plan for the "right" projects—those that offer the greatest value and contribution to the strategic interests of the organization.[6] As Dianne Bridges has written, "Doing the right thing starts with developing a strategic focus and ends with project selection. Doing the right things *right* (and quickly) is project management."[7] Just as it is beyond the scope and charter of individual project managers to manage a portfolio of projects, it is beyond the scope of a Level 2 project office to manage a corporate-wide portfolio. That leads to the need for a Strategic Project Office and is, in fact, one of the primary reasons for the existence of the SPO.

Project Selection and Prioritization

After your organization's focus is established and understood (the process of strategic management), projects are selected and resources are placed where it matters.

Portfolio management begins with the selection of the portfolio. The SPO is the "voice of the projects" on the executive-level steering committee that must decide which of the many opportunities to pursue in light of a limited amount of resources. The decision of which projects to authorize is complex and depends on a number of factors, such as return on investment, fit with the current portfolio, desire to introduce a new product line, availability of resources, and many others. This is a classic executive decision, involving many decision criteria and alternatives. The first task for the committee is to select a decision support tool to help organize and simplify the decision process. A number of corporations have developed their own proprietary tool, such as the NCR Risk and Opportunity Assessment Model, but there are commercially available tools that will get the job done. Decision tools that lead the decision maker or group through a series of steps help to identify the decision criteria, establish the relative importance of these criteria, and compare the possible projects to one another to produce a ranked list of projects.[8] Once the Committee decides which opportunities to pursue, the list must be compared to available resources to determine how many of the desired projects can be undertaken, given resource constraints.

The selection process involves identifying opportunities; assessing the organizational fit; analyzing the costs, benefits, and risks; and developing and selecting a portfolio. Portfolio management is concerned with *fit, utility,* and *balance.* If done effectively, portfolio management will ensure optimum use of people and resources.

Figure 9.3 provides a visual snapshot of the *fit, utility, and balance* paradigm. Almost every organization uses this thought process to build a portfolio of projects. The organization may first identify opportunities; then assess the organizational fit; analyze the costs, benefits, and risks; and finally develop and select a portfolio. It is the methods and techniques employed that differ. Invariably, at some level of sophistication, all organizations will understand the fit and utility of their projects and make some attempt to establish a mix of projects.

Fit. The first major element of portfolio management is to identify opportunities and determine if those opportunities are in line with the corporate strategic direction. In a sense, this may be the identification and initial screening of projects before more in-depth analysis is conducted. The questions to ask are: What is the project? Does the project fit within the focus of your organization and the business strategy and goals? Several strategies to consider include the following:

- *Develop a process to identify opportunities and make it easy to follow.* Many individuals have an aversion to complex processes and

Figure 9.3. The Fit, Utility, and Balance Paradigm

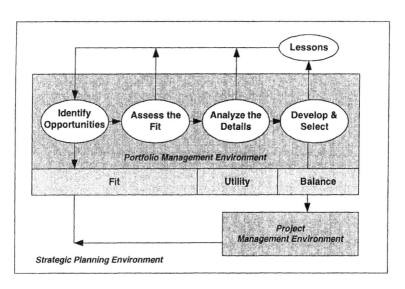

bureaucratic paperwork. Establish an avenue for communicating ideas. Make the process simple and easy to use. Identify a team to review the opportunities and assess the fit within the strategic direction and business goals.

- *Establish a template for project justification as part of the process.* The ideas need to have some substance and content; otherwise it will be difficult to screen the projects. The template may include things such as a description of the project, what will be done, the project's sponsor, the link to organizational direction and business goals, and a top-level description of the project's costs, benefits, and risks.

- *Establish minimal acceptance criteria as part of the process.* The individuals submitting ideas and the review team should understand the minimal acceptance criteria. There should be basic requirements a project must meet before being considered for further analysis and funding. Such requirements may include the link to strategic direction, business threshold minimums (e.g., return on investment or cost/benefit ratio minimums), compliance with organizational constraints (e.g., existing technology architecture), and completion of the project justification paperwork.

- *Reward ideas and suggestions—give credit where credit is due.* Most employees love recognition for their ideas and suggestions. Take the time and interest to formally acknowledge ideas that meet the "fit" test. Always give credit where credit is due.

- *Make sure clear strategic direction and business goals have been established.* Since strategic focus becomes the foundation for selecting projects, the strategic direction and business goals should be clearly established. These may be reflected in the vision statement, mission statement, statement of principles, organization objectives, and/or strategic plan(s).

Utility. The second major element of portfolio management is to further define the project (if needed) and to analyze the details surrounding its utility. The utility of a project captures the usefulness of the project and its value and is typically defined by costs, benefits, and associated risks. The questions to ask are: Why should this project be pursued? What is the usefulness and value of the project? Several strategies to consider include the following:

- *Establish criteria and develop a model to support decision-making.* Multiple projects vie for resources and funding, and somehow a decision has to be made on which ones to select. To help in the decision-making process, establish common decision criteria and measure each project against the criteria. Since most decisions are based upon multiple factors, weight each criterion to establish the relative importance of each item. This will identify what is most significant to the organization, and each project can be measured against the criteria that are important.

- *Make sure accurate data are available to make decisions.* Your organization should have a reliable accounting system that collects and accounts for resources (expenditures, revenues, and manpower). Information from the accounting system may be necessary to forecast project costs and benefits. Your organization should have reliable, up-to-date market, technical, and manufacturing information. Since project portfolios include both new projects and ongoing projects, your organization should have a system to track the status of ongoing project activity.

- *Establish a process to analyze the project information.* The purpose of this process is to analyze the project information to ensure data validity and consistent application of the decision criteria. It is important to go through this process before selecting the portfolio to eliminate any controversy over the data and key assumptions while in the midst of developing the portfolio (the next area).

- *Uniformly apply the methodology across the organization.* Although this seems a little stifling, the criteria and weights should be identified, defined, and completely documented. The process established should ensure project teams consistently interpret the criteria and its related measures and/or probabilities. An analogy can be made to performance reviews and the use of criteria and performance scales. For example, different managers may have different definitions of an "excellent" rating. In order to ensure fairness for all employees, it is imperative the organization clearly defines all performance levels so managers consistently interpret and apply the scales.

Balance. The third and last major area of portfolio management is the development and selection of the project portfolio. The questions to ask are: Which projects should be selected? How does the project relate to the entire portfolio, and how can the project mix be optimized? Several strategies to consider include the following:

- *Establish a process that will help optimize the portfolio, not just the individual projects.* Industry approaches for developing portfolios range from simple ranking based on individual project financial returns to more complex methodologies that take into account the interrelationships between projects. Regardless of the chosen method, the objective should be to optimize the portfolio, not necessarily the individual projects (assuming you have more than one project opportunity). The appropriate method is dependent upon an organization's strategic direction, guiding principles, capabilities, limitations, and complexities. When developing and selecting the portfolio, the organization needs to consider all types of projects such as research, new product development, information technology, and business improvement. Remember that relative comparisons are being made, not specific comparisons.

- *Establish portfolio decision meetings to make decisions.* Separate decision meetings and teams should be established to make portfolio decisions using the validated project information. Typically, senior leadership, in the form of the steering committee and with the input of the SPO, makes the portfolio decisions. The meetings and reviews are normally held in conjunction with the corporate planning schedule.

Three Predominant Goals. Organizations establish different sets of criteria and varying importance for each criterion. Although the specifics may be different, there is a tendency within industry to place emphasis on one or more of three specific goals when selecting project portfolios. The three goals are: maximization of value, development of a balanced portfolio, and alignment with strategic objectives.[9] The point is that the criteria and weights will help in the selection of project portfolios and typically industry selects a method that emphasizes one of these predominant themes.

Resource Allocation Decisions

Historically when priorities changed, the project manager found out by noticing that a key resource had been reassigned. Most of these types of resource conflicts are resolved within the SPO, but if the SPO director can't resolve resource allocation issues, they can be brought to the attention of the steering committee for resolution. Keep in mind, however, that the steering committee does not make day-to-day management decisions. It *steers*. Depending on the "personality" of the committee, it can be more or less active in the hands-on management of projects. It is not unusual for the committee to want weekly, and sometimes even more frequent, updates on high-priority projects.

Resolving the issues raised by resource allocation is a primary goal of the successful SPO. When projects and departments are all vying for the use of a certain facility, the skills of a certain programmer or planner, or the funds in a certain pool, only an organization with a bird's eye view of the entire corporate landscape can make decisions that are fair and reasonable.

In one organization, we worked with the steering committee to produce a prioritized list of its top 100 projects. The committee found, much to its surprise, that the company only had enough money for 53 of the projects, yet all 100+ had been formally chartered. The process led to cancellation of 47 projects and much less angst among the project managers who had been competing for unavailable resources.

Methodology Deployment

A project management methodology is essential in portfolio management. Once the methodology is written, it must be deployed and enforced. This implies periodic process audits by the SPO to ensure it is being used properly. The SPO itself is a user of the methodology in its role as overall portfolio manager. For all project managers and the portfolio selection team, training must be provided, along with specific guidance on use of the various tools and templates provided in the documentation.

Measurement

The SPO ensures that individual project status is reported and controlled, that individual status is integrated with portfolio objectives in each business unit and across the enterprise, that tradeoffs are made for the benefit of the entire organization, and that relevant information is passed up the chain to senior management. The metrics used to measure performance vary slightly among organizations, but normally address, at a minimum, cost and schedule variance, scope and quality deviations from plans and specifications, and customer satisfaction. See the discussion of the project dashboard in Chapter 8.

Portfolio Management: Best Practices

New Product Development

Hoechst-AG uses a scoring portfolio model with 19 questions within five major categories to rate projects. The five categories are: probability of technical success, probability of commercial success, reward to the company, business strategy fit, and strategic leverage (ability of the project to leverage company resources and skills). Within each of these five factors are a number of specific characteristics or measures which are scored on 1-10 scales by management (e.g., strategic leverage, synergy with other operations within the corporation, absolute contributions to profitability). The criteria and scoring approach is a particularly effective model and purported to be one of the best. [10]

Research and Development

The Weyerhaeuser Corporate R&D program has put new processes into place to align and prioritize R&D projects. The program has three types of activities: technology assessment (changes in external environment and impact to the company); research (building knowledge base and competencies in core technical areas); and development (development of specific commercial opportunities). Four key inputs are considered when establishing priorities: significant changes in the external environment; long-term future needs of lead customers; business strategies, priorities, and technology needs; and corporate strategic direction. Lessons learned are be patient, it takes time to engage company business leaders; get the project leaders involved so they understand the criteria and rationale; and put processes in place that encourage staff across technical areas to be involved.[11]

Information Technology

A construct was developed to help organizations choose between IT projects. The criteria center around four areas: customer (commitment in terms of need); strategy (alignment with company goals and objectives); technology (ability to meet technical requirements); and delivery (ability to successfully deliver the project). Strategy is further broken down into profitability (measuring the IT project's cost savings), process improvement (ability to improve business processes or save time), and employee satisfaction (satisfaction of employees working the IT project). Technology is broken down into core competency (organization capability to perform the project), cost competitiveness (ability to provide a competitive solution), and integration (with existing technology). Delivery is broken down into schedule, budget, and quality reflecting the organization's ability to complete on schedule, within budget, and deliver a quality solution. The relative importance of each criterion is determined using a simple spreadsheet or the pair-wise comparisons of the Analytical Hierarchy Process (AHP). It is recommended to establish twelve to fifteen criteria to support IT decision-making.[12]

Strategy Tables

At Eli Lilly, strategy tables are used to develop alternative portfolios and compare alternative strategies. The strategy table represents different combinations of projects and different courses of action for each project, thus providing an array of portfolios for selection. The benefits of examining multiple portfolios versus simply ranking projects are 1) the focus is on the portfolio of opportunities versus individual opportunities, 2) relationships between opportunities are considered, and 3) alternative courses of action are determined and evaluated.[13]

Project Alternatives

SmithKline Beecham examines a range of alternatives for each candidate project before they assess the value of each project. In doing so, the organization has gone away from a single plan of action with one viable option to four project alternatives with four viable options. Each project team must develop at least four alternatives: the current plan (follow existing activity), a "buy-up" option (have more to spend); a "buy-down" option (have less to spend); and a minimal plan (abandon project but preserve as much as possible). The approach has been beneficial to the company, which cites an experience in finding a new alternative that could create more value for less money. The benefits to creating project alternatives include 1) the formation of new ideas, 2) the creation of new chances for projects that would not survive under their current plans, and 3) the opportunity to help teams to understand the elements of their development plans (they have to think it through to determine options).[14]

Risk-Reward Bubble Diagrams

At 3M bubble diagrams are used to visually depict project portfolios. Generally, two axes are drawn dividing the space into four quadrants. Each axis stands for a key characteristic that describes the portfolio. The most popular diagram is a risk-return diagram (such as the probability of technical success and reward). In this case, the separate quadrants stand for different combinations of the risk-return relationship (low risk, low return; high risk, high return; low risk, high return; high risk, low return). Each project is assessed and placed within a quadrant, resulting in a visual depiction of the portfolio. There is really no prioritization of projects, but rather a display of information to help in portfolio decisions. 3M adds another level of complexity to portray uncertainty and probabilities. The size and shape of each bubble on the diagram is adjusted to reflect project uncertainties. The bubble diagrams help decision-makers visualize the total portfolio.[15]

Real Options versus Static Cash Flows

Option Space Analysis employs a more dynamic approach to portfolio management versus following a predetermined plan, regardless of what happens. In theory, this analysis approach takes into account uncertainty in business and active strategic planning. The method uses a volatility metric and a value-to-cost metric versus the conventional discounted cash flow. The volatility metric measures how much things can change before an investment decision is made and the value-to-cost metric measures the value of what's being built with the costs needed to build them. Using the metrics, opportunities can be categorized into invest now, maybe now, probably later, maybe later, probably never, and invest never.[16]

Project Manager Competency and Professional Development

Research tells us that project goal achievement is influenced by four basic groups of factors: the superior project manager, the project office organization, the host organization, and the external environment. For purposes of generalized discussion, the project manager influences approximately 50% of project success, the project office organization about 20%, the host organization 20%, and the external environment 10%.[17]

As the component with the most influence on the probability of project success, a superior project manager has the ability to overcome nearly any *controllable* obstacle—and research indicates that the dominant events related to project success are generally in the controllable category. The project manager also is the key factor in recognizing and mitigating the impact of *uncontrollable* events. The project office organization might be non-existent, the host organization could be weak, and adverse conditions might be encountered in the external environment. Nevertheless, the superior project manager will minimize these obstacles and work to achieve project goals.

The consensus of the literature agrees that the project leader is a major determinant of the organization's capability to achieve goals.

This is usually obvious when a project is in trouble. A responsive action taken by many organizations is to install a superior project manager. Some companies often have special names for these individuals, such as a "smoke jumper."

Several studies have quantified the impact of leadership on teams and organizations. The broad competency groupings that compose the superior project manager are: (1) character, traits and background, (2) professionalism consisting of leadership and management skills, and (3) project-specific skills comprised of the application of structured methodologies and procedures. According to the standards identified by the Top 500 Project Management Benchmarking Forum relative to project manager character, traits, and background, the best practice project manager:

- Is recognized by stakeholders as the single most important factor in project goal achievement

- Is truthful in all dealings and relationships

- Has a four-year college degree

- Is PMP® (Project Management Professional) certified

- Exhibits eagerness to organize and lead groups

- Exhibits evidence of a strong desire for goal achievement (degrees, certifications, ranks, and other goals achieved)

- Has above-average intelligence

- Is even-tempered

- Has faith that the future will have a positive outcome

- Has confidence his or her personal performance will result in a positive outcome.[18]

Obviously, the SPO has a stake in hiring, identifying, promoting, and rewarding the most competent project managers. In addition, as the center of project management within the organization, the SPO can serve as an incubator of future project talent. The other areas of the organization will look to an SPO to both provide excellent project management mentors and to develop their staff into superior project personnel.

Figure 9.4. Project Manager Tasks

Time planning, monitoring & controlling
Managing external stakeholders
Scope monitoring & controlling
Integrative monitoring & controlling
Cost planning
Cost monitoring & controlling
Organization structure
Managing internal stakeholders
Communication
Technical performance
Managing client
Strategic direction
Project definition
Procurement
Integrative planning
Closing
Risk monitoring & controlling
Quality monitoring & controlling
Team selection
Quality
Team development
Lessons learned

2.5 2.75 3.0 3.25 3.5 3.75 4.0

Source: L. Crawford, "Project Management Competence for the New Millenium, Proceedings of 15th World Congress on Project Management, International Project Management Association, 2000.

Competency Identification

In seeking to identify the competencies that should be required in a company's project managers and team members, the SPO has a wide range of research on which to draw. Work by Lynn Crawford, which contributed to the Australian government's official competency requirements for project managers, is widely available in project management journals and on the Web (see Figure 9.4). In addition, the Project Management Institute has been engaged for the past two years in an international standards project to identify competency requirements for project managers. At this writing, this project is not yet complete, but ongoing details on their findings are posted on the PMI Website.

Due to the evolving nature of the competency research, it would be difficult to provide the reader with a hard and fast list; see Tables 9.1 and 9.2 for some suggestions, but be aware that differing industries and types of projects will call for differing competencies. The establishment of a standard internal competency checklist for your organization is a critical first step for an SPO, however. We hope that the resources provided in this chapter and in our bibliography will assist the reader in preparing this important document. Without internal guidelines as to the skills and competencies required of project personnel, none of the most critical human resource issues—from hiring to career development to termination—can be equitably resolved. [19, 20]

Career Pathing

Once the competency checklist is established, the SPO works closely with an organization's HR department to develop position descriptions and grades and to establish a career path and promotion path combining project management assignments, years in the profession, training, and certification.

Recent job satisfaction research has revealed that one of the primary reasons project managers leave a company is the lack of a clear career path. Formerly, the only way project managers, who were primarily technical staff, could rise in the organization was by leaving their technical specialities and project management skills behind to climb the supervisory and administrative ladder, positions which were often a poor fit with the project manager's temperment, abilities, and talents. With the evolution of the project office, career project managers can now look forward to managing projects, managing other project managers, directing a project office, participating on the steering committee, and even in some cases rising to corporate executive status based on the performance of the projects under their care. However, this path must be incorporated into the company HR documentation and made known to project managers and others in the organization or it remains only a possibility, not a policy. See Figure 9.5 for an example of the professional development path for project managers, based on a program developed by the PM College.

Table 9.1 A Project Mentor's Competency Checklist

	Needs Improvement .... Excellent				
	1	2	3	4	5
COMPETENCIES					
Integrator	☐	☐	☐	☐	☐
Educator	☐	☐	☐	☐	☐
Expeditor	☐	☐	☐	☐	☐
Coach	☐	☐	☐	☐	☐
Problem solver	☐	☐	☐	☐	☐
Quality manager	☐	☐	☐	☐	☐
Risk taker/risk manager	☐	☐	☐	☐	☐
Conflict manager	☐	☐	☐	☐	☐
Partnering	☐	☐	☐	☐	☐
Visionary	☐	☐	☐	☐	☐
Information powerful	☐	☐	☐	☐	☐
Flexible	☐	☐	☐	☐	☐
SKILLS REQUIRED					
Facilitation	☐	☐	☐	☐	☐
Listening	☐	☐	☐	☐	☐
Team building	☐	☐	☐	☐	☐
Negotiation	☐	☐	☐	☐	☐
Coaching	☐	☐	☐	☐	☐
Presentation	☐	☐	☐	☐	☐
Interpersonal	☐	☐	☐	☐	☐
Communication	☐	☐	☐	☐	☐
Conflict management	☐	☐	☐	☐	☐

Note: The table contains a list of competencies and skills required to deliver the highest quality project management mentoring expertise to our client. Take a minute and rate yourself on each competency and skill and then establish a personal development plan for improving those areas that need improvement.

Table 9.2 Mentor Quality of Service Delivery

	Needs Improvement .... Excellent				
	1	**2**	**3**	**4**	**5**
DOES YOUR PROJECT MENTOR*					
Seek out your requirements priorities, and expectations	☐	☐	·☐	☐	☐
Effectively support your project and/or program	☐	☐	☐	☐	☐
Treat you with respect and understand your situation?	☐	☐	☐	☐	☐
Solicit, listen to, and resolve your concerns?	☐	☐	☐	☐	☐
Provide timely advice?	☐	☐	☐	☐	☐
Deliver quality information and guidance?	☐	☐	☐	☐	☐
Display flexibility in responding to your needs?	☐	☐	☐	☐	☐
Keep you informed?	☐	☐	☐	☐	☐
Would you select this mentor for future projects?	☐	☐	☐	☐	☐

Note: In performing as a mentor, ask yourself the following: "What would be my client's response if asked these questions in regard to me?" Then rate yourself again to determine where you need to improve.

RATE YOUR MENTOR ON THE FOLLOWING**					
Project management	☐	☐	☐	☐	☐
Project planning	☐	☐	☐	☐	☐
Project scheduling	☐	☐	☐	☐	☐
Communication skills	☐	☐	☐	☐	☐
Interpersonal skills	☐	☐	☐	☐	☐
Judgment	☐	☐	☐	☐	☐
Team participation	☐	☐	☐	☐	☐

**Note: If your client is asked about your knowledge, skills, and abilities in the following areas, what would be the response?

Figure 9.5 Professional Development Path

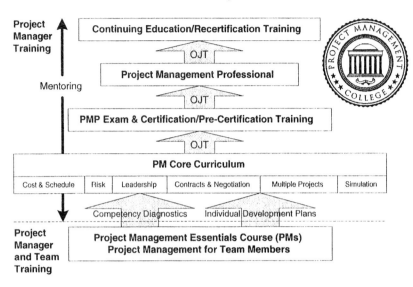

A Note on Mentoring

Providing expert advice and practical help in the form of mentoring to project managers is one of the core functions of a project office. Mentors from the SPO spend much of their time helping others. Although basic information about mentoring was provided in Chapter 3, we would like to provide some real world, practical information here to help those in the SPO who actually perform this critical function. Much of the material presented comes from PM Solutions' *Mentoring Guide* used on engagements to establish our own guidance and best practices for conducting mentoring as consultants.[21]

Mentoring is the most effective way to bring new project managers up to speed quickly. Why? Mostly because practical experience is the best teacher. Once the basics are learned through training, project management expertise is gained from on-the-job training. Experience, under the tutelage of a mentor, is the best teacher and the best way to bring new project managers up to speed in a hurry.

Mentors from the Strategic Project Office use the project management methodology—a solid process for managing projects—and bring experience and lessons learned from real projects, along with innovative tools that help produce successful project results.

Guiding Principles

A mentor is defined as someone who is *"a wise or trusted counselor or teacher."* With this definition in mind, the goal of each project management mentor is to provide the highest quality service and support to project managers by imparting to them wisdom, gained through experience and continued learning, in a trustworthy manner. To achieve this goal, it is necessary that each engagement reflect the highest level of integrity, professionalism, individual expertise, and team interaction based on trust. Each individual is responsible for ensuring that the full benefit of his or her knowledge and experience is brought to bear upon project mentoring, while ensuring there is an atmosphere of trust created between the mentor and the project manager. Sharing of professional knowledge and judgment to the fullest extent possible is essential to the successful accomplishment/completion of any engagement.

Except under unusual circumstances, no individual staff professional working alone or in isolation is capable of providing a product that has the level of quality and completeness required to deliver excellence in performance. A single individual, working in isolation without benefit of collective organizational knowledge and experience, cannot achieve this excellence and will not be considered as doing business in an acceptable manner. Virtually without exception, this method of operation will result in delivering a poorer quality product to the project manager. All deliverables must reflect the best efforts and collective knowledge, skills, and expertise of the entire professional staff.

Mentoring support within the SPO will only grow and maintain its leading edge technology through the sharing of project information and ongoing interaction. Thus, each project mentoring situation should also be an enhancing growth experience for each member of the professional staff. Each professional will gain in knowledge not only from exposure to the project manager's environment, but also from insights provided by other members of the staff through their specialized perspectives. Collectively then, the project manager, the SPO, and the mentor all gain and grow from the experience.

The SPO, as the repository for the specialized approaches, tools, and techniques of project management, possess more knowledge, collectively, about project management than any single individual. The SPO is obligated to ensure that its professionals are knowledgeable in these tools and techniques and their effective use. Therefore, it will be necessary for the SPO to plan for the incorporation of some time for training and development for each professional. Furthermore, each professional is responsible for contributing his or her specialized knowledge and understanding to the SPO database.

Types of Mentoring Assignments

If the mentoring assignment is a large one, the SPO will field a team of experts, organized under a team leader, in a fashion similar to the organizational style of external consultants brought into the firm. The team leader is responsible for the scheduling and workload of the professional staff and the production of quality work.

Mentoring work is classified in six general areas: (1) project mentoring, (2) project management, (3) project planning, (4) project administration, (5) professional development, and (6) project audits.

- *Project mentoring* is the process of providing project management expertise to both internal and external project managers and project teams. Each individual is expected to maintain a high level of proficiency and knowledge in the areas assigned and to display that knowledge and proficiency during engagements and project reviews. Tasks will be defined for each project. Project mentors are not to be confused with project managers, who will have the full responsibility for project planning and execution. Project mentors may be assigned to individual projects or groups of projects, depending on project size and/or complexity. In this role, the mentor is responsible to counsel and advise the program/project managers throughout the five phases of the project: initiating, planning, executing, controlling, and closeout. The team leader will make project mentoring assignments.

- *Project managers* are individuals assigned to specific projects to bring forth the benefits defined in the project goals. While the SPO mentors do not normally engage in the full-time management of individual projects, it may sometimes be necessary to step into that role to recover projects that have drifted out of control, manage projects due to temporary incapacitation of the project manager, or to initiate projects pending assignment of a full-time project managers. While assigned to the project, the mentor/project manager will have the full responsibility for project planning and execution.

- *Project planners* are individuals assigned to roles and responsibilities that support project planning. They are tasked with developing, maintaining, and analyzing project plans, schedules, and other project data.

- *Project administration* is the recording and reporting of activities performed on the mentoring assignment and will be submitted weekly to the team leader. Individuals may also be tasked with writing specific reports of activities for a project or other work group as defined by the team leader. When support is required during startup or when a shortage of project administration resources exists, it may be necessary for the mentor to step in and (1) define the project administration requirements for a project, (2) set up specific templates for administration of the project, (3) develop the administrative processes for the project, or even (4) assist in maintaining initial project documentation during project startup.

- *Professional development* of the SPO mentor pertains to attaining a higher level of knowledge and expertise regarding the theory and practice of project management. To be effective, each member of the SPO consulting staff is expected to know all of the organization's services and products. Furthermore, each member of the consulting staff will be assigned as the resident expert or point of contact for a particular area or areas (e.g., project scope, time, risk, cost, quality, integration, human resource, or communications management). That individual will be expected to maintain a current and thorough knowledge of that subject and ensure that all relevant reference materials in the specialist's technical library are also kept current. In addition, each member of the professional consulting staff is expected to stay informed about state-of-the-art project management techniques, tools, and methodologies by reviewing technical literature. Each individual is expected to share his or her knowledge by occasionally conducting a brief seminar for the staff. The development of tools to support the SPO consulting effort and the research employed to support this development are included in this area.

- *Project audit* is a critical internal project review, particularly in a complex project. It is at this point that the collective wisdom of the SPO professional staff can be most helpful in developing the best possible solutions. This internal project review may contain:

  - Review of data collection (Are there any gaps?)

  - Review of findings and recommendations (Are they supported? Are they complete? Is the logic sound? Can we anticipate client reaction? Have all elements of the proposal been considered?)

THE STRATEGIC PROJECT OFFICE is a relatively new phenomenon in organizations; as such, few best-practice examples are available to use as templates. By providing a standard organizational methodology for planning, executing, staffing, prioritizing, and learning from all the projects that comprise today's organization, the SPO gives organizational life a coherence that has long been lacking. The development of the SPO as a feature of the modern organization will be, I feel, one of the most exciting trends in organizational development this decade.

Endnotes

1. Robert Block, *Politics of Projects*, Prentice-Hall, Inc., 1983.
2. Nolan Eidsmoe, "The Strategic Program Management Office," *PM Network*, Dec. 2000.
3. Software Engineering Institute, *Capability Maturity Model for Software*, 1993.
4. Jeannette Cabanis-Brewin, "Project Management Metrics: Moving Toward a Balanced Approach," *Project Management Best Practices Report*, Sept. 2000.
5. Robert S. Kaplan and David P. Norton, *The Balanced Scorecard*, Harvard Business School Press, 1996.
6. Lowell D. Dye and James S. Pennypacker, *Project Portfolio Management: Selecting and Prioritizing Projects for Competitive Advantage*, Center for Business Practices, 1999.
7. Dianne Bridges, "Project Portfolio Management," *Project Management Best Practices Report*, Dec. 1999.

8. See http://www.palisade.com/html/expert_choice.html for information on Expert Choice.

9. Robert G. Cooper, Scott J. Edgett, and Elko J. Kleinschmidt, *Portfolio Management for New Products*, Reading, MA: Perseus Books, pp. 19-20, 1998.

10. Robert G. Cooper, Scott J. Edgett, and Elko J. Kleinschmidt, "Portfolio Management in New Product Development, in L. Dye and J. Pennypacker, ed., *Project Portfolio Management*, Center for Business Practices, 1999.

11. Gilbert L. Comstock and Danny E. Sjolseth, "Aligning and Prioritizing Corporate R&D," *Research Technology Management*, p. 20, May-June 1999.

12. Bruce Miller, "Linking Corporate Strategy to the Selection of IT Projects," *Project Management Institute 28th Annual Seminars & Symposium Proceedings*, p. 56, 1997.

13. C. Thomas Spradlin and David M. Kutoloski, "Action-Oriented Portfolio Management," in L. Dye and J. Pennypacker, ed., *Project Portfolio Management*, Center for Business Practices, 1999.

14. P. Sharpe and T. Keelin, "How SmithKline Beecham Makes Better Resource-Allocation Decisions," in L. Dye and J. Pennypacker, ed., *Project Portfolio Management*, Center for Business Practices, 1999.

15. Robert G. Cooper, Scott J. Edgett, and Elko J. Kleinschmidt, "Portfolio Management in New Product Development, in L. Dye and J. Pennypacker, ed., *Project Portfolio Management*, Center for Business Practices, 1999.

16. Timothy A. Luehrman, "Strategy as a Portfolio of Real Options," in L. Dye and J. Pennypacker, ed., *Project Portfolio Management*, Center for Business Practices, 1999.

17. Frank Toney, *The Superior Project Manager*, Marcel Dekker/Center for Business Practices, 2001.

18. Frank Toney, op. cit.

19. Paul O. Gaddis, "The Project Manager," from *The Harvard Business Review* collection of articles entitled *Project Management*, by the President and Fellows of Harvard College, 1991.

20. Lynn Crawford and Fran Gaynor, "Assessing and Developing Project Management Competence," *Proceedings of the Annual Project Management Institute Seminars and Symposium*, PMI , 1999.

21. *Mentoring Guide*, PM Solutions, Inc., 1999.

Chapter 10

Changing the Organizational Culture

IT'S A FAMILIAR STORY: A company faces competitive pressure to improve its performance. Maybe projects are over budget; maybe it's chronic late finishes. It could be poor technical performance or missed releases and late product deliveries. The result is the same—customers are not happy and the company is losing business. The prescription of the '90s is to turn to a project management approach to improve performance and regain market share. Organizations have tried training programs, external project management consultants, "thou shalt" policy letters making new methodologies mandatory, yet they have not achieved the anticipated improvements in project performance. While these are all necessary parts of the whole prescription for wellness, they will not, in isolation, cure the problem. One important element is missing: the creation of a project culture. And money alone won't buy it. A "culture" is a set of shared beliefs, values, and expectations, not simply of set of procedures. It is much more difficult to put into effect than policies and procedures, but it can be changed. This chapter explains, in simple terms, how to change your existing organizational culture to a project culture. Let's begin by defining exactly what we mean by "culture," then delving into the specific steps you can take to change your culture.

Climate or Culture—Which Do You Change?

What's the difference between climate and culture? Culture has already been defined as a set of shared beliefs, values, and expectations. A climate, on the other hand, consists of the tangible things that make up a culture, such as policies, procedures, habits, and routines—all the things that define how things are done in the organization. For example, the compensation structure of the organization—how people are rewarded—is a matter of climate. If quantity is rewarded over quality, the practice will be to crank out as much work as possible without regard to errors. On the other hand, if people are rewarded for producing a quality product every time, and even have the power to shut down an assembly line when defects are detected, the practice will be to produce quality. This practice will lead to a change in culture—one where employees believe what the organization's leadership believes in and values: quality.

A project example illustrates the point further. Let's say the company project management methodology says to create a risk management plan—an issue of climate—but management never asks to see it. The message is clear—don't waste your time doing risk plans. On the other hand, if management requires the risk plan to be updated and presented at every project status meeting, the message is clear—management values and rewards risk planning. This change in the way things are done, a change in climate, leads to a shared value, that risk planning is an important part of the organization's culture. In fact, years later, when someone asks why risk planning is done so religiously, one might give the response that "it's just the way we do things here," not knowing the origin or evolution of the practice that led to the climate which changed the culture.

Changing the culture will not occur through declarations, new mission statements, or a big party, unless these proclamations are backed up by changes in the everyday practices and procedures that define what people should do, how they are evaluated, and how they are rewarded. These changes in the way things are done will lead to a new belief that the new way is the right way, a matter of culture. We demonstrate from our experience in the project management field that improvements in the way projects are managed leads to bottom-line success. Another way to think about it is to "act as if" the desired belief system were already in place to bring about the desired change. After improving project management practices and providing members a chance to see that improved practices lead to success, individual's belief in the merit of improved project management process will follow. Before long the organization will naturally assume that the most effective and efficient way to manage complex undertakings is to organize and execute them as projects.

Organizational Needs: Flexibility And Creativity

Companies today need employees who can think fast on their feet, innovate, take responsibility, and "go with the flow" of change. Yet although these are the characteristics companies are seeking, too often they are the characteristics least rewarded.

Companies frequently speak of vision, but express their vision as a concrete set of goals and objectives, solidified into rules. A vision must be the inherent way we function, the essence of what we are, the way we feel about ourselves as a unit and as individuals. If we know only what the goals and objectives are, anything new that does not match our expectations throws us into confusion and chaos. It is the difference between the internal and the external. We must always be able to evaluate situations and opportunities according to the core spiritual and emotional assumptions of the organization.

Goals and objectives can create tunnel vision. As the organization transitions from a functional to a project culture, we must constantly re-evaluate and re-consider.

- Do our goals focus efforts so much that we are unable to see opportunities?

- Do they keep us from making the paradigm shifts necessary to anticipate the needs of customers or make it possible for employees to soar?

- Do they lock us into only the assumptions that were available when we set them?[1]

Creating a Project Culture—From the Top

We have established that the culture cannot be changed unless the practices that make up the organizational climate are changed and rewarded. In the project management context, this entails establishing a whole set of new behaviors, starting with creation of a project management methodology, defining what is required, when it is required, and how to do it. A complete set of instructions, forms, templates, and tools is necessary to ensure consistent, repeatable performance across the organization. Next, a training program, tailored to the new methodology but grounded in the project management body of knowledge, is necessary to teach and reinforce use of the methodology. Finally, management must *require* consistent application of the methodology and reward successful project behaviors. This is usually thought of as bringing in a project on time, under budget, according to specifications, ensuring a satisfied customer, but can also include knowing when to kill a bad project.

Specific Guidance on Changing Your Culture

Schneider, Brief, and Guzzo have published an excellent paper entitled "Creating a Climate and Culture for Sustainable Organizational Change" that lists six steps to implementing what they refer to as "total organizational change (TOC)."[2] In it, the authors suggest following a six-step process to introduce any TOC into an organization. We've added an initial step to make it a seven-step process:

1. Assess the need for change. Do you even *need* to change the organizational culture? Chances are if you are reading this book and considering implementing project management across the organization, the answer is yes. But to be sure, perform an assessment (see Chapter 2) to determine your level of project management maturity. If you are at Level 1 of the Project Management Maturity Model, just beginning to define processes and practices, you should read this chapter carefully before "beating your head against the wall" trying to get everyone to embrace a new way of thinking.

2. Ensure the organization is prepared to handle a major organizational change. By "prepared" we mean the level that people in the organization believe that the change is necessary and that management will support the change. And beyond that, we also mean the actual level of commitment senior management will give to the change. Schneider et al. phrase their discussion in terms of trust.

If the organization's management is not trusted, any attempt to change will be treated with skepticism on the part of the organization's members. We have all heard statements like "this is just the flavor of the day;" "this too shall pass;" "this will last about a year then we'll be into something else;" "this is just like TQM—here today, gone tomorrow." These are statements that reflect distrust in the organization's leadership. To put it bluntly, change will be difficult in an organization where the walls are papered with Dilbert cartoons. On the other hand, such a place probably needs the changes discussed in this book more than most! Ask the following questions before attempting to install a Strategic Project Office:

- Is employee morale high? High morale is usually associated with a high level of excitement and commitment about belonging to the organization.

- Does the senior leadership have a history of successfully implementing major changes? If so, people will naturally assume that the pending change to a project management approach has been well thought out and that senior management will see the change through.

- Is management known for tackling tough decisions and doing the "right thing?" If so, management will be respected for its integrity and perseverance.

On the other hand, if the answer to these questions is no, any attempt to implement the sweeping changes necessary to implement an SPO will be met with skepticism. It is advisable not to attempt the change until trust is established—something that will not happen overnight.

3. Is the proposed change consistent with existing organizational climate and culture? Major changes will have a greater probability of success if they are undertaken in incremental steps that are consistent with the existing organizational culture. Change that is consistent with the existing culture will be seen as user friendly and nonthreatening, and will be more likely to be accepted than change that is radical in nature. For example, if your organization is structured as a vertical, functional bureaucracy, where all the power is vested in functional management (a traditional functional organization structure), then changing to a cross-functional, lean, project environment in one major step will be difficult and time consuming. Implementing a Strategic Project Office will cause quite a stir, as functional managers are asked to share power with a "new kid on the block." Radically changing the culture will require a significant amount of time, effort, and attention in such an organization.

On the other hand, if your organization is already managing projects, issuing project charters, and empowering project managers to reach laterally across the organization for resources and support, then establishing a project office will be seen as the next logical step to improving the practice of project management. Even if you have experienced project failures, often a strong move by management to do something about it is seen as a positive step.

In either of these cases, it is inadvisable to go from no project management processes to a Strategic Project Office in one step. In deciding how ambitious to get in changing the culture, consider the following four dimensions of organizational climate:

- The nature of relationships. Are they contentious? Is conflict the order of the day? Or do people work collaboratively toward solutions, freely sharing information?

- The nature of existing hierarchies. Is the organization rigidly structured or is the structure flexible and agile?

- The nature of the work itself. Is most of the organization's work project or process oriented? Does the work have a defined start and end; can specific objectives be established; are resources from more than one department involved? If so, the work can be classified as project work. Otherwise, it is continuous in nature and not suitable for the project management approach.

- The focus of support and rewards. Are people rewarded for achieving results or just showing up and putting in their time? This question addresses one of the fundamental differences between bureaucratic and entrepreneurial organizations. Project management rewards those who can bring projects in on time, within budget, according to customer expectations.

The proposed change to a project culture should be examined, and the impact on each of these dimensions analyzed, to gain an appreciation for the effort that will be required to bring about the change.

4. Plan the change in as much detail as possible. Nature abhors a vacuum. If information about the change—what is happening and why—is not continuously shared with the rest of the organization, the rumor mill will defeat you. For example, in working with one of our clients engaged in establishing a project office in its IT division, we found in a joint meeting of senior management that the project office implementation team had not been keeping members of the CIO team (a group of senior IT managers) informed of the status of the implementation effort. As a result, they assumed the effort was having difficulty or had even been canceled. Without their support, there was literally no chance of success. Following the meeting, the implementation project manager made it a point to personally keep all key managers informed.

Following some common sense guidelines will help you with this step:

- Formulate and widely communicate the plan for the change you are considering.

- Specify, in writing, the objectives of the change. Use the same guidelines used in formulating project objectives—they should be SMART: specific, measurable, agreed to by stakeholders, reasonable, and time constrained.

- Follow up dissemination of the objectives with written systems, methodologies, and procedures for the change. Let's say you are trying to publish a new project management methodology as part of your effort to change the organizational culture. You must first ensure that you establish a cross-functional team to help you write and review the methodology. You must also make sure the team members keep their managers informed of progress—make sure they are excited, on-board, and feel a sense of ownership for the new guidelines. And make a special effort to apprise management at every opportunity. One final thing— find out how to get information out directly to everyone in the organization affected by the change.

- Follow up written methodologies and procedures with support systems and rewards for following the new practices. The support will come from the new project office In a Level 3 Strategic Project Office, the project manager reward system will be driven by the project office with significant input and influence from functional management. Team member performance will primarily be determined by functional management with input and influence from project management. Work closely with functional management and human resources to structure rewards (and they don't all have to be monetary) for those who follow the new practices and who achieve better results.

In short, specify why the change is necessary—what is threatening the current organization and how the proposed change will defeat the threat. Spend time and money developing the methodology, processes, and policies. Distribute the methodology and other literature widely. Make it clear to people that they will receive training, will be expected to implement the new practices, and will be rewarded for doing so. Going halfway with this step will lead to disaster.

5. Ensure the reward system is structured to motivate employees to focus on implementing the project management methodology. People are smart. They figure out what the organization rewards and they focus their energy on doing those things well. Almost everything else is ignored. Management must determine specifically what behaviors will be rewarded in advance and tie appropriate behavior to both financial and non-financial rewards. Project management is a well-defined set of processes and activities, captured, published, and distributed around the world by the Project Management Institute as *A Guide to the Project Management Body of Knowledge*.[3] In changing to a project culture, these practices, articulated in a project management methodology document, will be required. We've already discussed how, by implementing these practices and achieving success, the organizational culture will be changed over time. But unless management insists upon, and rewards, behavior associated with the consistent application of this approach, it will fail—and all the time, effort, and money devoted to implementing the change will have been wasted. More important, the organization will not achieve project success, which will probably spell disaster in a very competitive marketplace.

6. Allocate resources to maintenance of the new system. To ensure the change to a project culture is sustained, resources must be allocated to maintenance of the new culture. The maintenance and support of this new approach comes from top management, and is operationalized through the project office. The project office, as we have seen, supports the practice of project management and, therefore, the culture, by becoming a center of excellence; by providing organization-wide support in a variety of ways; by owning the project management process and publishing the methodology; by providing a home office for project managers; by providing mentors to projects throughout their life cycles; by training project managers, team members, and other managers; and by performing the many other activities covered in Chapter 9.

7. Monitor the progress and effectiveness of the change to the organization and adjust as necessary. This step is fundamental project management practice. For example, in developing risk mitigation strategies, the project team develops the strategies, implements those that become necessary, checks to see if the strategies are effective in reducing risk, and adjusts the strategies to ensure they are effective. In a similar manner, when management is implementing a change to a project culture, it must check periodically to ensure the desired behavior is, in fact, occurring. If not, either changes to the practices must be made or more emphasis put on changing and rewarding the behaviors. Either way, performance must be monitored and variance minimized to bring about lasting change. To monitor progress, the project office might consider a simple graphic, such as that shown in Figure 10.1, to guide its long-term effort. It might also be advisable to periodically reassess project management maturity to measure real improvements in project management practices, artifacts, and results.

Measuring for Results

Daniel Tobin, in his book *Re-Educating the Corporation*,[4] identifies the need to create relevance, value, quality, and measurement criteria in order to transition successfully to a new corporate culture.

Relevance

If the employees do not find that the proposed change is relevant to their current working environment, they will not support it. To make a change relevant, the context in which that change is perceived must be changed. For example, Tobin suggests that functional and project managers' performance measurements reflect the value now placed on teamwork.

Value

Employees need to understand the value that the change has to their work and their performance measurements. Tobin cites the ex-

Figure 10.1. Assessing Effectiveness of Change

Pilot Phase	Deployment	Functional	Integrated	World Class
Definition Responsibilities Training Data needs Process Champion identified	Consistency Tools PM role Project manager qualification Selection Training	Consistency PM process Data Tools Project manager capabilities Broad authority Certification Mentoring	PM structure PM tools widely used Project managers certified Performance improvement	PM capability used as benchmark by others PM directory contributes to best-in-class performance

Monitor progress and adjust as necessary

ample of departmental employees who, if they are to adopt team-related work methods, must view the teamwork as a way of making their jobs easier or making them more effective in their work. Unless they perceive the value added by teamwork, no amount of training will persuade them to work as a team.

Measuring

A functional-to-project organization transition should be measured by results which are based upon a definition of quantifiable objectives. As such, the entire program needs to be measured in its entirety the individual pieces should not be evaluated as an end onto themselves, but rather in how they support the overall transition effort.

Change Processes

Typical approaches to dealing with change and transition in an organization are anticipatory, attempting to predict the future and manage to that potential reality, or reactionary, waiting for situations to occur and responding accordingly. Neither is likely to succeed. The following approaches can lead to a more long-reaching and effective change and transition implementation.

The Scenario Approach

We can't predict the future, yet we all spend a great deal of time attempting to do just that. It is much more productive to question,

"What are potential scenarios that might occur? What are strategies we can use to deal most effectively with each of them? What resources will we need; what skills will be required; what critical competencies do we have right now that we can build upon?"

The trouble with planning based on predicting the future is that it implies we can control the future, creating an illusion of certainty. "I've thought it out, made my plans, therefore this is the way it will happen." From these illusions specific objectives are established and from that point on, any contradictory evidence is ignored. These internal contracts too often form an impenetrable box that isolates us from reality. It is like the old saying, "Don't confuse me with the evidence. My mind's made up."

The perception of order can create an artificial sense of stability; in reality it is the most unstable environment of all for it lulls people to a passive state where they are least of all prepared to deal with the unexpected, which surely will occur.

The scenario approach, on the other hand, is based on plural possibilities for the future. It encourages questioning; it recognizes the reality of ambiguity and expects change. It creates a "memory of the future" that prepares people to deal effectively and confidently with whatever occurs, and makes much more likely the possibility to direct the course of events in the most positive direction. It also teaches people to be effective problem solvers and it reduces fear of the unknown, critical attributes for individuals and companies in the 21st century.

Scenario planning demands that everyone look outside their own immediate interests into the broader world outside: social values, technology, economics, environmental issues, political thinking, changing cultures, etc. It encourages relationship awareness and network building—the foundation for synergy. It is the essence of project organizations who form a successful partnership between their internal managers and their project managers.

A Project Management Approach to Change

Any change that is significant enough to engender transition within the company is significant enough to be considered a project. For example, going from a functional to a project organization will require:

- A defined scope (the magnitude of how business operations will be modified)

- Associated cost parameters (are new systems required, are new personnel required?)

- Risk issues (opportunity risk as well as the risk of not being competitive)

- Quality issues (ensuring that the same quality of service/product is offered throughout the transition)

- Designated time frame constraints (will this occur over one month, six months, or one year?)

- People who will be involved and need to be managed (how will roles and responsibilities be defined, will this require reorganization within the company, will new skills need to be learned?)

- Major communications issues (how do we communicate with our existing customers, our employees, our stakeholders?).

The problem with most corporate change and transition is that it is poorly managed. Some changes are treated like a project (business process re-engineering is a notable example), but most are not. The attitude of management tends to be one of "survival of the fittest," and then they wonder why productivity sinks. Employees need to understand the value and rationale behind corporate change and transition. They need to understand how, when, where, and why this is occurring. Project management is an ideal way to manage all corporate change and transition by defining what will occur, when it will occur, how it will occur, and where it will occur. By developing respect on all sides (employee, customer, and corporation), the organization puts itself in a position for successful change and transition.

How does an organization move forward with a business or personnel change in the most productive manner?

- Begin with defining the project parameters of the change.

- Develop a project plan, elicit comment and feedback, and get buy-in from those who will be affected.

- Baseline the project plan and manage the customer expectations of the end deliverable.

Figure 10.2 looks at organizational change from a project management perspective.

Readying The Troops For Battle

Besides developing a solid project plan and managing it, we can prepare people for cultural change by helping them to do the following:

- **Accept Ambiguity.** *"Lets wait until we know for sure before we make a decision"* were no doubt the last words of the dinosaurs. The need for certainty must be replaced with, not just an acceptance, but a firm belief in the power to evolve in a positive way with whatever the future holds.

- **Prepare for Possible Scenarios.** The reality is that we constantly create possible scenarios for the future. David Ingvar, the head of the Neurology Department at the University of Lund, Sweden, calls this the *"memory of the future."* The human brain automatically attempts to make sense of the future by testing possible plans of action; therefore, when the situation actually occurs, there is a "memory" of how the choices were sorted before it occurred.

- **Have Fun in Order to Survive.** Creativity, imagination, insight, and intuition are most likely to occur when we're having fun, when we're not taking ourselves or our activities too seriously, when we feel free to react naturally, to just be.

- **Forget Consensus—Conquer Through Collaboration.** Consensus guarantees mediocrity, because it focuses on reaching agreement rather than emphasizing deeply held convictions, which most often exist because people have expertise or knowledge in a particular area. Collaboration focuses on people's strengths, and creates synergy.

- **Adapt to Life in the Chasm.** The gap between the known and the proposed, between our knowledge of the past and our image of the future, can seem like a huge chasm. How does one learn to live with optimism and faith in oneself and in the organization's ability to make a safe bridge across? First, by acknowledging the reality of the gap. Second, by looking for congruence between the sides, most often based on values. Third, by being excited by the possibilities.

- **A Task is for Today—A System is For Always.** The workplace is shifting from one of obedience and domination, to one of co-operation, mutual respect, and shared responsibility. Networks of collaborative relationships are creating transformational learning based on integrated systems of people working together. In a rapidly changing world, it's not enough to learn a skill; we must create structures and processes in order to reach higher levels of performance. We must have a system, rather than a task perspective. It's big picture thinking. It involves asking such obvious questions as, "Are we going about this in an effective way?" "We seem to be jumping all over the map in this discussion. Let's take a moment to focus on identifying the problem." "What is the scope of our project?"

Rules for Successful Culture Implementation[5]

The success factors examined here can be summarized in a set of rules for organizational culture change. The more rules that are followed, the greater the chances for successful implementation.

- Become a learning organization. Embrace new ideas, new concepts, new techniques, and make them available to everybody.

- Establish clear communications processes and media.

- Record and praise accomplishments and heroes who support and demonstrate the concepts required in the new culture.

- Establish a flexible, central structure which provides a critical core for all implementation efforts.

- Accept risk and proceed judiciously. Strive to extend the culture throughout the organization, despite the inherent risk of change.

- Know and publish boundaries for the culture. Ensure a common understanding of what the culture is intended to be, and what it isn't.

- Evaluate and prove the economic value of the culture.

- Involve everyone.

Figure 10.2 Organizational Change from a Management Perspective

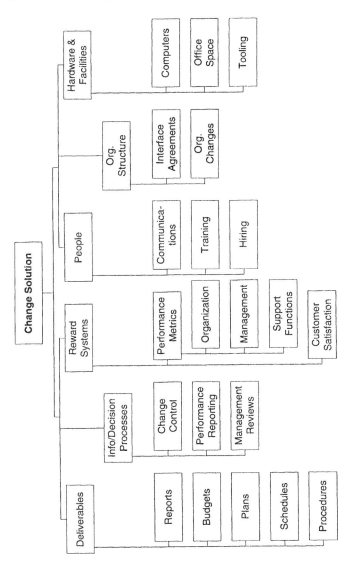

Source: Cheryl J. Walker and Jean Erickson Walker, "Transitioning Functional Organizations into Project Organizations," *Proceedings of the Project Management Institute Annual Seminars and Symposium*, PMI, 1999.

Overcoming Barriers to Change

In her excellent paper on change management in the project organization,[6] C.J. Walker discusses how entrenched divisions of power in a functional organization pose barriers to change.

People And Power

One of the major obstacles in transitioning from a functional to a project organization is the perception that functional managers must give up their power base. To become a project organization means that project managers become, in effect, temporary managers of resources. Their decisions directly affect the organization as a whole and the functional managers become leaders of resource pools with the responsibility for developing and managing human skill sets which will then be "on loan" to projects.

To ease this transition, create fluid roles and responsibilities that integrate functional managers into the total organization. Their focus in the past has largely been reactive, identifying and responding to internal drivers and fulfilling current business needs. Today's companies require functional managers who are capable of focusing on the big picture, proactively anticipating future needs and actively participating in multiple areas and projects at the same time. As projects become the organization's driving force, project managers must negotiate with functional managers to acquire skilled and flexible resources to fill specific short-term project needs. In addition, the organization must allow the functional managers the latitude to staff appropriately to meet both the ongoing operational needs and the project needs of the organization, and there must be an acknowledgement and reward system built into the process that recognize the value and importance of supporting project needs. The functional managers and the project managers must work together as a management team, developing a workforce that is flexible and mobile.

The second step is recognizing the impact to the individual when the organization changes from a functional focus to a project focus. The basic premise of project management is that a clearly defined venture with known objectives and goals will be completed in a finite period of time. Once the starting gun goes off, the project manager is expected to lead the way down a direct path to the goal line. This can create a major destabilizing force, distracting people from their ongoing priorities and causing resentment throughout the organization.

The third step is understanding the evolutionary nature of projects. New evidence will emerge throughout the life of the project, changing initial assumptions and requiring paradigm shifts that substantially change the comfort level of employees.

The project manager must be sensitive not only to directing the activities of the project, but to gaining the support of the people. Futurist Joel Barker describes three stages in the life of a paradigm and defines the people most likely to be comfortable in each stage.

- *Paradigm Shifters* realize the current paradigm does not solve all the problems; they determine the issues and create the new paradigm.

- *Paradigm Pioneers* lead the implementation of the change; they establish the parameters and rules and provide the impetus to move the organization forward.

- *Paradigm Settlers* institutionalize the change; they root it, refine it, and ensure excellence in operating under the new system.

A project responds to a defined need, lifts the element up out of the ongoing work of the organization, solves it, and reinserts it back into the organization. The organization is changed by this process. Invariably, the paradigm has "Shifted," the "Pioneers" have left, and too often the "Settlers" are asked to proceed without having been involved in the change. They are expected to integrate the change into ongoing systems, and to create excellence without having the opportunity to develop the required skills.

The project cannot be isolated from the functional work of the organization. Therefore, the project manager must be integrated into the operation, serving as the transition guide, working directly with functional managers to identify those employees who will be most comfortable and thus most productive in each stage, pulling the "Settlers" into the project early enough for them to identify and develop the skills they will need later in order to ensure excellence and their willingness to accept the new paradigm.

The fourth step is understanding the impact that organizational culture has on project success. In a January 1995, *PM Network* article, Dan H. Cooprider said, "Culture is the key ingredient of a company's success. Discovering, defining, and changing that culture is the business challenge of the 90s.... As more attention is placed on corporate culture and more projects are undertaken to change or manipulate that culture, project managers will have a corresponding need to understand and manage aspects of culture pertinent in their project."[7]

The Impact Of Change On People

As functional organizations transition to project organizations, there will be a significant impact on the people of the organization. Change includes three distinct time periods: the *Ending*, the *Transition Period*, and the *New Reality*. Employees over these last years have become so immured to the multitude of changes taking place in all aspects of their lives, they are reacting in several ways, based on their own personal styles:

- Ignore it and it will go away.

- Embrace it immediately; whatever it is, it's new.

- Wait and see.

- Don't bother me with it, I'm busy.

- I'm too tired and discouraged to deal with anything new; I'm out of here.

In the majority of cases, it is seen as someone else's problem, and the employee feels powerless and disenfranchised.

A key factor to effective change is to provide a foundation of stability that forms the basis upon which all decisions are made, and then to apply specific strategies and procedures consistently when a change is implemented. Stability is provided by the vision and values of the organization; however, consistent implementation is provided through project management training throughout the organization.

There must be a clearly defined *Ending*, which communicates the reason the organization is moving to a project organization, the relationship between organizational goals and the proposed change, and specific steps for implementation, including each employee's involvement. The *Ending* cannot be ambiguous.

There must be understanding that a *Transition Period* will take place; expectations must be explained, and a time line presented and visible, with current updates when the *New Reality* will be in place. The fact that the company will not return to a functional structure must be expressed clearly and frequently. Awareness that employees will react in different ways makes it critical in this period for leaders to be more visible, more communicative, and more reassuring than at any other time. Opportunities for informal discussions and transition and communication style assessment and training by outside consultants can be extremely useful. Procedures for feedback, questions, and suggestions should be implemented and continued well after the *New Reality* is in place.

The 15-15-70 Rule

In any organization, there is a small percentage of people who are constitutionally incapable of dealing with change. Their strength is in providing continuity in a stable organization. Forcing them to undergo the disruption endemic in a dynamic organization is destructive to them and to everyone else in the organization. Therefore, it is critical to identify the change potential of employees and to make it possible for them to leave the organization in a positive manner.

- 15% of the employee body will eagerly accept any change, just because it is new. They will lead the transition and thrive on the challenge, because it is their nature to do so. In fact, their productivity and probability of staying with an organization long term will largely depend upon the opportunity for new challenges. They are the *Shifters* and the *Pioneers*.

- 15% will be extremely uncomfortable with change. In a stable organization, they are often valued as *Settlers*, providing excellence by refining the details of the operations and ensuring consistency. They will do everything in their power to prevent change from upsetting these established routines.

- 70% range between these extremes and can be integrated successfully into the new system with proper coaching. The challenge of project managers and internal managers is to work closely to identify them and assist them in the transition.

Using Language to Create Community

Nearly 40% of the workforce is now contingent labor. It is projected to reach 60% early in the new millennium. Therefore, less than half of the employee body will be "residents," the rest will be visitors, outsiders who move in and out, without ties to the company's long-term goals or to each other.

Language is a critical factor in establishing a sense of community, expressing its values, beliefs, and assumptions, and bonding people. It includes the industry/company terminology that is used to explain procedures and give instructions, the assumptions that are not verbalized but are nevertheless there (including those critical to safety), the implications that show the relative importance of what is being said, and simple casual conversation that makes people comfortable with each other.

If 60% of your workforce speaks numerous "foreign" languages, how can they be expected to function effectively? Project management can provide a common "language" and procedures:

- Company-wide education in project management methodology

- Introductory seminars for new employees and contingency workers to smooth the transition and immediately create a community that speaks the same language, rather than taking the risks inherent in language translations

- Encouraging managers to identify work that can be handled as projects and providing opportunities for each of their employees to gain experience in the methodology

- Consciously incorporating project management language in all in-house communications

- Providing a project partner for all outsourced projects, to work directly with the project manager on integrating the change into the organization

- Including cultural change in the scope statements for projects managed internally and externally

- Assuming that everyone in the organization is a stakeholder in every project and ensuring communication that is open, easily available and constant.

You Made It!—Signs of a Project Culture

How can you tell if you have achieved the goal of creating a project culture? One way is to reassess project management maturity using the same assessment tool originally used for the assessment of the need for change. An abbreviated method is to use the following checklist. An organization with all five of these elements up and running is well on its way to achieving success:

- A standard project management methodology, deployed throughout the organization and used by all project teams

- A meaningful, attractive career path for project managers

- Effective education, training, and certification for project managers, and training for team members, managers or project managers, and senior executives

- Ongoing support through a Strategic Project Office at the corporate level

- A standard suite of software tools to support project managers.

We might want to include a sixth element—integration of software systems throughout the enterprise—as discussed in Chapter 8. An integrated system provides project managers, managers, and other stakeholders with all the information necessary for real-time project planning, execution, and control. Software will not create a project culture, but it can support and reinforce the behaviors that make up a culture.

Endnotes

1. Cheryl J. Walker and Jean Erickson Walker, "Transitioning Functional Organizations into Project Organizations," *Proceedings of the Project Management Institute Annual Seminars and Symposium*, PMI, 1999.

2. Benjamin Schneider, Arthur P. Brief, Richard A. Guzzo, *Creating a Climate and Culture for Sustainable Organizational Change*, Organizational Dynamics, Spring 1996.

3. PMI Standards Committee. *A Guide to the Project Management Body of Knowledge*, PMI, 1996.

4. Daniel Tobin, *Re-educating the Corporation*, pp. 235-42, 1993.

5. Nicholas Schacht, "Project Management Culture: An Anthropological Perspective," *PM Network*, pp.53-56, Sept. 1997.

6. Walker, op.cit.
7. Patrick Brown, Sheila Grove, Richard Kelly and Satyendra Rana, "Is Cultural Change Important in Your Project?" *PM Network*, pp. 48-51, Jan. 1997.

Appendix A

Project Management Maturity Model

THE SOFTWARE ENGINEERING INSTITUTE (SEI), operated by Carnegie Mellon University and sponsored by the U.S. Department of Defense, has done much work over the past decade in under standing the areas of organizational expertise necessary in order to help organizations to consistently produce quality software products.

SEI says that "For most organizations, the ability to estimate and predict accurately the results of their product development activities from a viewpoint of cost, schedule, and quality is a fundamental business goal. Case studies from the software engineering community and elsewhere suggest that addressing issues of process management, measurement, and institutionalization improve the organization's ability to meet its cost, quality, and schedule goals."

It is certainly the objective of each PM Solutions client to meet its cost, quality, and schedule goals in the management of projects. As indicated in the above quote, in order to do so, they must address these issues as related to project management:

- **Process Management**—There must be a repeatable, quantifiable process in place throughout the organization.

- **Measurement**—The PM methodology must make the measurement of scope, quality, schedule, and cost a natural part of running the project.

- **Institutionalization**—The processes must be precipitated by the organization's upper management and applied uniformly throughout the organization.

So the question is: How can an organization know how "good" they are? There must be a *standard* against which to measure. That was the concept behind SEI's Capability Maturity Models (CMMs). In 1993 SEI published their Capability Maturity Model for Software, Version 1.1. This has become the de facto standard model for assessing and evaluating process maturity in the software industry.

Unfortunately, there had been no accepted standard project management maturity model. PM Solutions has seen this need, and has created such a model.

The underlying structure for our PMMM is the nine Knowledge Areas within the *PMBOK® Guide* (PMI's *A Guide to the Project Management Body of Knowledge*). Why? The *PMBOK Guide* has two different frames of reference for addressing the whole PM body of knowledge:

- PM Processes. This approach looks at the management of projects as a set of five tightly integrated, repeatable processes. These processes can be decomposed into a set of Activities and Tasks necessary to successfully manage a project. Another way of saying this is that this forms the basis for a PM *methodology*.

- PM Knowledge Areas. This approach looks at the management of projects as a set of eight interwoven sets of skills/expertise, with a ninth set of expertise (integration management) that binds them together. A project manager needs to wear each of these nine hats at some time throughout the project (as if she or he is nine different people), and needs knowledge/expertise in all areas.

So this second (knowledge area) approach focuses on knowledge, skills, and expertise. In other words, as the project managers within an organization increase their expertise, knowledge, and skills in these areas, the organization overall becomes more *mature* in its practice of project management and is able to execute the processes more effectively.

Given that we are focusing on a specific business *organization* in addition to the pure theoretical practice of project management, we determined that there are three additional "special interest" knowledge areas in which the organization needs to develop maturity in order that successful projects may flourish. They are project office, management oversight, and professional PM development. These are essential ingredients in making any project organizational structure truly become institutionalized in any business environment. While they are not true knowledge areas in the context of "project management" knowledge, they are critical supporting ingredients that will lead organizations down the path toward optimizing their project management processes. In order to maintain consistency with the *PMBOK Guide*, we have woven these additional areas into the *PMBOK Guide* framework as shown below:

- Project integration management (includes project office)

- Scope management

- Time management

- Cost management

- Quality management (includes management oversight)

- Communications Management

- Project human resource management (includes professional PM development)

- Risk management

- Procurement management

Each of the nine knowledge areas has been decomposed into its major areas of focus (generally 3-5 areas), which we call "components." The *Amercan Heritage Dictionary* defines *mature* as "having reached full natural growth or development (*n*.)," or "to bring to full development (*v*.)." To define and measure maturity in Project Management we must specify levels of growth and development in the requisite skills. We have defined five levels of PM maturity, intentionally consistent with SEI's CMM. They and their definitions are described in detail in a subsequent section. The SEI CMM model has been chosen because it is commonly known and accepted, and is representative of the general evolution that knowledge and processes should exhibit within organizations. Its applicability in the general sense is broader than just to software. Additionally, many organizations are already familiar with the SEI structure and implementation processes. Given

Figure A.1 CMM for Software version 1.1

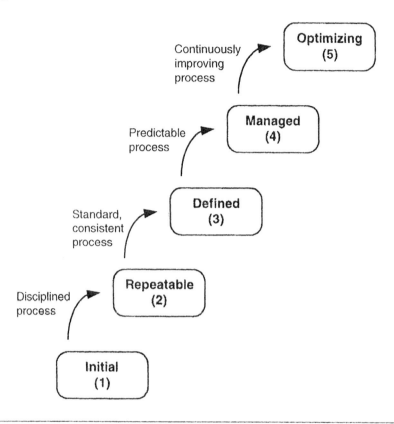

the model's relatively broad applicability, it makes sense to leverage this learning already completed by many organizations to the maturity of project management.

Comparing PMMM and SEI's CMM

When the PMMM was created, we decided to use SEI's CMM as a guide. SEI's model uses five levels (see Figure A.1).

The meanings of the levels of SEI's CMM are:

- **Initial.** The software process is characterized as ad hoc, and occasionally even chaotic. Few processes are defined, and success depends on individual effort.

- **Repeatable.** Basic project management processes are established to track cost, schedule, and functionality. The necessary process discipline is in place to repeat earlier successes.

- **Defined.** The software process for both management and engineering activities is documented, standardized, and integrated into a standard software process for the organization. All projects use an approved, tailored version of the organization's standard software process for developing and maintaining software.

- **Managed.** Detailed measures of the software process and product quality are collected. Both the software process and products are quantitatively understood and controlled.

- **Optimizing.** Continuous process improvement is enabled by quantitative feedback from the process and from piloting innovative ideas and technologies.

SEI's Software CMM says: "Maturity Levels 2 through 5 can be characterized through the activities performed by the organization to establish or improve the software process, by *activities performed on each project,* and by the *resulting process capability across projects*" [italics added for emphasis].

This would lead one to suspect that there is a mapping between the CMM and our PMMM. SEI goes on to say: "Software process improvement occurs within the context of the organization's strategic plans and business objectives, its organizational structure, the technologies in use, its social culture, and *its management system.*" [italics added for emphasis].

In fact, a close inspection of both CMM for Software and our PMMM shows a direct mapping. The levels are very similar, with the significant differences between the two within the implementation details and characteristics defining the levels (see Figure A.2).

PM Maturity Model Definitions

The meanings of the levels in the PM Solutions PM Maturity Model are as follows:

Level 1: Initial Process

Although there is a recognition that there are project management processes, there are no established practices or standards, and indi-

Figure A.2 Mapping CMM to PMMM

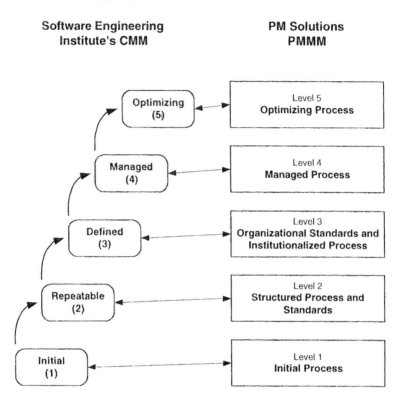

vidual project managers are not held to specific accountability by any process standards. Documentation is loose and ad hoc. Management understands the definition of a project, that there are accepted processes, and is aware of the need for project management. Metrics are informally collected on an ad hoc basis.

Level 2: Structured Process and Standards

Many project management processes exist in the organization, but they are not considered an organizational standard. Documentation exists on these basic processes. Management supports the implementation of project management, but there is neither consistent understanding, involvement, nor organizational mandate to comply for all projects. Functional management is involved in the project management of larger, more visible projects, and these are typically executed in a systematic fashion. There are basic metrics to track project cost, schedule, and technical performance, although data may be collected/ correlated manually. Information available for managing the project is often a mix between summary level data and detailed level data.

Level 3: Organizational Standards and Institutionalized Process

All project management processes are in place and established as organization standards. These processes involve the clients as active and integral members of the project team. Nearly all projects use these processes with minimal exception. Management has institutionalized the processes and standards with formal documentation existing on all processes and standards. Management is regularly involved in input and approval of key decisions and documents and in key project issues. The project management processes are typically automated. Each project is evaluated and managed in light of other projects.

Level 4: Managed Process

Projects are managed with consideration to how the project performed in the past and what is expected for the future. Management uses efficiency and effectiveness metrics to make decisions regarding the project and understands the impacts on other projects. All projects, changes, and issues are evaluated based upon metrics from cost estimates, baseline estimates, and earned value. Project information is integrated with other corporate systems to optimize business decisions. Processes and standards are documented and in place to support the practice of using such metrics to make project decisions. Management clearly understands its role in the project management process and executes it well, managing at the right level, and clearly differentiating management styles and project management requirements for different sizes/complexities of projects. Project management processes and standards are integrated with other corporate processes and systems.

Level 5: Optimizing Process

Processes are in place and actively used to improve project management activities. Lessons learned are regularly examined and used to improve project management processes, standards, and documen-

Figure A.3 PMMM Hierarchy

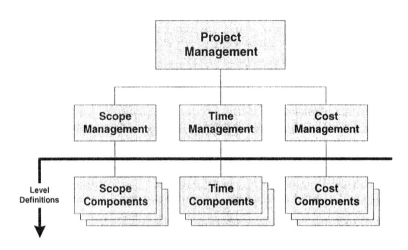

tation. Management and the organization are not only focused on effectively managing projects, but also on continuous improvement. The metrics collected during project execution are used to understand the performance of not only a project , but also for making organizational management decisions for the future.

In this appendix each knowledge area of the PM Maturity Model (PMMM) is defined at each level of maturity. In order to provide as complete definition as possible, the entire process of project management has been broken down into its knowledge areas (see the *PMBOK Guide*) and these knowledge areas have been broken down into their specific components (along with the additional special interest subcomponent areas mentioned earlier). In our full Project Management Maturity Model, progressive "maturity" is described, level by level, for each component. This can be viewed as in Figure A.3.

Note that definitions of component maturity are *grouped by level* within knowledge area. Achievement of a given knowledge area level by a client organization is *cumulative*—that is, for each succeeding PMMM level, the assumption is that all criteria for the preceding levels for that knowledge area are being (or have been) fulfilled. So Level 5, for example, assumes that Levels 1-4 are being fulfilled, plus Level 5.

The following subsections define each knowledge area of the PM Maturity Model (PMMM) at each level of maturity.

Project Management Maturity

Project Integration Management

The purpose of project integration management is to (1) coordinate project activities and integrate all efforts into a project plan; (2) integrate, analyze and report the project results in carrying out the project plan; (3) control changes to the baseline plan; and 4) collect, integrate, and organize project information in a project information system.

- Level 1. There is recognition of the need for accepted processes, but there are no established practices or standards. Individual teams or parts of the organization may have their own way of doing things in an ad hoc, informal fashion. Documentation of the processes is loose and makes it difficult to repeat the activities elsewhere. Management is aware of the importance of project integration and on an ad-hoc basis asks for information on work results.

- Level 2. There are basic, documented processes in place for developing project plans and integrating, analyzing, and developing the reports on work results. Summary-level information is consolidated into reports. The focus is on summary status and performance reporting for the triple constraint items (scope, time, cost). Although the processes are in place, they are not considered an organizational standard. Management supports the efforts and is involved on large, high-visibility projects, but not on a consistent basis.

- Level 3. Additional processes are developed and documented for creating project plans, reporting information on work results, controlling changes, and evolving the project information system. Project plans now include management plans from most knowledge areas. Both summary and detail-level information is consolidated into reports. The status and performance reporting goes beyond scope, time, and cost and includes areas such as risk, quality, and procurement. Change control processes are used to control cost and schedule changes, in addition to scope changes. There is a coordinated effort within the organization to have a common information system setup for individual project teams. The project management processes are considered standard practice for projects. Management supports project management, and is actively involved, particularly on large, visible projects. Management monitors status, performance, and changes and responds with corrective actions, as required. Systems are becoming more integrated; the project information systems are integrated with the project office. Management fully supports project integration efforts and has institutionalized the procedures and standards related to integration activities.

- Level 4. All processes are in place, documented, and being utilized by all projects. Processes and standards are integrated with other corporate processes and systems. Integration includes incorporating project plans and program plans into organization strategic plans. In addition, the reporting process and project information system are integrated with the project office, finance/accounting, strategic planning systems, and risk management process. There is a mandate to comply with the organizational project management processes and procedures. Management takes an "organizational view" of projects. Projects are managed with consideration as to how the project performed in the past and what is expected for the future. Management uses efficiency and effectiveness metrics to make decisions regarding the project. All projects, changes, and issues are evaluated based upon metrics from cost estimates, baseline estimates, and earned value. The metrics are used to understand the performance of a project during execution for making management decisions for the future.

- Level 5. Improvement procedures are in place and utilized. Lessons learned are regularly examined and used to improve documented processes.

Project Scope Management

Scope management is the set of processes required to ensure that the project includes all the work required, and only the work required, to complete the project successfully.

- Level 1. There is a very general statement of business requirements which is reduced to a requirements list by the project team. Documentation and management of all elements (issues, changes, etc.) is very loose and ad hoc. Although there is an awareness of the need for managing project efforts, there are no standards in the organization for project management. Management is generally aware of the scope of the initiatives, but typically is only aware to the point of definition of a few key milestones.

- Level 2. There is a basic project management scope process in place. There is a process to involve management in the project scope management process, but not all management is participating in this process. Many of the projects in the organization are utilizing the standard PM process to identify and manage project scope. Although organizational management is involved in PM processes on the larger, more visible projects, there may not be consistent management involvement across all projects, nor an organizational mandate to utilize the basic PM processes on all projects. Management is supporting the project management processes, and the scope management process in particular.

- Level 3. There is a full, rigorous project management process documented and standardized for the organization; this process is in use by nearly all of the projects. All project management processes involve the clients as active and integral members of the project team. This team develops requirements, scope, and so on. The team as a unit seeks management input and approval of key decisions and documents; management is actively and integrally involved in key project decisions and issues. Stakeholder management is involved in the scope management process. The process requires, and management is actively participating in, key decisions where they pertain to project scope issues.

- Level 4. All project management processes are in place, being actively used on all projects, and are the normal (assumed) method of performing projects. There is an "organizational view" of all projects—even from within any single project. *Each project is evaluated and managed in light of other active projects.* WBS methodology is mandated to be an integral part of planning and evaluating issues, changes, etc. There is in place a matrix relating to the complexity of projects, by which the project manager can determine the level of scope detail and complexity it is necessary to go into for a given project. *Organizational management:* (1) understands its role in the PM process; (2) is regularly involved in the project management process; (3) manages at "the right level" (delegating when appropriate and managing at a lower level when necessary); (4) holds the project managers and the project teams accountable for deployment against a comprehensive project management process on appropriate levels of projects (that is, on large complex projects all steps of the project management process should be performed, all PM deliverables created, etc., but on smaller, simpler projects a scaled down set of steps and deliverables should be followed); (5) is managing against the "improved process," not against the "basic process."

- Level 5. The organization now has its focus not only on effectively managing all projects, but also on *improving the manner* in which future projects can be managed—that is, on process improvements. Projects are managed with *high utilization of value considerations.* Effectiveness and efficiency metrics are regularly calculated and tracked. There is a clear understanding of a project's value to the organization; all changes, issues, etc., are evaluated based upon effectiveness and efficiency metrics. Scope determinations are made at the appropriate level of management based upon quantitative metrics determined by the project team.

Project Time Management

The overall purpose of time management is to develop the project schedule, manage to that schedule, and ensure the project completes within the approved time frame. Time management involves defining project activities, sequencing the activities, developing the schedule, and controlling the plans during project execution.

- Level 1. There is recognition of accepted processes, but there are no established practices or standards. Individual teams or parts of the organization may have their own way of doing things in an ad hoc, informal fashion. Documentation of the processes is loose, which makes it difficult to repeat the activities elsewhere.

Management is aware of the importance of time management and has periodically asked for schedule metrics.

- Level 2. There are basic, documented processes in place for identifying project activities, sequencing the activities and establishing dependencies, developing summary schedules, publishing and distributing reports, and monitoring basic schedule metrics. Although the processes are in place, they are not considered an organizational standard. Management supports the efforts and is involved, but not on a consistent basis. Basic metrics exist for schedule information (milestone percent complete) although they may be collected and correlated manually. Additional processes are developed and documented for activity definition, schedule development, and managing and controlling the schedule. A mix of summary and detailed information is developed and collected. Project management processes are considered standard practice for large, visible projects. All documented processes are repeatable. Management supports project management, but is only consistently involved on large, visible projects.

- Level 3. All processes are in place and documented. The processes are considered an organizational standard and are being utilized for nearly all of the projects. The activity definition process is expanded to include activity templates. Activity sequencing is expanded to include external dependencies and activity network templates. The schedule control process is expanded to include schedule performance analysis. The schedule integration process is developed and implemented with program schedules. Metrics are collected and analyzed in areas such as the number of project activities, type of external dependencies, duration standards, capability factors, resource dedication factors, and schedule performance and efficiency. Management fully supports the schedule management processes and has institutionalized the procedures and standards. Processes and standards are integrated with other corporate processes and systems. Integration includes organization-wide integration of projects with key dependencies established and monitored. In addition, the schedule development, schedule baselining, and cost control processes are integrated with the project office, finance/accounting, strategic planning systems, and risk management process. There is a mandate to comply with the organizational project management processes and procedures. Management takes an "organizational view" of projects.

- Level 4. Projects are managed with consideration to how the project performed in the past and what is expected for the future. Management uses efficiency and effectiveness metrics to make decisions regarding the project. All projects, changes, and issues are evaluated based upon metrics from the schedule baselines, planned status, actual status, and schedule performance efficiency. The metrics are used to understand the performance of a project during execution for making management decisions for the future.

- Level 5. Improvement procedures are in place and utilized. Lessons learned are regularly examined and used to improve documented processes.

Project Cost Management

The overall purpose of cost management is to determine the total costs of the project, manage to those costs, and ensure the project completes within the approved budget. Cost management involves identifying required resources, estimating the cost of those resources, developing a project baseline, comparing progress against the baseline, and controlling costs.

- Level 1. There is recognition of accepted processes, but there are no established practices or standards. Individual teams or parts of the organization may have their own way of doing things in an ad hoc, informal fashion. Documentation of the processes is loose, making it difficult to repeat the activities elsewhere. Management is aware of the importance of cost management and has periodically asked for cost metrics.

- Level 2. There are documented processes in place for identifying generic key resources (labor categories, hours, equipment, and material), generating and documenting project cost estimates, publishing and distributing reports, and monitoring basic cost metrics. Although the processes are in place, they are not considered an organizational standard. Management supports the efforts and is involved on large, high-visibility projects. A basic cost-estimating template exists. Metrics exist for basic cost information (planned budget, percent complete) although they may be collected and correlated manually. Additional processes are likely to exist for resource cost planning, historical cost database development, earned value techniques, cost reporting, and cost performance analysis. Summary and detailed information is developed and collected. Project management processes are considered standard practice for large, visible projects. All documented processes are repeatable.

- Level 3. All processes are in place and documented. The processes are considered an organizational standard and are being utilized by nearly all projects. The cost estimating process is expanded to include analysis of alternatives. The performance measurement process is expanded beyond simple variance analyses. The cost change control system is in place and implemented. All processes are repeatable. Systems are becoming more integrated: resource requirements are uploaded into the project office's resource repository, project baselining is integrated with the project office's automated scheduling system (or something comparable), and cost reporting is easily accomplished. Metrics are collected and analyzed on the types of resources, cost estimates, and project performance and efficiency. The project teams reconcile "estimated" actuals versus accounting actuals from corporate financial/accounting systems. Management fully supports the cost management processes and has institutionalized the procedures and standards.

- Level 4. Processes and standards are integrated with other corporate processes and systems. Integration includes the resource planning process with the project office and human resources management process. In addition, the cost estimating, cost baselining, earned value, and cost control processes are integrated with the project office, finance/accounting, strategic planning systems, and risk management process. Actuals are provided by the corporate financial/accounting systems and analyzed by the project teams. There is a mandate to comply with the organizational project management processes and procedures. Management takes an "organizational view" of projects.

- Level 5. Improvement procedures are in place and utilized. Lessons learned are regularly examined and used to improve documented processes. Projects are managed with consideration as to how the project performed in the past and what is expected for the future. Management uses efficiency and effectiveness metrics to make decisions regarding the project. All projects, changes, and issues are evaluated based upon metrics from cost estimates, baseline estimates, and earned value. The metrics are used to understand the performance of a project during execution for making management decisions for the future.

Project Quality Management

The overall purpose of quality management is to satisfy the customer, to conform to requirements, to ensure fitness for purpose, and to ensure the product is fit for use. It is that set of activities/tasks that are required to ensure the project satisfies all the needs for which it was undertaken (and which are documented in the statement of work), and includes a focus on quality management from the perspective of product, processes, and the people needed to make quality an effective and efficient aspect of successful project completion.

- Level 1. Management has an awareness of the need for quality management, but there are no established practices or standards. Management is considering how they should define "quality."

- Level 2. A basic organizational quality policy has been adopted which management encourages the use of on large and high-visibility projects. Management is supportive (but on an inconsistent basis) of the time required to add quality to a project, such as defining and implementing quality control metrics into a project. The organization's quality policy has been bolstered to state the organization's quality objectives, the level of quality acceptable to the organization, and the roles/responsibilities of members of the organization for executing the policy and ensuring quality. Management takes an active role in ensuring that quality standards are accounted for and applied to most projects.

- Level 3. The quality process is now well documented and is an organizational standard; most of the projects follow this standard. Management signs off on the quality plan and final testing for all projects and often participates in quality reviews. Quality has a program focus—that is, how well does the product perform within the context of all other products/systems in the immediate domain of the product? Management supports the development of a quality department and has identified one or two people whose focus is organizational project quality standards and assurance.

- Level 4. Organizational management has mandated that all projects follow the quality planning standard processes. Nearly all of the projects employ them. Quality is viewed from an organizational perspective—the quality of the product is evaluated in light of all other products/systems in the environment and how well it will meet the business objectives. There is an established quality office within the organization responsible for quality standards and assurance to quality processes for all projects.

- Level 5. The quality process includes techniques/methods/ guidelines for feeding improvements back into the process. The quality process focuses on the use of metrics in making benefit/ cost comparisons, effectiveness and efficiency decisions, and final decision on the quality of the product.

Project Human Resource Management

The overall purpose of human resource management is to identify the requisite skill sets required for specific project activities, to identify individuals who have those skill sets, and to assign roles and responsibilities for the project, managing and ensuring high productivity of those resources, and forecasting future resource needs.

- Level 1. There is recognition within the organization of the need for a human resource project management process consisting of identifying resource requirements and "reserving" them, however there is no established practice or standards. This ad hoc process is used to determine how many people would be required to accomplish project activities and define who is available. In general, the "warm-body" concept applies, which means that there is an assumption that any person can serve in whatever capacity necessary. Documentation is loose and may exist in the form of a list of people working on a project. As such, informal project teams may exist in an ad hoc sense. Metric data exist only from the standpoint of who worked on the last project, but is not required.

- Level 2. There is a documented, repeatable process in place that defines how to define, acquire, and manage the human resources in the form of suggested inputs, tools and techniques, and outcomes. Formal teams are established on large projects that are held accountable to follow the human resource management process. Management expects the project manager to have a project management human resource plan in place for large projects. Project team evaluations are conducted and project managers are expected to provide line management with a performance report for the individuals at the end of the project. Processes are readily available and integrated with other project planning elements.

- Level 3. All projects are expected to follow the human resource planning process, which has been institutionalized. External stakeholders and customers are considered an integral part of the project team.

- Level 4. All projects are expected to follow the human resource planning process, which has been mandated. Management expects the project managers, project office, and line managers to work cohesively in resource pool management and prioritization. Decisions relating to each project are evaluated in light of other projects. Project team evaluations and performance reporting for the individuals at the end of the project play a significant role in individual performance reviews and measurements. Project teams work in conjunction with other corporate processes and systems.

- Level 5. An improvement procedure exists whereby the project management human resource planning processes and standards are periodically reviewed and enhancements are incorporated.

Project teams identify and support improvements to the process. At the conclusion of each project, lessons learned are captured, evaluated, and incorporated into the process to improve the process and documentation. Management is actively involved in the resource management and prioritization process and reviews and supports improvements. Functional line management of other corporate processes and systems are aware of, support, and are involved in overall resource pool management and prioritization for projects and maintenance requirements. Resource pool management and the prioritization process are integrated such that management can see how resources are being utilized to ensure high productivity of resources. Project team evaluations and performance reporting contribute to overall project efficiency and effectiveness for enhanced resource utilization and corporate career path standards.

Project Communications Management
The overall purpose of communications management is to manage the project data process from collection to categorization to dissemination to utilization and decision-making.

- Level 1. There is an ad-hoc communications process in place whereby projects are expected to provide informal status to management, when called upon to do so.

- Level 2. A basic communications management process is established whereby stakeholder communication needs and project constraints and assumptions are identified, project status and progress reporting are distributed on a regular basis, and there is a notification of phase and overall project completion. Large, highly visible projects are encouraged to follow the process and there is documentation supporting how the process should work. Management understands the need for regular communication of project activities in order to have the needed information to make good decisions and supports the collection of project status. The focus for communications is on summary status and progress reporting for the triple constraint items (scope, schedule, cost). Projects are launched through project requests from a client. Formal acceptance from the customer is obtained for project deliverables. The communications management process is fully documented and the process is repeatable. Communications templates exist and are readily accessible and integrated with other project planning elements. Management values the output of communications management and requires utilization of project management tools and techniques to communicate project outcomes and the triple constraint parameters.

- Level 3. The communications management process has been institutionalized and a formal communications management plan is expected for most projects, including conducting informal variance/trend analysis. Management is actively involved in reviewing and acting upon communications reports from individual projects. Project performance reviews are conducted. Key management is involved in reviewing and approving any changes that impact the triple constraints.

- Level 4. The communications management process is mandated for all projects and a formal communications management plan is expected for all projects, including formal variance/trend analysis. Project communications management plans are documented and integrated into the overall corporate communications structure.

- Level 5. An improvement process is in place to continuously improve project communications management. Lessons learned and improvements are documented into repeatable processes. Management is actively involved in project reviews and process enhancements. There is a project communications improvement procedure in place. Functional management is aware of, supports, and is involved in project communications and uses the information to evaluate the impact of projects on functional operations. Efficiency and effectiveness metrics are incorporated into projects as part of defining value-added communications about project progress.

Project Risk Management

The overall purpose of risk management is to identify, analyze, respond, and control risk factors throughout the life of a project. Risk management is understanding the risk events, assessing their impact to the project, determining the best way to deal with them, developing and executing a plan, and monitoring progress.

- Level 1. There is recognition of the need for accepted processes, but there are no established practices or standards. Individual teams or parts of the organization may have their own way of doing things in an ad hoc, informal fashion. Documentation of the processes is loose, making it difficult to repeat the activities elsewhere. Management is aware that risk management has importance.

- Level 2. Risk management processes are developed and documented for identifying, and quantifying risks, developing a risk response, and reporting risks. Project team members generally understand macro- and some detail-level risks, and most projects are expected to determine strategies for dealing with the risks. Teams use a structured approach to quantify the impact of the risks in an effort to rank their importance. Risk lists are compiled to track and monitor progress. The risk management processes are considered standard practice for large, visible projects, and recommended for all other projects. All documented processes are repeatable. At least 50% of all projects are using the processes. Management supports risk management, but is only consistently involved on large, visible projects and gets involved in other projects if the risk is critical and of great magnitude. Risks are examined and controlled on a project-by-project basis.

- Level 3. The risk processes are considered an organizational standard and are being utilized by nearly all projects. The risk identification process is expanded to include efficient ways for teams to identify risks (e.g., checklists, automated forms, etc.). In addition, teams are asked to identify symptoms of risk (risk triggers) for incorporation into the historical database. The risk quantification process is expanded to identify more advanced procedures for quantifying risks and multiple criteria to prioritize risk items. The risk response development process is enhanced with templates. All processes are repeatable. A risk control system is developed and established. Systems are becoming more integrated: risk information and status is provided to project integration (see also the project integration knowledge area). Metrics are collected and analyzed, such as the types of risks and success rate in mitigating the items. Management fully supports the risk management processes and has institutionalized the procedures and standards. Risks are examined and controlled on a program basis.

- Level 4. All processes are in place, documented, and being utilized by at least 90% of all projects. Processes and standards are integrated with other corporate processes and systems. Integration management includes the risk management process with the project office, cost management, time management, finance/accounting, and strategic planning processes. There is a mandate to comply with the organizational risk management processes and procedures. Management takes an "organizational view" of projects.

- Level 5. Improvement procedures are in place and utilized. Lessons learned are regularly examined and used to improve documented processes. Projects are managed with consideration of how similar projects performed in the past and what is expected for the future. Management uses efficiency and effectiveness metrics to make decisions regarding the project. All projects, changes, and issues are evaluated based upon metrics from cost estimates, baseline estimates, and earned value. The metrics are used to understand the performance of a project during execution for making management decisions for the future.

Project Procurement Management

Procurement management is the processes and actions undertaken by the project manager and/or project team to acquire goods and services in support of the project. It also includes activities in managing the contract throughout the period of performance and closing the contract upon completion. All these processes and actions must be taken within the constraints of the organizational structure and policies of the overall organization. Generally the process involves contracting with an outside vendor to acquire goods and services in a timely manner, in the appropriate quantity, and within a defined quality standard. In fact, the term "contracting" is often used interchangeably with "procurement."

- Level 1. There is no project procurement process in place, but the organization does recognize that there may be value in having a defined procurement process. Some project managers recognize the need to go through the process of procuring outside goods and services in a methodical manner, although these methods are ad hoc and inconsistently performed. Contracts are managed at a final delivery level.

- Level 2. There is a basic process documented for procurement of goods and services from outside the organization, but this process is not a standard practice. Its use for large or high-visibility projects is encouraged. The procurement organization drives the process with some input from the project team, organizational management, and the client. Contracts are managed at a final delivery level with key milestones and interim reporting. The process for procurement is considered standard practice for large, highly visible projects, and all other projects are encouraged to use it. The process is specific and documented, although the analysis used is rather informal. Organizational management is more involved, with input from the client department. The process now involves the project team and capitalizes upon its technical knowledge. Contracts are managed at an appropriate level of detail with regular periodic reporting.

- Level 3. The procurement process is considered an organizational standard, and is used for more than 75% of all projects. The client is directly and integrally involved in the analysis and decision to make or buy. The procurement is run with a much more "program" view—that is, management views other projects and products in the program when making its decisions. The project team and purchasing department are now fully integrated in the procurement process. Contractors/vendors are asked to comply with applicable project management processes and structure that is standard throughout the organization.

- Level 4. Organizational management now mandates compliance with the procurement process for all projects. Make/buy decisions are now made with an organizational perspective. The vendor is integrated into the organization's reporting mechanisms.

301

- Level 5. An improvement procedure exists whereby the project management procurement processes and standards are periodically reviewed and enhancements are incorporated. The project manager and project teams identify and support improvements to the process. At the conclusion of each project, lessons learned are captured, evaluated, and incorporated into the process to improve the process and documentation. The procurement process is evaluated based upon efficiency and effectiveness metrics. Management is actively involved in obtaining strategic alliances with approved vendors who have a reputation for delivering high quality products or services in a timely manner and supports improvements to the process for "just-in-time" delivery.

Appendix B

Project Management Assessment and Recommendation Report
For Company XYZ

Background

Company XYZ is a service bureau for the processing of Mutual Fund services. The organization is the business definition and development department of Company XYZ. Their Line of Business (LOB) partners and corporate staff are located in Delaware.

Company XYZ has gone through a significant growth period over the past several years, expanding their business solutions and customer base. The target organization, for whom this report has been developed, had to support this business growth, which called for new development, many enhancements to existing systems, and adding several outside packages to their system mix. It also increased the size of the infrastructure in people and systems.

The Sr. Vice President, (name), has recognized that there is a problem in the planning and management of projects within the department.

The continued business has brought many new employees on board. These employees differ significantly from the current population, in that they are more educated and have had other work experiences. Various long-time employees have a strong loyalty to Company XYZ and use their own loosely structured processes to get the job done.

PM Solutions was engaged by Company XYZ to address their project management methods, techniques, and practices by providing the following:

1. Assessment of current project management practices/methodologies

2. Summarization of assessment and recommendations for improvements

3. Presentation of a 2-day Project Management Essentials course.

The PM Essentials class was delivered successfully on May 10th and 11th, 1999. This document represents the culmination of Steps 1 and 2, above.

The purpose of this assessment is to determine the areas of project management in which Company XYZ requires improvement, and to understand those areas in which Company XYZ has the greatest strengths, or "best practices".

The assessment was accomplished in two phases:

- Survey questionnaire

- Personal interviews.

Survey Questionnaire

The PM HealthCheck[SM] survey or questionnaire is a self-assessment instrument designed to provide a means of determining the health and strength of the project management practices being applied in the organization and on projects. It consists of ten candid, introspective questions on each of the nine major knowledge areas covered in the Project Management Institute's *A Guide to the Project Management Body of Knowledge (PMBOK Guide)*. These areas are:

- Scope management

- Time management

- Human resource management

- Communications management

- Risk management

- Quality management

- Cost management

- Procurement management

- Project integration management.

The survey questionnaires were completed by 28 people, between April 16th and 23rd, 1999.

Personal Interviews

Seventeen people and the Senior Vice President were interviewed on-site at Company XYZ on May 4th, 5th and 6th, 1999. They included a random sampling of all employees who had completed the questionnaire and represented all segments of the department.

The interviews focused on individuals' background and experiences, organization strengths and weaknesses, validation/understanding of individuals' questionnaire results and issues, and what was needed for the individual to be successful.

The results of the surveys and interviews are provided in the summary following. Nearly everyone interviewed was very candid and concise. There is a recognized need for improvements and that there are better project management techniques and practices, *but most importantly, the attitude is generally one of openness and willingness to change.* This attitude is a critical success factor that is pivotal to the success of project management improvements.

Summary

This section summarizes the findings of the HealthCheck^{SM} and the subsequent interviews, and provides recommendations.

This report is brief and to the point. Supporting detail has not been documented in this report due to time and budget constraints.

In *The Chaos Report* by Standish, it is reported that only 16% of IT projects are successful. The reasons these 16% are a success is typically:

- Clear requirements

- User involvement

- Executive management support

- Proper planning

- Realistic expectations.

The above research is noteworthy, as the lack of the listed attributes above are the some of the reasons for the issues at Company XYZ.

- Clear/concise requirements are the exception.

- User involvement is not consistent and requirements often change throughout a project.

- There is no incentive for developing consistent, repeatable processes that will ensure effectiveness, efficiency and user delight.

- The business analysts establish expectations with little regard to input from systems and programming.

It is important to note that there are pockets of effective planning, primarily from new personnel who have used consistent project management methodologies.

On both the HealthCheck survey and the interview sessions Company XYZ personnel confirmed senior management's belief that there are *Critical* concerns in the area of project management. Perhaps the clearest portrayal of the nature and gravity of the problems can be seen in the chart shown below, which summarizes the survey results. Note: a complete set of charts from the HealthCheck survey and a copy of the actual survey are contained in the appendices.

Each person's questionnaire results were grouped by "job category" (CIO, business analysts and team leaders) or business unit (FSA, accounting and transfer). The scores from all categories were used to find an overall average, which is shown on the following charts as 1.6. In terms of meaning, this translates loosely to "Intensive Care" to "Critical" when plotted against the PM Solutions Maturity Model. In this writer's opinion this situation demands immediate attention.

The noticeable "gap" between team leaders and the balance of the organization (below) is notable, as it is representative of poor communications processes and/or a lack of clear understanding of roles and responsibilities.

The interview process supported the findings of the survey.

There were a number of areas perceived by the interviewees as strengths and which were recognized as a credit to the management team:

- Good people with a lot of pride

- Business knowledge

Figure B.1 PM HealthCheck Summary by Grouping

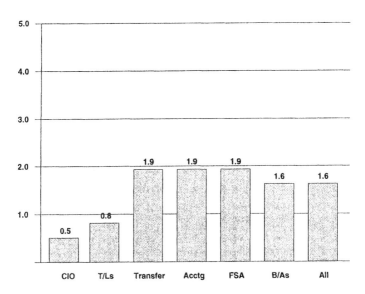

- Technical skills
- Projects completed on time (usually)
- Loyalty
- Commitment to get things done
- Customer orientation (customer accommodation)
- Variety of work
- Do a lot with little
- Low turnover.

Likewise, there were a number of areas perceived by the interviewees as weaknesses:

- Poor communication (horizontal and vertical)
- Lack of consistent methodology/standardization for business operations (not organized to be project efficient)

Figure B.2 PM HealthCheck Summary for All Responses by A of K

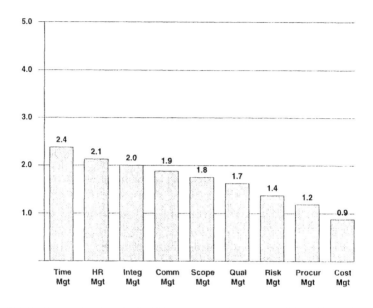

- No consistent approach for requirements definition (note: effort is currently underway to develop a tool/template to address this)

- Business unit's relationship with systems and programming

- Lack of historical project data

- Lack of enterprise resource information/allocation/management (work prioritization, competition for resources, assignment of workloads, etc.)

- Lack of effective tools/techniques (e.g. estimating)

- Poor or non-existent change control

- No good tool for project status or summarization across the organization

- Lack of risk analysis/management

Figure B. 3 PM HealthCheck Gap—T/Ls versus All Others

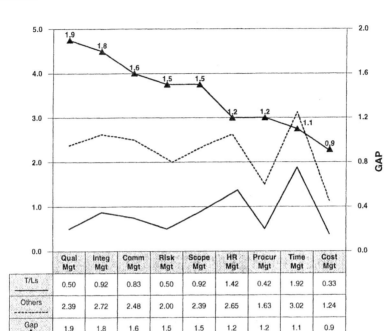

	Qual Mgt	Integ Mgt	Comm Mgt	Risk Mgt	Scope Mgt	HR Mgt	Procur Mgt	Time Mgt	Cost Mgt
T/Ls	0.50	0.92	0.83	0.50	0.92	1.42	0.42	1.92	0.33
Others	2.39	2.72	2.48	2.00	2.39	2.65	1.63	3.02	1.24
Gap	1.9	1.8	1.6	1.5	1.5	1.2	1.2	1.1	0.9

- Unclear roles and responsibilities, accountabilities and performance requirements
- Lack of consistent QA processes and practices
- Poor project management expertise/knowledge
- Recognition by headquarters, isolation
- Design and architecture of current applications.

Given the fact that many people mentioned the same areas, we conclude that most people in the organization understand that there are better ways in which to plan and manage projects and to conduct business. They appear to be looking for improvements in communication, a set of common practices that are institutionalized and supported by management in addition to guidance and direction on deployment.

Note: The scope of the assessment did not allow for interviews with "users and/or customers." As a result, this is a "gap" in this report. The customers and users of the organization's processes are critical suppliers of key inputs and their perception of problems/issues is important in addition to a clear definition of their expectations.

Summarization of Findings

- There is recognition by management that there is a need for improving organizational capabilities.

- Loyalty to the department is very noticeable and is a significant reason for operational successes.

- The organization is populated with many good people who take pride in getting things done with little, in the face of formidable odds.

- A majority of the organization recognizes the need for change and appears to be ready to embrace it.

- Communication or lack thereof, both horizontal and vertical, is a major issue.

- There are no consistent, repeatable and/or accepted processes utilized within the organization.

- Crisp, committed requirements definition for projects, signed off by customers, is an exception.

- New employees have experienced organized projects in their previous employment and are disillusioned by the lack of organization and standards.

- Many of the current employees, particularly the lead programmers, programmer analysts, and team leaders have been in the organization for 10–25 years. They have little or no standard against which to base their current job.

- New employees brought into management positions, face difficulty in being accepted into the organization.

- While the term "team" was used on occasion, there is no evidence of effective teaming occurring.

- There is a strong desire to improve the current environment but little motivation to "take the lead." People do not feel empowered.

- Each S&P team leader manages their group with varied levels of skills.

- People are not motivated to work to standards.

- Job descriptions exist but serve little value and appear to be used only for pay banding.

- A systems life cycle (SLC) process exists and was found to contain processes that could be modified to meet the department's needs, but is not used and numerous interviewees were not aware of its existence.

- There are no clear and consistent definitions of roles and responsibilities. This has resulted in some people carving out the role they want to fill within the organization.

- Financial accountability is not defined at the project level nor is there clearly defined success measures that performance (project team or individual) can be measured against.

- People are not recognized for their hard work and meeting deadlines. They are expected to do what is necessary to meet deadlines, which have been imposed from outside their group.

- Systems and programming has little say in setting deadlines, estimating the time necessary to get work done, or defining the work that needs to be done.

- Cross training or movement within the organization does not occur. There is little structured emphasis on career development.

- Successes are not celebrated or shared openly nor are there department activities to re-enforce teaming and bonding.

- There is a team working on a new requirement documentation tool but little knowledge this is occurring. The tool needs to be surrounded by a process.

- Many of the department's successes are based on personal relationships and crisis management.

- There are no consistent performance reports or an "executive dashboard" with key performance metrics.

- Relationships between the department and the lines of business (LOBs) are generally weak. The perception is the LOBs do not have a high regard for the department.

- The organization is not structured effectively for efficient execution of business requirements.

Recommendations

The four primary areas that need immediate care:

- Communication

- Methodologies/processes

- Organization development/department operations

- Training.

The following are recommendations to improve the department's performance and are all deemed vital.

Establish Communications With and Within the Department

- Develop a communication plan for the organization.

- Conduct department meetings monthly. Introduce new employees, recognize successes and discuss new business.

- Conduct line-of-business meetings on a regular basis to discuss issues, resolve problems, establish procedures, update, etc.

- Establish a simple newsletter, to be distributed on a periodic basis.

- Have department get together periodically, outside of the work environment, to celebrate successes, reinforce worth and encourage bonding.

Improve Methodologies/Processes

- Establish a clear definition of what a project is and is not.

- Develop and deploy a standard *project management methodology* tailored to the department's needs. It should contain the project management processes and also templates for the major deliverables from the project management process. It should be made clear within this guide how small projects should be handled (are there certain steps that can be left out, etc.) It should be made clear to all, both within the department and in the client areas, that this methodology is the cornerstone for success. Ensure the first edition is simple to use so people are not overwhelmed or use it as an excuse for "getting in the way of getting the job done."

- Develop a process for requirements definition immediately.

- Devise and institute a change management process which must be utilized on every project.

- Devise and institute a risk management process which must be utilized on every project

- Company XYZ needs a portfolio management process. The organization should create a detailed, documented process for managing the project portfolio. We recommend that the responsibility for managing the portfolio rest with a project office. This includes managing project requests, prioritization, etc.

- Company XYZ has a systems development life cycle (SDLC) standard in house although it has not been institutionalized and used. Company XYZ should tailor and adopt this as a standard operating practice.

- Develop a sign-off process at project closure (sign-off by line-of-business and operations) and ensure that experiences and lessons learned are shared.

Organization Development/Department Operations

- Establish a standards department, with responsibility as a service organization to the project and support teams, which provides expert knowledge, advice and assistance in quality management, project management and process management.

  - Project prioritization

  - Leadership and appropriate structure to improve individual project performance

- Department-wide resource management, resource procurement, and project deployment

- Work-plan setup, review, monitoring

- Standardized systems development methods and frameworks

- Risk management across the portfolio

- Knowledge management and sharing of best practices

- Consistent project management practices throughout the department

- Increased number and capacity of project managers

- Portfolio view of major projects

- Coordination of process change/continuous improvement

- Coordination of department-wide planning and budgets.

• Formally assign empowered project managers and establish budgets for all projects.

• Establish a project and service call prioritization process and dedicate resources to a help desk function to handle service/ support calls exclusively and support them with the service call/ support process.

• Consider modifying the organization structure to place appropriate resources, supporting a specific line of business, into the same functional unit

—— Or ——

• Form project teams at the inception of a project, assign an empowered project manager and place control of the resources under the project manager until the project is closed.

• Establish clear and consistent roles and responsibilities. Establish standards of performance. Establish clear accountabilities and performance objectives for all positions that support the overall goals and objectives of the organization. Reward accordingly. Ensure that career development objectives are defined and processes are implemented to encourage professional development.

- Establish a recognition program. Allocate discretionary dollars to managers/team leaders to recognize their employees. Teach managers how to recognize people. Manage by wandering around. Know what people are doing and how they feel. Measure the satisfaction of all associates on a regular basis.

- Establish a management infrastructure, annual operating budgets and other management requirements to appropriate levels to promote accountability

- Develop a business plan and recommendation for charging back all work to the LOBs. Perceived value will improve as will efficiency. The current practices re-enforce bad business behavior.

- Reconsider the plan to move quality assurance out of the organization. The quality of the deliverable and all the testing should be the responsibility of the project teams and the project manager.

Training

- Company XYZ has conducted training in project management essentials. The learning from this class must be put to practical use throughout the department.

- The business clients need to be trained in the methods and value of project management. It is our suggestion that they be provided a "Project Management Essentials" overview to promote interaction and understanding between the department and business client personnel.

- Company XYZ should conduct training in their project planning/control tool (MS Project 98). This will reinforce knowledge already acquired by some of the personnel and provide critical skills for others.

- Company XYZ should consider an advanced project management training course after the *Project Management Handbook* is deployed and formal assignment of project managers is implemented.

- Establish a comprehensive orientation program for new employees.

Recognizing that funding for all improvements immediately is not practical, we recommend a prioritization list be developed and that the list becomes the basis for the milestones of a project plan designed to improve the efficiency and client satisfaction of the department. A shared objective should also be established, across the management team, to implement (develop and deploy) the milestones of the project, on schedule.

Note that PM Solutions has the capability of performing many of the functions in the above list of recommendations. Examples:

- Creation or tailoring of a project management methodology

- Training on project management (single courses or an entire curriculum leading to a Masters Certificate in Project Management)

- Training on a variety of project management tools

- Project manager mentoring

- Integration of project management processes with an SDLC

- Project office tailoring and mentoring.

Recommended Action Plan

Step I—Communication

- Implement "quick fixes" immediately e.g. schedule and execute monthly/quarterly department meetings and LOB team meetings, with crisp agendas. (ASAP)

- Establish facilitated sessions with small groups of associates to "listen" for requirements and solicit input. (ASAP)

- Establish a cross-functional team, chaired by human resources or a neutral facilitator. The mission and objective of the team is to develop and deploy a comprehensive communication plan for the organization and supporting processes by October 1. (Jul–Sep 1999)

• Develop an orientation seminar/tool for new employees.

Step II—Project Management Training, Methodologies/Processes

Phase I

• Develop a crisp, user-friendly requirements definition process immediately, working closely with key stakeholders, and implement throughout the organization. (Jun–Jul 1999)

• Provide PM Essentials course to the balance of the organization and selected LOB partners. (Jul 1999)

• Provide MS Project 98 course to all project managers as well as team members who have a need-to-know. (Jul–Aug 1999)

• Develop a standard project management methodology and a process guide (*Project Management Handbook*) tailored to the department's needs. (Jul–Sep 1999)

• Develop curriculum requirements for project management training and establish a schedule to satisfy requirements. (Aug–Oct 1999)

Phase II

• Pilot and deploy the Company XYZ project management methodology
  - Pilot the process on 2 projects (Sep 1999)
  - Gain commitment from all teams (Sep–Oct 1999)
  - Deploy the new process throughout the organization and measure compliance (Oct–Dec 1999)

• Provide project management mentoring to select project teams to enhance knowledge and skill transfer. (Sep 1999–Q2 2000)

• Build or contract for courseware to satisfy the PM curriculum requirements defined in Phase I. (Oct–Dec 1999)

• Implement the PM curriculum throughout the organization and celebrate / reward levels attainment. (Year 2000)

Figure B.4 Organizational Development Schedule

	1999							2000	
	Jun	Jul	Aug	Sep	Oct	Nov	Dec	Q1	Q2

STEP 1

Communications
Improvements

STEP 2 - Phase I

Requirements
definition process

Elementary
training

Develop PM
methodology

PM curriculum
requirements

STEP 2 - Phase II

Pilot new PM
methodology

Commitment and
general deployment

PM Mentoring

Curriculum
development/delivery

STEP 3

Organization
development

Step III —Organization Development/Department Operations

• Establish a standards department, with responsibility as a service organization to the project and support teams, to provide expert knowledge, advice and assistance in project, process and quality management. (ASAP)

• Establish clear and consistent roles and responsibilities. Establish standards of performance. Establish clear accountabilities and performance objectives for all positions, that support the overall goals and objectives of the organization. Reward accordingly. Ensure that career development objectives are defined and processes are implemented to encourage professional development. (Q3 1999)

• Establish a management infrastructure, annual operating budgets and other management requirements at appropriate levels, to promote accountability. (Q4 1999)

The PM Solutions Assessment Team wishes to thank (names), and those associates in the organization who gave their valuable time to complete the survey questionnaires and participate in the interviews. The frankness and understanding of the issues is very encouraging.

Appendix C

Project Management Templates

Contents

- T.1 Project Determination Checklist
- T.2 Project Request Form
- T.3 Scope Statement Checklist
- T.4 Project Charter Template
- T.5 Project Binder Contents Checklist
- T.6 Project Logistics Checklist
- T.7 Kickoff Meeting Agenda
- T.8 Project Risk Log
- T.9 Project Issues Log
- T.10 Project Planning Process Checklist
- T.11 Weekly Project Status Report Template
- T.12 Customer Sign-Off Checklist
- T.13 Scope Change Request/Impact Template
- T.14 Project Change Log
- T.15 Project Control Checklist
- T.16 Project Closeout Checklist
- T.17 Project Closeout Report Template
- T.18 Project Lessons Learned Template
- T.19 Project Sign-off Form

T.1 PROJECT DETERMINATION CHECKLIST

DOCUMENT PREPARATION INFORMATION

PROJECT NAME	PREPARED BY (PRINT)	DATE PREPARED	PROJECT ID

CUSTOMER INFORMATION

CUSTOMER	CONTACT

The following characteristics help determine whether the potential work opportunity is a project. The more items checked, the more likely the opportunity is a project.

☐   The opportunity is unique.

- Generally, a project is a stand-alone, one-of-a-kind effort requiring a customized solution. A project is not just one piece in a series of similar or identical efforts.

☐   The project is similar to other projects that have successfully used project management services.

- Typically, projects have a clearly defined starting point.

☐   The opportunity has a clear ending.

- A project will end at a clearly defined point in time. It is not self-perpetuating.

☐   The opportunity meets a specific business need.

- A project must focus on specific, objective goals. The most valuable opportunities are those that are consistent with our core business and strategic directions.

☐   The opportunity requires a quick response to meet the business need.

- Opportunities requiring quick, accurate responses are often best managed as projects.

☐   The opportunity requires coordinating and managing several or many interdependent elements, organizations, and/or resources.

- The greater the number of activities or elements required for the opportunity, the greater the need for project management.

☐   Pursuing the opportunity will consume resources.

- If an effort does not consume financial, physical, and/or personnel resources, it does not qualify as a project.

BUSINESS CASE INSTRUCTIONS

Part 1. Executive Summary
Provide a succinct, stand-alone description of the overall business case, including the background, proposed solution, and justification for the project.

Part 2. Decision Required
Summarize the decision required and the information needed to make that decision.

Part 3. Background
Provide the background on the problem or opportunity and clearly state the business need, including the current situation, why the current situation fails to satisfy the requirement, and the specific business need

Part 4. Proposed Solution
Explain the proposed solution to the problem or opportunity and the benefits to be derived.

Part 5. Justification
Provide narrative and financial analyses.

- Narrative: Describe the justification for the project in terms of strategic alignment, regulatory compliance, or financial benefits.
- Financial Analysis: Provide fundamental financial statements (income statement, balance sheet, cash flow statement, etc.) to allow a thorough financial evaluation of the opportunity. Include annual revenue, net operating profit, cumulative discounted cash flow, internal rate of return, return on investment, and net present value.

Part 6. Change Management
Discuss the process to be used to control change to the project scope and the project plan. Consider the following:

- Implementation: If the implementation of the project will be unique or complex, provide an overview of the implementation plan.
- Communications: Define who will be responsible for communicating the solution, and outline how the solution will be communicated.
- Support: Explain how the hardware, software and process will be supported.
- Technology Overview: Describe any unique technical requirements and proposed technical solution.
- Training: If new tasks or new jobs will be introduced to the business, outline the training that will be required.

Part 7. Risks and Issues
List the primary risks and issues, and state how they have been addressed. Estimate the likelihood of success for the project, including quantitative data to support your estimate.

Part 8. Market Analysis (if applicable)

- Target Market: Identify the target market. Identify existing market, customer, or operational needs. Describe the reason(s) for the needs. Define any market entry and/or exit barriers.

323

- Market Segmentation and Size: Segment the market where possible. Determine the size of each market segment. Estimate the demand for the product or service. Identify market uncertainties that may affect estimates of demand.
- Customer Description: Describe the customer and the availability and sources of customer funding. Describe how the selection is made and what factors influence the customer's decisions. Describe the customer's short-term "hot buttons" and long-term requirements. Describe what architecture the customer currently has in place.
- Existing Products and Services: Identify the existing competing products and/or services that either do or could meet the customer's needs.

T.2 PROJECT REQUEST FORM

DESCRIPTION OF REQUEST
Description of requested function(s):

Business group(s) or area(s) affected:

Benefits that will be achieved:

Business reason for this project:
☐ Stay in business (MANDATORY)
☐ Return on Investment *(Include ROI analysis with this form)*

I request that Information Technology undertake this project.

Project Initiator: Date:

T.3 SCOPE STATEMENT CHECKLIST

DOCUMENT PREPARATION INFORMATION

PROJECT NAME	PREPARED BY (PRINT)	DATE PREPARED	PROJECT ID

CUSTOMER INFORMATION

CUSTOMER	CONTACT

The scope statement should be no more than two pages long. It should completely but concisely describe the project and, at a minimum, address the following elements:

☐ Customer identification

☐ Description of the customer business need

☐ Overview of our approach to meeting the customer business need, including the following:
- A description of the hardware to be used in the solution
- A synopsis of the software to be used
- Identification of any services to be provided as part of the solution

☐ Discussion of how our proposed solution meets the business need and how that solution fits in with the overall customer strategy

☐ Identification of the internal organizations that will participate in the project

☐ Identification of the third-party organizations that will participate in this project

☐ Identification of the project sponsor or owner

☐ Statement of the time frame in which the project will be implemented

☐ An estimate of total project price or cost

T.4 PROJECT CHARTER TEMPLATE

PROJECT PARTICIPANTS

PROJECT NAME

PROJECT SPONSOR IT PROJECT MANAGER

BUSINESS AREA PROJECT MANAGER

OTHER PARTICIPANTS

PROJECT DESCRIPTION
Business Background:

Project Scope (detail both what is *in* and *out* of scope):

Objectives (in business terms):

Deliverables:

Constraints:

Assumptions:

We agree that this is a viable IT project. We authorize the beginning of the planning process.

Project Sponsor: Date:

IT Senior Manager: Date:

PROJECT CHARTER INSTRUCTIONS

PURPOSE
The project charter formally recognizes the existence of a project. It describes the project at a high level and explains the business need for the project. The charter is completed by the IT project manager, with input from the business area project manager. It is approved by the business area executive (the project sponsor) and the IT senior manager. The charter authorizes the project manager to expend company resources in planning the project. With an approved project charter, the project is added to the IT budget and project portfolio.

ORIGINATION AND TIMING
The IT project manager completes the project charter upon receipt of a project request from a business area project manager. The project charter must be approved by both the project sponsor and an IT senior manager.

FIELD AND INSTRUCTIONS
Project Name: Enter a brief name to describe the project.

Project Sponsor: This is generally the executive of the business area for which this project is being undertaken. This person will be responsible for budgeting the funds to undertake the project, and will have final authority to approve project completion.

Business Area Project Manager: The primary business area liaison with the IT project manager. This person is responsible for the business unit's project-related activities.

IT Project Manager: The person in IT responsible for planning and managing the project.

Other Participants: In addition to the sponsoring business area, indicate other business groups that will have crucial responsibilities for the project.

Business Background: Give an overview of the business reasons for the project.

Project Scope: Using business terminology, give a general description of the project scope (provide details in the following sections). Indicate both what is *within* the anticipated scope and what is *outside* the scope. Consider these topics:

- Systems
- Communications
- Infrastructure
- Business locations

Objectives Using business terminology, list specific business objectives that the project is anticipated to achieve.

Deliverables: List the specific deliverables expected from the project and how these will fulfill the objectives. The deliverables should be as tangible as possible.

Constraints: List factors that will limit the project team's options. For example, a predefined budget range is a constraint that is very likely to limit the team's options regarding project scope and staffing levels.

Assumptions: List factors or situations you will assume for the purposes of planning the project. For example, if the availability date of a key resource is uncertain, the team should make a reasonable assumption about the date of availability and list this as an assumed or contingent factor in the plan.

T.5 PROJECT BINDER CONTENTS CHECKLIST

DOCUMENT PREPARATION INFORMATION

PROJECT NAME	PREPARED BY (PRINT)	DATE PREPARED	PROJECT ID

CONTENTS	LOCATION Where is the document stored?	UPDATE INFORMATION When was the document created? Updated?
• Project Charter		
• Business Case		
• Kickoff Meeting Documentation		
• Completed Checklists and Documentation from Initiating Processes		

Project Plan
Include key Project Plan elements and other Project Plan elements that will be used extensively in managing the project.

- Work Breakdown Structure
- Project Schedule
- Project Budget
- Staffing Plan
- Risk Management Plan
- Communication Plan
- Change Control Plan

Execution and Control
- Status Reports
- Scope Change Requests

Closing
- Lessons Learned Documentation
- Project Closeout Report

Meetings
- Agendas
- Minutes
- Issue/Action Item Logs
- Presentations

T.6 PROJECT LOGISTICS CHECKLIST

DOCUMENT PREPARATION INFORMATION

PROJECT NAME	PREPARED BY (PRINT)	DATE PREPARED	PROJECT ID

Facilities

- Office and workspace: Ensure that adequate office and workspace is provided for each individual assigned to the project and working at the project location.
- Furniture: Provide the requisite furniture, such as desks, chairs, tables, file cabinets, and bookshelves.
- Security access: Ensure that project team members have access to the project workspace. This may require providing keys and/or identification badges.
- "Comfort" space: Ensure that project team members have access to restrooms, break or kitchen facilities, and other common support facilities.

Equipment

- Computers and workstations: Provide adequate numbers of personal computers or workstations, with appropriate software and printers for the project team members assigned full time to the project.
- Calculators: Provide calculators, if required.
- Copy machines: Provide copy machines to support small copy jobs. Large reproduction jobs should be handled according to standard operating procedures.
- Fax machines: Provide a sufficient number of fax machines to support the project team.
- Telephones and telephone service: Obtain telephone installation sufficient to support the project team—typically, a telephone for each full-time project team member or the equivalent. Ensure that local and long-distance telephone services are provided.
- Project-specific hardware: Provide other hardware or equipment items specific to and necessary for project implementation, including test equipment, specialized computer hardware, and other items.
- "Comfort" equipment: As necessary, provide coffeemakers, a refrigerator, or other equipment that will support team members' comfort.

Supplies

- General office supplies: Provide an adequate supply of pens, pencils, writing paper, Post-it notes, tape, staplers, and other office supplies.
- Computer supplies: Provide computer supplies, including disks, paper, ink or toner cartridges, and other necessary items.
- "Comfort" supplies: Obtain adequate "comfort" supplies, including coffee

and its condiments, other refreshment supplies, toiletries, and anything else that may be appropriate.

Other Resources

- Administrative support: Arrange for the necessary administrative support, including personnel to answer the telephone and take messages and perform routine administrative tasks.
- Reproduction support: To accommodate large copying jobs, ensure access to reproduction support that can print, collate, and bind with sufficient speed and efficiency.
- Production support: If necessary, provide access to editorial, word processing, and clerical support to assist in document production.
- Graphics support: Arrange for graphics or artistic support as required by the project
- Order processing
- Project office support

T.7 KICKOFF MEETING AGENDA

DOCUMENT PREPARATION INFORMATION

PROJECT NAME	PREPARED BY (PRINT)	DATE PREPARED	PROJECT ID

SPONSOR/CUSTOMER INFORMATION

SPONSOR/CUSTOMER	CONTACT	PROJECT NUMBER

ANNOUNCEMENT INFORMATION

TO	FROM	DATE

MEETING INFORMATION

DATE	START TIME	END TIME	LOCATION

MEETING PURPOSE

CALLED BY	PHONE	FAX	E-MAIL

SPONSORED BY	PHONE	FAX	E-MAIL

AGENDA ITEMS	**PRESENTER**	**TIME**

Welcome and Introductions

Project Overview
    Project Charter Elements
    The Project Requirements
    The Proposed Solution
    Project Accomplishments to Date

Executive Perspective

Project Deliverables

Project Schedule

Team Roles and Responsibilities

Special Issues

Summary

Close

T.8 PROJECT RISK LOG

PROJECT NAME:

Type of analysis (original or revised):

Date of analysis or revision:

Risk Area	Potential Impact	Probability Code (1-5)	Impact Code (1-5)	Risk Level (H/M/L)	Mitigation Strategy	Trigger Point or Event
•						
•						
•						
•						
•						
•						
•						
•						
•						
•						
•						
•						
•						
•						
•						
•						

Codes: 1=Low 5=High
Attach additional documents to complete the sections.

PROJECT RISK LOG INSTRUCTIONS

PURPOSE

The purpose of the project risk log is to document the identified risks for the project. Risk factors or events represent something that may happen, or a situation that may develop, to the detriment of the success of the project. The possible detriment from risk could range from rendering the project not viable to reducing the value of some of the delivered benefits.

The project risk log is a format in which to describe and analyze risks and to offer action plans to mitigate or eliminate risks. The log provides a reference source for both information technology and other project participants and supports their need to be apprised of and evaluate the risks.

ORIGINATION AND TIMING

Project managers should begin considering project risk factors from the time of the initial project request. Actual documentation of project risks usually begins with the statement of work. The original project risk log should be included in the project risks section of the statement of work so that those connected with the project can gain understanding of the risks and your plans to respond to the risks.

The project risk log is created and maintained by the IT project manager. In many cases the log will be a "living document," updated with appropriate frequency. Risk factors change, and the update frequency will depend on the project and the risk factors. In some cases, the log may be produced weekly in conjunction with the project status report. In all cases, the project manager should go through the risk log each time the project status report is prepared, examining each potential risk (especially the "Trigger Events").

RISK ANALYSIS GUIDELINES

On the next page are some of the major risk categories to consider. Use the guideline information below, the project risk log definitions, and the project risk matrix to complete the information in the project risk log.

Major Risk Categories

Some major risk categories are outlined here:

Business risks, if they materialize, will adversely impact the corporation's operations by decreasing revenues, increasing costs, or inhibiting our ability to increase revenues or decrease costs. Some examples are:

- Financial (cost overrun)
- Schedule (delay in application deployment)
- Scope (an expanding requirements list)
- Operational readiness and support (for the current, transition, and target environment)

Technical risks, if they materialize, will adversely impact the corporation's IT organization in efficiently supporting business applications, result in re-work and additional investment in a targeted solution, or cause schedule delays in the deployment of a targeted solution. Some examples are:

- Application software incompatibility
- Improper configuration/design
- Inability to support co-existent environments

Resource risks, if they materialize, will adversely impact the ability of the project to be efficiently and effectively executed. Some examples include:

- Lack of technical skills (or inappropriate skill mix)
- Inability to back-fill
- Permanent infrastructure and back-fill personnel turnover
- Delay in obtaining external consultants

Among other elements of risk to consider: customer and market shifts that may impact the value of the project deliverables, vendor stability and changes in the vendor organization, changes in the broad technical environment (as in networking or communications technology), and risk of change in the corporation's organizational environment.

RISK ANALYSIS—BRIEF EXAMPLES

Risk: The package implementation may not be completed before the year 2000.

Potential Impact: Lack of a Year 2000 compliant application on January 1, 2000.

Mitigation: Closely monitor project plan; determine go/no go checkpoints; develop contingency plan.

Risk: An accelerated project may result in some requirements being missed.

Potential Impact: Missed requirements may result in scope changes during the project that extend the completion date.

Mitigation: Conduct thorough requirements gathering sessions with all appropriate parties; closely manage the change request process.

Risk: Lack of appropriate technical skills.

Potential Impact: Project tasks may take longer to complete.

Mitigation: Train project team members early in the project.

PROJECT RISK LOG—DEFINITIONS
Field and Instructions

Risk: Describe the risk factor or event: something that might happen, or a situation that may develop, to the detriment of the project.

Potential Impact: State how the risk would affect the project.

Probability Code: Indicate the probability that the factor or event will occur by entering a code from 1-5. (1 represents the lowest probability and 5 the highest.)

Impact Code: Indicate how much impact occurrence would have on the project by entering an impact code from 1-5. (1 represents the lowest impact and 5 the highest.)

Risk Level: Use the project risk matrix shown below to relate the probability and the impact and thereby determine the risk level (high/medium/low). Sort the log by risk level, with the factors having the highest risk level shown first.

Risk Mitigation: Strategy: Document the preventative actions planned to mitigate or eliminate the risk factor. If the mitigation strategy is contingent on a trigger point or event, indicate the point or event in the next column.

Trigger Point or Event: Define the situation or event that would cause the mitigation strategy to be invoked. (For example: projected project cost overruns exceed 5%, or the vendor fails to deliver sub-system B by the specified date.)

RISK LEVEL DETERMINATION

Refer to the probability and impact codes from the project risk log and the project risk matrix shown below. Find the intersection of the probability row and the impact column. The type of shading at the row and column intersection indicates the risk level: high, medium or low. Record each item's risk level on the project risk log. Sort the log by risk level, with the factors having the highest risk level shown first.

Project Risk Matrix

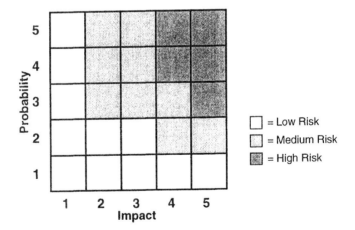

T.9 PROJECT ISSUES LOG

Project Name:

ISSUE NO.	STATUS (O, I, C)

PRIORITY (H, M, L)	

TYPE	

DATE LOGGED	LOGGED BY

ASSIGNED TO	TARGET DATE

ISSUE DESCRIPTION

RESOLUTION (& SUPPORTING DOCUMENTS)

DATE CLOSED

ISSUE NO.	STATUS (O, I, C)

PRIORITY (H, M, L)	

TYPE	

DATE LOGGED	LOGGED BY

ASSIGNED TO	TARGET DATE

ISSUE DESCRIPTION

RESOLUTION (& SUPPORTING DOCUMENTS)

DATE CLOSED

PROJECT ISSUES LOG INSTRUCTIONS

PURPOSE
The purpose of the project issues log is to document and manage issues relating to a project. "issues" are problems or questions arising in the course of the project that need to be defined, researched, evaluated in terms of scope and impact, and resolved in order for a project phase or task to proceed.

An effective issues resolution process resolves problems and questions as quickly as possible and includes escalation procedures to the appropriate management or committees. Issues must be documented, and the log provides a reference source for both information technology and the other project participants, and supports their need to be apprised of and evaluate the issues.

ORIGINATION AND TIMING
The project issues log and issues management process are described and implemented by the IT project manager once work begins on the statement of work. Procedures for documenting, communicating and resolving issues are also described in the statement of work. The process and procedures may differ depending on the project.

The frequency of producing the project issues log is documented in the statement of work. Typically, the log will be produced weekly in conjunction with the project status report.

FIELD AND INSTRUCTIONS
Issue No.: The issue number is the identification number you assign to the issue when you record it. Use a sequential numbering scheme that you will apply to all issues for the project (beginning with "1" is fine). Enter the issue number on supporting and reference documents in order to cross-reference them with the issues log.

Status: Status options

O = Open

I = In Process

C = Closed

Priority: Priority options

H = High (issue will impact schedule and/or cost if not resolved; project manager involved; escalation may be required)

M = Medium (issue may impact schedule and/or cost if not resolved; project team is involved in resolving)

L = Low (issue will not impact schedule and/or cost if not resolved, but the issue needs to be resolved and its priority may increase over time)

Type: The classification of an issue. Possible types are scope, testing, design, etc.

Date Logged: The date the issue was entered into the log.

Logged By: The person who initially entered the issue into the log.

Assigned To: The person who is to investigate and resolve the issue.

Target Date: The date by which the issue is to be resolved. The date selected should minimize any negative impacts to schedule and/or cost.

Issue Description: A complete description of the issue. Specify the areas affected, ramifications and impact of the issue. If you need more space, create an additional description document and use the issue no. to cross-reference it to the log.

Resolution (and Supporting Documents): When an issue has been resolved, this field should contain a complete history and state how the issue was resolved. If applicable, refer to supporting documents.

Date Closed: The date on which this issue was formally closed. After this date, no further attention will be paid to this issue.

T.10 PROJECT PLANNING PROCESS CHECKLIST

PROJECT PARTICIPANTS

PROJECT NAME   PROJECT ID/NUMBER

PROJECT SPONSOR   DATE

PROJECT MANAGER   BUSINESS AREA PROJECT MANAGER

ASSESSMENT QUESTIONS TO REVIEW NEAR THE COMPLETION OF THE PHASE

☐ Has a master schedule been developed that identifies all major events throughout the project life?

☐ Are all stakeholders in agreement with the master schedule?

☐ Is the master schedule achievable? If not, have all stakeholders been informed?

☐ Is there agreement from all functional organizations for the execution of the defined project tasks?

☐ Has a project network (WBS) been developed that includes all project tasks?

☐ Has the critical path been identified?

☐ Does the critical path satisfy the master schedule with sufficient contingency for surprises?

☐ Are all team members committed to the planned approach to project execution?

☐ Have detailed schedules been developed for the individual tasks of the project?

☐ Are the performing organizations signed up and committed to the execution of these tasks as described?

☐ Have project risks been evaluated at all levels with appropriate risk-management actions incorporated into the planning for project execution?

☐ Does a documented project plan exist for review by interested parties?

T.11 WEEKLY PROJECT STATUS REPORT TEMPLATE

TO: (INCLUDE APPROPRIATE ADDRESSEES)

FROM: DIVISION OR BUSINESS UNIT NAME

PROJECT NAME

STATUS REPORT FOR WEEK ENDING __ __/__ __/__ __ __ __

Project Name (Enter a short description of the project and the outcome.)

Activities and Accomplishments for Period Ending ___/___/_____(List the week's activities and accomplishments that have been achieved for this project.

Plans for Week Ending ___/___/_____ (State the current week's objectives and significant activity for this project.)

Target Dates (List any new, changed or significant target dates.)
           Task   Target Date

Assumptions (List any assumptions.)

Issues (List any issues, new or open, that require an action plan.)

Risks (List any new or continuing risks associated with the project. Always include risks documented in the project charter.)

Note: Include project schedule showing delays to the critical path. Include other project status graphics as necessary to support information in this report.

T.12 CUSTOMER SIGN-OFF CHECKLIST

DOCUMENT PREPARATION INFORMATION

PROJECT NAME	PREPARED BY (PRINT)	DATE PREPARED	PROJECT ID

CUSTOMER INFORMATION

CUSTOMER	CONTACT

SIGN-OFF

DELIVERABLE	REF.	PARA.	PAGE	COMMENTS	DATE	INITIALS
•						
•						
•						
•						
•						
•						
•						
•						
•						
•						
•						
•						
•						
•						

T.13 SCOPE CHANGE REQUEST/IMPACT TEMPLATE

DOCUMENT PREPARATION INFORMATION

PROJECT NAME	PREPARED BY (PRINT)	DATE PREPARED	PROJECT ID

PROPOSED CHANGE

BASELINE DESCRIPTION

Give an in-depth explanation of the original system design and architecture. Explain why this was originally the selected solution.

CHANGE DESCRIPTION

Define the product or technical design changes that must be carried out to implement the change request. Identify all WBS elements and work packages affected by the change. If additional resources are required or if resources must be shifted, show the impact on the existing work package implementation.

REASON FOR CHANGE

Describe circumstances resulting in need for change request. Include timing, personnel involved, and summary of the issues.

BUDGET IMPACT

State the cost to complete this change request. Identify and analyze projected financial consequences of making the requested change. Estimate cost differentials as precisely as possible, and include a recommendation on any changes in the customer's obligations.

SCHEDULE IMPACT

State the impact on the project schedule of this change. Include references to the critical path. Discuss workarounds to preserve schedule if possible.

LIST TASKS AND OTHER RELEVANT INFORMATION NEEDED TO COMPLETE THE SOLUTION

TASK	START DATE	END DATE	DURATION	RESOURCE(S)
Task 1	99/99/99	99/99/99	99 d	Resource 1, Resource 2
Task 2	99/99/99	99/99/99	11 d	Resource 1

AUTHORIZATION – PROJECT MANAGER

NAME (PRINT)	SIGNATURE	PHONE	DATE

AUTHORIZATION – BUSINESS SPONSOR

NAME (PRINT)	SIGNATURE	PHONE	DATE

T.14 PROJECT CHANGE LOG

Project Name:

CHG NO.	CHANGE DESCRIPTION	DATE SUBMITTED	DATE CLOSED	DISP* DISP*	CHANGE IMPACT**	DURA- TION	RESEARCH HOURS	LABOR HOURS
1								
2								
3								
4								
5								
				TOTAL				

*Disposition Code

   A = Change accepted in project

   C = Change rejected or withdrawn

   X = Estimate adjustment

**Change Impact Code

   H = High, extremely important or imperative to change

   M = Medium, important, but we can operate without this change

   L = Low, desirable, but with little impact if change is not made

PROJECT CHANGE LOG INSTRUCTIONS

PURPOSE
The project change log serves two purposes: (1) it provides a summary record of all the project change requests that have been submitted for the project, regardless of the disposition of the change request, and (2) it serves as a management reference for approved changes in project scope, deliverables, cost, or duration. This log and the project change request form provide a reference source for both information technology and the customer or user, keeping them apprised of the change requests and the disposition of those requests.

ORIGINATION AND TIMING
A project change request form must be completed prior to entering a change request in the project change log. See the "Project Change Request Form and Instructions" for more information.

The IT project manager completes the project change log. The frequency of updating and distributing the project change log is documented in the statement of work. Typically, the change log will be published weekly in conjunction with the project status report.

RELATED FORMS
- *Scope change request/impact template.* A detailed description of a project change request. The scope change request/impact template is completed prior to entering the change in the project change log.

FIELD AND INSTRUCTIONS
Chg. No.: The change number is the identification number you assign to the change request when you record a change in the project change log. Use a sequential numbering scheme that you will apply to all changes for the project (beginning with "1" is fine). Enter the change number on the project change request form in order to cross-reference the change request form with the change log.

Change Description: Briefly describe the change based on the information in the project change request form.

Date Submitted: Date on which the change request was submitted to the IT project manager.

Date Closed: Date on which this change request was accepted, rejected, or withdrawn. If accepted, the work and schedule impact of the change should be incorporated in the project plan.

Disposition: The disposition code records the final disposition of the change:
A = Change accepted in project
C = Change rejected or withdrawn

X = On hold or pending

Change Impact: This code indicates the impact of this change on the business group or area:

H = High (extremely important or imperative to change)

M = Medium (important, but we can operate without this change)

L = Low (this change is desirable, but with little impact if the change is not made)

Duration (days): Enter the estimate for the duration (in days) that this change will add to the project schedule.

Research Hours: Enter the number of hours that will be (or have been) spent to research this change.

Labor Hours: Enter here the number of person-hours that this change will add to the project.

Total: As changes are incorporated in the project, calculate the total for each of the impact metrics (duration, research hours, and labor hours).

T.15 PROJECT CONTROL CHECKLIST

PROJECT CONTROL QUESTIONS

Check when complete response is logged in project binder

☐ Where is the project with respect to schedule?

☐ Where is the project with respect to cost?

☐ Where is the project with respect to meeting specifications?

☐ Where is the project with respect to overall objectives and goals?

☐ Where are the WBS elements (at desired level of evaluation) with respect to schedule?

☐ Where are the WBS elements with respect to costs?

☐ Where are the WBS elements with respect to meeting technical requirements?

☐ Where are the WBS elements with respect to project goals and objectives?

☐ What project areas are running well?

☐ What project areas are running poorly?

☐ What opportunities are evolving from the project?

☐ What concerns are developing with the project?

☐ Is the project still in line with organizational objectives?

☐ Is the customer satisfied with progress?

☐ Is the project team satisfied?

☐ Have outside sources examined project progress?

☐ Is the project team functioning well?

☐ Is the project still a strategic fit for the organization?

☐ Does the project remain profitable or cost effective?

☐ Are project management tools being applied to the project on a regular basis?

☐ Is the risk management plan being followed and updated?

T.16 PROJECT CLOSEOUT CHECKLIST

DOCUMENT PREPARATION INFORMATION

PROJECT NAME	PREPARED BY (PRINT)	DATE PREPARED	PROJECT ID

PROJECT

Check off when complete response is logged in project binder.

☐ Are any deliverables outstanding?

☐ Are there any internal outstanding commitments?

☐ Have all costs been appropriately charged to the project?

☐ Have all work packages and work orders been completed?

☐ Have any incomplete work packages been documented and rationalized?

☐ Has management been notified regarding the availability of project personnel?

☐ Has management been notified regarding the availability of project facilities?

☐ Has the project plan been archived with all support data?

☐ Has agreement been reached with the project sponsor on disposition of remaining deliverables?

☐ Have suppliers been notified regarding any outstanding commitments?

☐ Are *all* parties aware of pending project closeout?

☐ Have operations and maintenance procedures been put in place and activated?

PERSONNEL—INTERNAL

☐ Have project team concerns regarding future assignment been addressed?

☐ Is the project team dedicated to remaining project commitments?

☐ Are motivating factors still in place for remaining tasks and obligations?

☐ Have personnel been reassigned or notified of reassignment methodology?

PERSONNEL—EXTERNAL

☐ Are efforts being made to ensure project sponsor interest remains high?

☐ Are efforts being made to ensure project sponsor attitudes and perceptions regarding the project are stable?

☐ Are shifting personnel issues being addressed with the project sponsor and management?

☐ Are key project (and project sponsor) personnel still being apprised of project status?

☐ Does a communication methodology exist to maintain relations between the customer and project manager?

T.17 PROJECT CLOSEOUT REPORT TEMPLATE

DOCUMENT PREPARATION INFORMATION

PROJECT NAME	PREPARED BY (PRINT)	DATE PREPARED	PROJECT ID

EXECUTIVE SUMMARY

Within each section of the executive summary, document changes that occurred during the project (for example: budget, staff changes, scope, etc.). Document the actual results of the project for staff time, budget, and schedule. Document the risks that were identified during project planning that actually occurred and how those risks were mitigated. Attach the lessons learned documentation. Summarize overall lessons learned from the project and recommendations for improvement in the last section of the report.

PROJECT SCOPE

RISK MANAGEMENT

SCHEDULE

STAFF TIME

COSTS

SUMMARY OF LESSONS LEARNED

T.18 PROJECT LESSONS LEARNED TEMPLATE

The purpose of this questionnaire is to help review the results from the project and to translate those results into lessons learned and recommendations for improvement. Attach this document to the project closeout report.

GENERAL QUESTIONS

- Are you proud of our finished product or system?
- What was the single most frustrating part of our project?
- How would you do things differently next time to avoid this frustration?
- What was the most gratifying or professionally satisfying part of the project?
- Did the project management methodology work? Which of our methods or processes worked particularly well?
- Which of our methods or processes were difficult or frustrating to use? What could be done to improve the process?

INTERGROUP COORDINATION

- What difficulty did we have in working with other stakeholders that were responsible for a task or set of tasks relating to the project?
- Did we have the right people assigned to all project roles? (Consider subject matter expertise, technical contributions, management, review and approval, and other key roles.) If no, how can we make sure that we get the right people next time?
- Did our stakeholders, senior managers, customer, and project sponsor(s) participate effectively? If not, how could we improve their participation?
- List team members or stakeholders who were missing from the kickoff meeting or who were not involved early enough in our project. How can we avoid these oversights in the future?

REQUIREMENTS DEFINITION

- Did our requirements definition identify all the project deliverables that we eventually had to build? Did the delivered product meet the specified requirements and goals of the project? If not, what did we miss and how can we be sure to capture necessary requirements on future projects?
- Did our requirements definition identify unnecessary deliverables? If so, how can we avoid this in the future?

PLANNING

- Were all team/stakeholder roles and responsibilities clearly delineated and communicated? If not, how could we have improved these?
- Were the deliverables specifications, milestones, and specific schedule elements/dates clearly communicated? If not, how could we improve this?

- Was the project budget met? How accurate were our original estimates of the size and effort of our project? What did we over or under estimate? (Consider deliverables, effort, and materials required)
- Describe any early warning signs of problems that occurred later in the project? How should we have reacted to these signs? How can we be sure to notice these early warning signs next time?
- Were risks identified and mitigated?
- Could we have completed this project without one or more of our vendors/contractors? If so, how?
- Were our constraints, limitations, and requirements made clear to all vendors/contractors from the beginning? If not, how could we have improved our RFP or statement of need?
- Were there any difficulties setting up vendor paperwork (purchase orders, contracts, etc.)? How could these have been avoided?

EXECUTING AND CONTROLLING

- Did key team members have creative input into the creation of the design specifications? If not, whom were we missing and how can we assure their involvement next time?
- Did those who reviewed the design specifications provide timely and meaningful input? If not, how could we have improved their involvement and the quality of their contributions?
- How could we have improved our work process for creating deliverables specifications?
- Were the members of our test group truly representative of our target audience? If not, how could we assure better representation in the future?
- Did the test facilities, equipment, materials, and support people help to make the test an accurate representation of how the deliverables will be used in the "real world?" If not, how could we have improved on these items?
- Did we get timely, high-quality feedback about how we might improve our deliverables? If not, how could we get better feedback in the future?
- Was our implementation strategy accurate and effective? How could we improve this strategy?
- Were our status reports produced on time? Were they helpful in monitoring the project? If not, why not?
- What worked well in the review and approval process?
- How did the process for managing change perform?
- Did our hand-off of deliverables to the customer represent a smooth and easy transition? If not, how could we have improved this process?

T.19 PROJECT SIGN-OFF FORM

I hereby certify that the above project has been completed. The following deliverables, listed in the project plan, have been completed (list deliverables from project plan and technical documents and any approved changes):

-

-

-

-

-

-

-

-

-

All issues have been resolved.

SIGNED	TITLE	DATE

SIGNED	TITLE	DATE

SIGNED	TITLE	DATE

Appendix D

Team Questionnaire for Capturing Lessons Learned

Give a rating for each question according to the legend.

1. PERSONAL

LEGEND
0 = DON'T KNOW   1 = STRONG NO   2 = NO
3 = MIXED OPINION   4 = YES   5 = STRONG YES

- Did you enjoy working on the project?
- Do you feel you have developed additional skills?
- Did you have the necessary skills to meet your objectives?
- Was the training on the project adequate?
- Did you find the work challenging/interesting?
- Additional comments for Question 1:

2. STANDARDS

LEGEND
0 = DON'T KNOW   1 = DETRIMENTAL TO THE PROJECT   2 = LITTLE VALUE
3 = SOME USE   4 = VERY USEFUL   5 = EXCELLENT

- Rate the value for the following standards:
  - Documentation standards
  - Turnover procedures
  - Status reports
  - Project walk-throughs
  - Team walk-throughs of subsystems
  - Project management standards and methodology
  - Other (please specify)
- Do you feel the standards were generally adhered to?   Yes/No
- What additional standards should the project have developed?
- Additional comments for Question 2

3. PROJECT/PRODUCT DEVELOPMENT ENVIRONMENT

LEGEND
0 = DON'T KNOW   1 = STRONG NO   2 = NO
3 = MIXED OPINION   4 = YES   5 = STRONG YES

- Did you have the proper equipment needed for the project?
- Did you have adequate software to do your work?
- Were the tools and utilities useful? If not, why?
- Was the office environment good to work in?
- Do you feel the recommended technical solution was a good choice?
- Additional comments for Question 3:

4. DEVELOPMENT

LEGEND
0 = DON'T KNOW   1 = STRONG NO   2 = NO
3 = MIXED OPINION   4 = YES   5 = STRONG YES

- Was the overall business design clear to you?
- Was the overall technical design clear to you?
- Did you know where to find documentation on the business and technical designs?
- Was the level of documentation on the project adequate?
- Was the documentation handled in a well-structured manner
- What procedures/methods would you use again?
- What procedures/methods would you NOT use again?
- Additional comments for Question 4:

5. TESTING

LEGEND
0 = DON'T KNOW   1 = FAILURE   2 = NEITHER FAILURE OR SUCCESS
3 = LIMITED SUCCESS   4 = SUCCESSFUL   5 = VERY SUCCESSFUL

- How well do you think the following was handled?
  - System testing
  - Turnovers
  - Defect reporting/fixing
  - Issues reporting/fixing
- Additional comments for Question 5:

6. COMMUNICATION

LEGEND
0 = DON'T KNOW   1 = FAILURE   2 = NEITHER FAILURE OR SUCCESS
3 = LIMITED SUCCESS   4 = SUCCESSFUL   5 = VERY SUCCESSFUL

- How successful/useful was the communication?
  - Between colleagues?
  - Between you and your direct supervisor?
  - Between you and the project manager?
  - Between you and the customer?
  - On overall project status?
  - On the objectives of the project?
  - On your objectives?
  - On your performance?
  - On the objectives of the development team?
  - On project decisions?
  - On project issues?
  - On team issues?
- Additional comments for Question 6:

7. PLANNING/SCHEDULING/STATUS REPORTING

LEGEND
0 = DON'T KNOW   1 = FAILURE   2 = NEITHER FAILURE OR SUCCESS
3 = LIMITED SUCCESS   4 = SUCCESSFUL   5 = VERY SUCCESSFUL

- How would you rate the overall project planning?
- How would you rate the overall project scheduling?
- Was it difficult to meet deadlines?
- Did you feel involved enough in planning/scheduling?
- Did you feel involved enough in estimation of your work?
- Did you feel comfortable in raising issues?
- Were issues you raised dealt with adequately?
- Did you feel the hours you worked were too long?
- If you worked long hours, did you feel pressured into it?
- Additional comments for Question 7:

8. METHODOLOGIES

- In your opinion, what methodologies did the project use?
- How well did they work?
- Why?
- Additional comments for Question 8:

9. SUMMARY

- What in your opinion were the three main project strengths?
- What in your opinion were the three main project weaknesses?
- In your opinion, was enough attention paid to quality in both the development process and the final product?
- Any other comments you would like to add?

THANK YOU!

Your input is valuable. It will enable us make improvements in future projects.

Bibliography

_____. 1998. "Risk Assessment Groups: Key Components of Project Offices." *PM Network* 12 (March):43–45.

_____. 2000. "Project Office: Does One Size Fit All?" *PM Network* (April):27–29.

Allen, Bruce. 2000. "What's in a CEO?" *Delta*. META Group.

Barnes, N M. L. and S. H. Wearne. 1993. "The Future for Major Project Management." *International Journal of Project Management* 11 (August):135–142.

Block, Thomas R. 1997. "The Project Office—Why More Companies Are Adopting IT to Help Manage IT Projects." *Proceedings of the Project Management Institute's 28th Annual Seminars & Symposium*. Newtown Square, PA: Project Management Institute.

Block, Thomas R. 1998. "The Project Office Phenomenon." *PM Network* 12 (March):25–30.

Block, Thomas R. 1999. "The Seven Secrets of a Successful Project Office." *PM Network* (April).

Bolles, Dennis. 1998. "The Project Support Office." *PM Network* 12 (March):33–38.

Bowe, Richard F. and Steve Devaux. 1996. "Achieving Enterprise Project Control." *PM Network* (February):31–36.

Bresnahan, Jennifer. 1996. "Mixed Messages." *CIO* (May 15):72–80.

Conway, Brendan and Richard Hunter. 1996. "Gartner View: Bewitched, Bothered and Bewildered." *CIO* (May 15):82, 84, 88.

Crawford, Kent J. 2000. "Are Your Project Management Processes in Place?" *Contract Management* 40 (June):8–14.

Crawford, Lynn. 2000. "Improving Performance Through Global Communications of Project Management Practice." *Proceedings of the Project Management Institute Annual Seminars & Symposium.* Newtown Square, PA: Project Management Institute.

Dinsmore, Paul C. 1999. *Winning in Business with Enterprise Project Management.* New York: Amacom.

Eidsmoe, Noland. 2000. "The Strategic Program Management Office." *PM Network* 14 (December):39–45.

Englund, Randall L. and Robert J. Graham. 2001. "Implementing a Project Office for Organizational Change." *PM Network* 15 (February):48–50.

Fabris, Peter. 1996. "Ground Control." CIO (April 1):41–52.

Frame, J. Davidson. 1996. "Understanding the New Project Management." Paper presented at ProjectWorld (August 7).

Goff, Leslie. 1997. "Project Management Skills Harmonize With Company's Goal to Bring Music to the 'Net." *ComputerWorld* (December 8):5.

Graham, Alan K. 2000. "Beyond PM 101: Lessons for Managing Large Development Programs." *Project Management Journal* 31 (December):7–18.

Hardy, Leigh and Tom Chaudhuri. 1999. Shortcut to Designing Your Project Management Office." *Proceedings of the 30th Annual Project Management Institute 1999 Seminars & Symposium.* Newtown Square, PA: Project Management Institute.

Hennings, Carolyn M. 1999. "Proposing a Program Office for a Service Organization." *Proceedings of the 30th Annual Project Management Institute 1999 Seminars & Symposium.* Newtown Square, PA: Project Management Institute.

Hobbs, Brian and Richard Coulombe. 1999. "A Project Office Maturity Model." *Proceedings of the 30th Annual Project Management Institute 1999 Seminars & Symposium.* Newtown Square, PA: Project Management Institute.

Kerzner, Harold. 1997. *In Search of Excellence in Project Management: Successful Practices in High Performance Organizations.* New York: Van Nostrand Reinhold.

Light, M. 1999. "The Enterprise Project Office: Beyond 2000." Research Note, Strategic Planning Assumption (November 1), *GartnerAdvisory*. Available online at http://gartner.jmu.edu/research/ras/83900/83954/83954.html.

Light, M. and T. Berg. 2000. "The Project Office: Teams, Processes and Tools." *Strategic Analysis Report* (August 1). Gartner Group.

Makulowich, John. 2000. "In a Dizzy Work Climate, Program Management Plays Vital Role." *Washington Technology* 14 (February).

McDermott, Richard. 2000. "Knowing in Community: 10 Critical Success Factors in Building Communities of Practice." *IHRIM Journal* (March).

Melymuka, Kathleen. "Project Management Top Guns Deliver." *ComputerWorld*.

Melymuka, Kathleen. "Spit and Polish." *ComputerWorld*:66.

Meredith, Jack R. and Samuel L. Mantel, Jr. 1995. *Project Management: A Managerial Approach, 3rd ed.* New York: John Wiley & Sons.

Meta Group, Inc. 1999. "Application Delivery Strategies in Conjunction With IT Performance Engineering & Measurement Strategies." *6th 1999 Trend Teleconference Transcript* (28 October), Stamford, CT: Meta Group, Inc.

Miller, Jean. 1998. "Project Office—One of the Fastest Growing Segments in Information Systems." *Proceedings of the 29th Annual Project Management Institute 1998 Seminars & Symposium.* Newtown Square, PA: Project Management Institute.

Murphy, Richard E. 1999. *The Role of the Project Support Office.* Available online at www.artemispm.com/w7154.html.

Perry, Scott S. and Louis Leatham. 2000. "The Case for a Full-Function Project Office." *The Business Forum.* Available online at www.bizforum.org/whitepapers/kanbay001.html.

Peters, James M. and William J. Honeyman. 2000. "The Mythical Project Office—Practical Ideas to Help IT Project Offices Succeed." *Proceedings of the Project Management Institute Annual Seminars & Symposium.* Newtown Square, PA: Project Management Institute.

Plevyak, Howard M. and James E. Pierce. 2000. "Managing the Colossal Project: How a Major Financial Institution Was Able to Successfully Design and Implement a Master Program Office and Enterprisewide Project Management Information System (PMIS)." *Proceedings of the Project Management Institute Annual Seminars & Symposium.* Newtown Square, PA: Project Management Institute.

Savioa, Robert. 1996. "Custom Tailoring." *CIO* (June 15).

Spender, J. C. and P. H. Grinyer. 1996. "Organizational Renewal." *International Studies of Management & Organization* 26 (Spring).

Stewart, Wendy E. 2001. "Balanced Scorecard for Projects." *Project Management Journal* 32 (March):38–53.

Storck, John and Patricia A. Hill. 2000. "Knowledge Diffusion Through 'Strategic Communities.'" *Sloan Management Review* 41 (Winter).

Sullivan, John. 2000. "The Hidden Roles of the Project Support Office." *PM Network* (February):17.

The Standish Group. 1995. The Chaos Report. Research paper.

Toney, Frank. 1999. "Project Office Structures: A Research Summary from the Top 500 Project Management Benchmarking Forum." *Best Practices Report* 1 (November):3–6.

Von Halle, Barbara and Dan Wahl. 1993. "We, the Miracle Workers." *Database Programming & Design.*

Wenger, Etienne C., and William M. Snyder. 2000. "Communities of Practice: The Organizational Frontier." *Harvard Business Review* 78 (January/February).

Whitten, Neal. 1996. "Defining the Indispensable Project Manager. *Power Snippets.*

Wysocki Jr., Bernard. 1996. "High Tech Nomads Write New Program for Future of Work." *Wall Street Journal* (August 19).

Index